The Russian Adoption Handbook

The Russian Adoption Handbook

How to Adopt a Child from Russia, Ukraine, and Kazakhstan

John H. Maclean

Writers Club Press
San Jose New York Lincoln Shanghai

The Russian Adoption Handbook
How to Adopt a Child from Russia, Ukraine, and Kazakhstan

Writers Club Press
an imprint of iUniverse, Inc.

For information address:
iUniverse, Inc.
5220 S. 16th St., Suite 200
Lincoln, NE 68512
www.iuniverse.com

John H. Maclean and his wife Brigitte have adopted twice from Russia. He is an attorney and can be reached at wassaw2@email.com

ISBN: 0-595-13194-8

Printed in Canada

For my two wonderful Leaps of Faith
Alexander and Catherine

Contents

Introduction

This handbook is written to assist those who have decided to adopt from Russia and its former Republics of Ukraine and Kazakhstan, now independent countries. Some of the comments and discussion are relevant to adopting internationally in general, however the focus is on Eastern Europe. Americans are now adopting almost 4,500 children a year from Russia. This places Russia ahead of China by a slight margin as the most popular country.

The main reason Russia has become so popular is simple. Compared to other countries, including the United States, the paperwork and process is easier. If you go through the steps, you have a very good chance of adding to your family within a few months. This is not to say that the process does not have its bumps in the road, and notice I did not use the word "easy," but "easier." Just that compared to other countries, Russia is not as difficult. Why adoption in the United States is so hard is beyond the scope of this book. However, if you have gone through the fertility nightmare, then the long wait for a domestic child, you will find the Russian, Ukraine or Kazakhstan process to be wonderful, just for their straightforwardness, if nothing else.

The purpose in writing this handbook is simply to provide a roadmap and to give you more control over the process. You will not find the answers to all of your questions in this book. But it will cover most of them. As to the remainder, between your agency and the Internet, you should be able to find the rest. Opinions expressed in this book all come with the caveat that they apply generally to situations. Exceptions will always exist

Finally, adopting is an art, not a science. Whether your experience in Russia is a happy one depends in some part on your expectations and demeanor. The Chinese have a saying that progress is two steps forward and one step back. You should expect that in adopting from Russia there might be a few bumps in the road, but there is nothing that you can not handle with a good attitude. You might not like the food. It might be colder than you thought. The Judge might ask you a question you didn't anticipate. Your homestay host doesn't speak English. The Embassy wants yet another piece of paper. In comparison to having and loving your child, it's all small stuff.

Now for the usual disclaimer. All opinions expressed in this book are those of the author. The information contained within these pages is intended to educate and not to serve as legal or medical advice on a particular problem. Discussions and links relating to websites, medical conditions and tax aspects of adoption are not intended to be endorsements or professional advice whether in this book or on the aforementioned websites. The companies and products referred to in this book maintain their trademarks and copyrights and no infringement is intended. They are simply mentioned for information only.

CHAPTER I

Background

Russia Today

The Russian Federation is twice the geographic size of the United States and is a country of 145 million people. It used to have more but Ukraine with 55 million is now a separate country. Kazakhstan also is a separate country and has 17 million people. While Russia seems to be exotic, it really is not. The flight to Moscow is just a little over 9 hours from New York. It takes the same amount of time as if you drove from Atlanta to Tampa.

Metropolitan Moscow contains about 20 million people, almost 15% of the population. The country is far larger than the United States. Once you leave the major urban areas, the population is quite thin. Both Moscow and St. Petersburg have about two months in the summer when the heat is unbearable. The winters are pretty rough on the other end of the scale. Welcome to Russia.

Notwithstanding the thinly spread population, Russia is an incredible melting pot of people. Generally speaking, pure Russians have a strong Finnish ethnicity. Yet in the central regions there is a strong Tatar mix. In the south and across the Urals, a more Asian background is prevalent. Yet all of this has been mixed together for a thousand years to produce a melting pot like no other. Generally, the Ural Mountains mark the boundary between European Russia to the west and Asian Russia to the east. The official breakdown of ethnicity is Russian 81.5%, Tatar 3.8%, Ukrainian 3%, Chuvash 1.2%, Bashkir 0.9%, Byelorussian 0.8%, Moldavian 0.7%, Other 8.1%.

The recent history of Russia follows a path no fictional book could write. Gorbachev succeeded Chernenko in 1985. In 1988 he began to loosen the reigns on the various Soviet Republics leading to their eventual independence beginning with the Baltic countries. In August 1991 the old timers and hardliners staged a coup. It appeared to be a close run thing at the time although comical afterwards. The coup was defeated when the military refused to participate in a bloodbath of their own people. Yeltsin was the hero of the moment and became President of the Russian Federation. Russia and eleven of the former Soviet Republics joined together to form the Commonwealth of Independent States ("CIS") in 1991. Putin, succeeding Yeltsin, became President in 2000.

Vast forbidden areas, once marked in red on official maps of the Soviet Union, were suddenly open for travel in 1992 when the United States and Russia signed the "Open Lands" agreement which allowed free travel throughout both countries.

Economically Russia is a mess. It had a brief period of prosperity in 1993-4, but has undergone two severe devaluations. The nascent middle class has had its hopes and expectations generated by the short lived economic boom, replaced by a feeling of hopelessness that things will ever get better. The national minimum monthly wage is $22, but each month an additional 10-15 million Russians earn less than that. The average monthly wage is about $60. About 73 percent of Russians grow some or all of their food. Fifty-five percent grow half of the food they eat. Russia imports almost all of its consumer goods. Russia has few exports other than natural resources such as gas, oil and heavy metals. Oil accounts for 40% of Russia's exports. As the commodity markets go, so does Russia's economy.

Yet despite all of the adversity, Russians persevere and are a very warm and generous people.

History of Russian Adoptions

The Russian Ministry of Education and Ministry of Health have jurisdiction over children's homes. The Ministry of Education has more to do with foreign adoptions. While adoptions in Russia began in 1991 with 12 adoptions, it really began to take off in 1992 when the Russian Education Ministry established a separate division that had access to the federal computerized database on children and dealt exclusively with adoption by foreigners. This division was responsible for selecting children for adoption, getting their papers ready, investigating the adoptive parents, and arranging for the children's departures abroad.

At that time, Russian law held that foreigners could only adopt children with documented health problems. As a result, Russian doctors often exaggerated concerns on health reports, knowing that it would mean a chance at a good life for that child. This process was changed with the institution of the "data bank restriction" in 1995, which is nothing more than a period of time within which only Russians can adopt a child. When the exclusive period ends, the child is cleared for international adoption.

The Education Ministry's division no longer exists, and in its place is the current system of adoption agencies in the adoptive country working with facilitators in Russia. Some of the facilitators are actually employees of the adoption agency and the agency may even have an office in Russia. Yet most work through independent facilitators. Facilitators are Russians who have good connections and good will with the federal and regional Ministries and the children's home directors and who shepherd you along through your Russian experience incountry. They will arrange for the driver, translator, and homestay. They will assist you on your travel around Russia whether by plane or train. They will take you to the children's home, work with the home's director and attend the court hearing with you.

Your agency probably began its adoptions in Russia in one of four ways. First, it may be an experienced international adoption agency and Russia is just another country in its long list of countries with which it works. Secondly, it may be an agency founded by people who did missionary work or gave medical help to Russia in the early 1990's and who returned to the States with the idea of helping the children. Thirdly, Russian émigrés may have founded the agency. Finally, the agency may have been founded by persons who have adopted internationally and wanted to start an agency.

Today the United States probably adopts the largest number of Russian children although Italy, France and Germany also adopt from Russia. For example, in St. Petersburg last year, foreigners adopted 529 children. While the majority, 262, went to homes in the United States, many of the children were placed with families in other countries— including 126 in Italy, 36 in France, 34 in Israel and 33 in Finland.

In 1992 the US Embassy in Moscow issued 324 visas to adopted children. In 1993 the figure doubled to 746. In 1994, the number was 1087. In 1995, it jumped to 2178. In late 1995 Russia issued a moratorium on adoptions as it was revising its laws. In 1996 the United States Embassy in Moscow issued 2,454 immigrant visas to adopted children. In 1997, 3,816 visas were issued, in 1998 4,491 and in 1999, 4,348.

Adoption Today

Russia allows adoption when it is in the best interests of the child. They do not like to have sibling groups split up, however, they will allow it when it is best for the children. To adopt a child, who has reached ten years of age, it is necessary to have the child's permission. While there is no law to this effect, the general rule is that parents must be under 55 years of age and there should be no more than 45 years separating the mother and the child's ages. This "unwritten" rule is not strictly applied and is barely a rule at all. Singles of either gender are permitted to adopt although men seem limited to boys only. Regions also have certain "rules." One region does not allow two unrelated children to be adopted within a year of the first adoption. Another region has no limit for couples but won't let a single parent adopt unrelated children at all.

There are very few young sibling sets available for adoption in Russia. Sibling groups under the age of 3 are rare. Most of the available kids are given up at birth by an unwed mother and adopted before the age of 1 1/2. That's usually not time enough for a sibling or, more likely, a half sibling to be born and identified as being related to the first child. Cases where young siblings are available would be where there is a birth of twins, or where parental rights were terminated because of abuse or neglect, or the parents have died. These are a minority of cases. Yet if your heart is on adopting twins, and you are willing to wait, then there is always a chance that twins can become available. Most sibling groups are ages 5 and older. Because of this most people who want to adopt young children, adopt unrelated children.

For unknown reasons, more boys than girls appear to be available for adoption. This does vary by Region, however it generally is true. The wait time for a girl can be longer.

The earliest an infant can be adopted in Russia seems to be around 6 months. Most infants are adopted between 8 months and a year. The difference is in how quickly your agency receives the referral from the Region's inspector and how quickly American families are "paper ready."

For the most part, the children are as healthy as American children are. By this I mean that once brought over to the United States and given proper vitamin enriched foods and love, Russian children respond like any American child. The severe attachment problems that were seen in some of the early Romanian adoptions do exist, but more so in older children than infants. Even with older children, it is only a minority that have these issues.

During the first 7 months of 1999 2,272 children were adopted. It was almost evenly divided between girls and boys with girls holding a slight edge. Couples adopted 89% of the children, single mothers 10%, and single fathers 1%. The largest number were in the 2-year-old range with the 1 and 3 year olds the second largest. After 3 the numbers are in the teens until the 9 year olds when they begin to drop below 10. The last age group is age 13. The total number of adoptions from Russia in 1999 was 4,348.

New Changes in Russian Adoption Law

On March 28, 2000, the President of Russia, Vladimir Putin, signed a series of decrees aimed at tightening control on adoptions. Some of these new regulations have been in the works since 1998 and some are new. Because these rules, as eventually implemented, may change certain practices outlined in the book, I have provided a preliminary review of the changes. The actually effect of these rules awaits their implementation which could vary by region. Ask your agency regarding how these new rules affect their Russian program.

The decrees outlaw the use of "middlemen" but do not define who is considered to be a middleman. This rule was actually discussed some years before, but there was no real consensus on what it really meant and so business went on as before using facilitators or "middlemen." Russian government officials have often alleged that intermediaries facilitate adoptions for foreigners by paying bribes to orphanages and bureaucrats. There has also been a perceived conflict of interest issue with persons who are in charge of the children actually being facilitators. Therefore, adoption agencies can now not employ people who also work for Russian State educational, medical, social service establishments or similar organizations that work with the children. Additionally, employees of Russian State adoption services, their spouses and close relatives are also prohibited from working for foreigners.

A special government commission headed by Education Minister Vladimir Filippov will oversee foreign adoptions and accredit adoption agencies. Once accredited under the new system, adoption agencies will be responsible for reporting back to the Education Ministry about the welfare of the children they have helped place in homes abroad. Since all adoptions must have post-placement reports anyway, this does not appear to be any real change.

The new rules also seem to prohibit sending any medical, video or other background information on any particular child to a prospective parent in the US. This is contrary to the previous practice although similar to how Ukraine and the city of Nizhny Novograd have handled adoptions. Regions appear to be interpreting this rule in different ways. Some regions are allowing this sort of information to be sent to prospective parents as in the past. Others are prohibiting the practice.

The new rules also ask that you register your child with the Russian Embassy upon returning to the States.

The other new requirement appears to be that you may have to make two trips. This is similar to the current procedure in the cities of Nizhny Novgorod and Novosibirsk. However, this does not appear to be an absolute rule, just an option for the regions to adopt. It will likely depend on the region and with 89 regions in Russia, there could be a wide variation. There has also been an indication that even in those regions now requiring two trips, they may go back to just one after the whole accreditation process is completed.

To illustrate how the adoption process varies between regions, some regions have not changed anything and everything is proceeding as before including referrals, videos and medical information. In these regions, one trip is all that is needed. In other regions, adoptions have completely stopped pending the accreditation process. The accreditation process has been under consideration for years as well so it is no surprise that the regulation finally came out. Be sure to check that your agency can meet the accreditation requirements. Even in those regions where there is a two trip requirement, there is variation. One region may send you several children's photographs and brief medical histories while you are in the States. You then travel to the children's home to meet them and choose. In others, you have no information until you arrive at the regional Department of Education.

There are also some new documents to add to your dossier. The first is the Commitment to Register the Child with the Russian Consulate or Embassy upon your return and the second is an agreement to allow your agency to conduct post-placement follow-up. Your agency will also have to make a commitment. These documents seem to be required by all of the regions. Some Regions have asked for others as well. You may also be asked to file a document officially asking for the exact date your child came off the registry. Some Regions also have asked for a medical report on any child that you have in your home and have asked for a document stating that you are proceeding to adopt independently. These documents have to be notarized and apostilled.

The requirement of registering the child may give you pause. However, other countries such as Ukraine have this requirement as well. All it means is that when you return to the States you send the Russian Embassy in Washington, D.C., a registration form with your address on it and the name of your child and their Russian passport. It doesn't change your child's status as your child or even as an American citizen once they obtain citizenship. If you think about it, the Russians already have this information from all of the dossier papers you had to file so this is just duplicative information.

Russia's Children's Homes

The number of children in Russia's orphanages is usually listed at 500,000 (about the same number as are in America's foster care system), but that figure is misleading, as many of these are not eligible for adoption. In Russia there are several types of orphanages for different children. Because most of the children are not real "orphans" in the sense that we use that word in America I will refer to the institutions as "children's homes". The reason they are not real "orphans" is because a great many of the children are placed with the state because the parents or family are simply too poor to support them at that time. This is not necessarily a permanent condition and the child may return to the family later. Also, the mother may have relinquished the child but other family members, like a grandmother, may periodically visit. If a family member shows an interest, then the child is not eligible for adoption at that time.

Some of the children have parents who are in prison and are simply waiting for their parent's term to end. These children are part of the 500,000, yet are obviously not eligible for adoption. Of course others are abandoned, or relinquished without any family visitation or have had their parents' rights terminated because of abuse or neglect. These are the children who are eligible.

The reasons children are relinquished to the children's home are as varied as snowflakes. Yet at the core, economics drives the majority. It is very hard to raise a large family in Russia under the current economic environment and if a surprise fourth or fifth child comes along the best alternative can be to relinquish the child. This is especially true if the woman is a single parent. It also cuts across classes and education levels. You can find birth mothers that are homeless, blue collar or college educated.

Russians consider being raised in a children's home in Russia a stigma. You would not be a happy Russian parent if you learned your son or daughter was marrying one. That label stays with you forever when you are looking for a job, housing, or school.

Sometimes you may find that your child is under some sort of quarantine. The disease season runs from October through March in a children's home. You may have heard the expression, "As fast as a cold through a day care." That is certainly the case in children's homes as well. Russian orphanages use quarantine to help prevent the spread of chicken pox, flu, measles, and other communicable diseases. It is a rather common measure. Sick children are hospitalized when they need more care than is available from the staff. They are often hospitalized for much less serious illnesses, such as bronchitis, than we would hospitalize our kids. The difference is that a parent can provide one on one attention and round the clock care for a sick child, but this is not available in a Russian's children's home.

What follows is a general description of the types of children's homes in urban Russia. You will, of course, find that exceptions exist.

Children from birth to the age of 4 years live in a "dom rebyonka" (house of the child). These homes belong to the (federal) Ministry of

Health (so the director is often a pediatrician). They are normally better equipped and are in a better condition than the other types of homes.

After their fourth birthday the children are evaluated in order to decide where they should continue to live. If the child has no delays or only minor developmental delays, he will go to a home from the educational system. They are called "dyetski dom" (children's house).

For school age children there are two different types of homes: those with an internal school (called "internat") and those without, which means, that the children living there visit external state/public schools. These schools (internal as well as external) could be regular schools or "vospomogatelnye schkoly" ("schools for backward children", or schools for children with learning disabilities).

The children could live there until their 18th birthday. But normally they will change to a PTU ("Prof-Tekh-Uchilishche", vocational school) at the age of about 15 or 16.

Homes for blind, deaf or physically impaired children also belong to the educational system. They are nearly all "internaty". Often the children living in the homes of the educational system are labeled as "umstvenni otstali" (children with learning disabilities).

Children with severe mental handicaps or with multiple handicaps live in homes of the social welfare system from their fourth birthday on. In these homes, called "dyetski dom/internat", the children are living in several different sections, according to their problems. The more problems a child has and the more severe they are, the less help the child gets. These are the homes you may have seen pictured in magazines and on television. There are also homes that have groups of about 15-20 children living in one room. These children are fed (more or less) and cleaned (better or worse), but they do not get any attention, occupation, education and only most basic medical therapy. The situation of these last children is terrible. The more severe the problems of the children are, the younger they die. Normally, no adoptions are allowed from these homes.

What I have described are the basic "types" of homes. Now as to "conditions," it is impossible to generalize about Russia's children's homes simply because there is one or more in every town. You can find good ones and bad ones and everything in between. Sometimes a rural home will be better than an urban one simply because food is more plentiful. Sometimes an urban one is better because it receives more money. Some homes are actually cottages where the children live in family like groups. In others the caregivers have not been paid and are uncaring. You simply can not generalize. No television show, no magazine story or newspaper is able to capture the true picture. You would actually have to visit many of the homes in a particular region to receive a generalized view.

Nevertheless, let me do a little generalizing, knowing that I will be inaccurate. Most of the homes do lack money. They do lack food. They do lack vitamins and medicine. They lack love. Because you might only have four caregivers to 30 children, life is scheduled. The children go to potty at the same time and eat at the same time. They sleep in a dorm or barracks like room. Beds are made up and tidy. The older children help with the younger ones. Their clothing and linen are well worn. The children do not receive as much stimulation as they need. Playground equipment is limited. The caregivers only have time to care for the children's basic needs and little time is left over for stimulation. Some children do not recover from this environment, but many, the "resilient rascals" as they are called, do rebound successfully. I have included in the back, descriptions of a few homes by people who have actually been there. This is for illustrative purposes only and is not intended to describe a typical children's home. There is no such thing.

CHAPTER II

American Paperchase

Begin Your Research

To complete a Russian adoption, parents must fulfill the requirements of their State, the United States Immigration and Naturalization Service and Russia. This may appear to be an endless paperchase and quite overwhelming at first. However, if you break down the process to its component parts, then it becomes just another manageable checklist. The checklist can be divided into three parts: Home study, INS, and Russia. If possible, you will find your stress reduced if you work on the home study and INS contemporaneously before choosing an adoption agency. The reason is that an agency may refer a child to you and you will then have the significant added stress of deciding whether to accept the referral while you are undergoing the paperchase.

But even before all of this you should do some research. Do not just jump in. Understand the process and some of the issues. Thanks to the Internet, there are hundreds of web sites devoted to Russian adoptions. Just type in "Russian adoption" on your search engine and you will be inundated with sites. The INS regulations governing international adoption can be found at 8 CFR 204.3, which can be found at this web site: *http://www.access.gpo.gov/nara/cfr/waisidx_99/8cfr204_99.html* The US Embassy has a good overview at *http://www.usembassy.state.gov /posts/rs1/wwwhci5.html*

Here are some very helpful web sites. This is by no means an exhaustive list. Your first stop might be to *http://eeadopt.org/* It is one of the best sites to visit. Its listserv is exceptional in the amount of information exchanged.

http://www.jcics.org/
http://www.iaradopt.com/toc.shtml
http://www.frua.org/index.html
http://travel.state.gov/adoption_russia.html
http://www.russianadoption.org/
http://adoption.about.com/msub_russia.htm
http://www.geocities.com/PicketFence/1045/adopt_bk.htm
http://www.ftia.org/russia/paperwork.htm
http://www.ftia.org/resources/ins.htm
http://www.rainbowkids.com/
http://www.geocities.com/Heartland/Lane/7410/index.html

http://www.adoptkorea.com/homestud.htm#I-600A (While this is a Korean adoption site, it has a lot of good information about the international process. Just remember that the actual Korean process is different from the Russian.)

http://www.adopt-sense.com/fees&forms.htm is an excellent Ukrainian adoption site and has good information on the American paperchase.

If you need INS forms or information you can retrieve them at http://www.ins.usdoj.gov/

Be aware that the I-600A and I-600 forms are of a particular color, orange and blue respectively. It is better to order those forms from the INS web site,or call them at 1-800-870-3676 or pick them up from an INS office. Your agency should also be able to send them to you. The INS and Visa Units in the various Embassies will now accept downloaded copies of forms on white paper. The INS has a general explanation of the adoption process at *http://www.ins.usdoj.gov/ graphics/howdoi/fororphan.htm*

Dr. Jenista has a good discussion of her view of the Russian adoption process at *http://eeadopt.org/home/jenista_hague.htm*. While her testimony illustrates some of the problems with international adoption, just remember that her conclusion is that "[t]he vast majority of intercountry adoptions have been tremendously successful, building happy "forever" families."

There are also many, many web sites where families tell their stories of adopting from Russia. I recommend reading a few of these just to get a feel for the process. Here is one such web site: *http://www.furman.edu/~treu/sasha/*

Finally, and you probably have already done this, do not fall in love with a picture of a child posted on the web. That child may not be available for adoption or might not be 6 months later when you are ready to travel to Russia. Someone else might adopt that child. It just adds to your stress in addition to all of the paperwork. Of course, it is a great motivator, and many people have adopted children that they first saw posted on the web. Just be careful. Protect your heart.

INS Overview

Whenever you deal with the INS you must remember that although you have paid your taxes, and your family may have come over on the Mayflower, you will not receive any special treatment from the INS just because you are an American. The INS does process the I-600A on an expedited basis, but do not expect them to answer any of your questions. There is no hotline or ombudsman. You will have to wait in line like everyone else.

You truly begin your international adoption journey when you file for pre-approval to adopt with the INS. This is actually pre-approval of the parents since you may not have accepted a child yet. The form is called the I-600A, the Application for Advance Processing of an Orphan Petition. It is orange. It is to be contrasted with the I-600, the Petition to Classify an Orphan as an Immediate Relative, which is the approval of the adopted child for a visa and which is filed at the time of your child's visa request at the US Embassy in Moscow. The I-600 is blue. The filing fee for the I-600A is $460. You will also need to include an additional $50 per person for fingerprinting. This fee is charged for each person living in your house over the age of 18. Therefore, if it is just you and your spouse living in the house, include an extra $50. If you are only adopting one child or a sibling group, then no additional fee is required when you file the I-600 in Moscow, other than the $335 visa fee.

Within four weeks of filing your I-600A, and sooner if you are lucky, you will be notified of where and when to go to be fingerprinted. An "official" INS fingerprint person will take your fingerprints. The INS used to allow you to submit them from your local police department, but no longer. They claim they had too many bad prints. You no longer bring fingerprint cards with you. The INS provides these cards to you when you are fingerprinted. Do not use hand lotion on the day you are fingerprinted as this may cause a problem.

Some offices, such as the Philadelphia INS, now use digital machines that take your fingerprints and send them out upon completion of your prints. No cards are needed.

On the I-600A at line 17 it asks you for the number of children you are adopting. You should put a number greater than you are currently considering. The same goes for your home study. The INS will actually go by the figure in your home study. Even so, both figures should be consistent. The reason for the higher figure is that many times people returning from Russia decide to increase their families by adopting again the following year. By already being approved for the higher number, you may be able to cut out a few steps the next year. Further, sometimes you find out late (as in while you are in Russia) that your child has a sibling that you want or need to adopt. Being already approved for more will certainly make the sibling adoption easier.

A perplexing problem in dealing with the INS can occur when you wish to adopt more than one child and they are unrelated. The rule should be that since the I-600A is for the parents, then only one form and fee is required at the time you file. However, some INS offices require you to file separate I-600As for each child and to pay separate fees. Other offices will only require one fee. Some offices make a distinction between filing one form for siblings versus separate I-600As for unrelated children. Other offices allow only one form if the children are in the same children's home or region. There appears to be little consistency between offices. Just do whatever your INS office tells you. Make sure you receive some sort of receipt or other evidence of having paid the second $460 or else the US Embassy will make you pay it again. Perhaps enclose a stamped return address envelope and ask that a receipt be mailed to you.

Even if you have filed only one form but are adopting two unrelated children, be prepared for the likelihood that you may have to pay an additional $460 for the other child when you obtain their visas at the US Embassy in Moscow. The reason for this is that the I-600 states that only one fee per sibling group is required as that is considered one adoption. However, since an I-600 must be filed for each unrelated child in order that they each obtain a visa, a separate fee logically follows. It really is all a question of whether you pay the fee up front or at the back end. If given a preference, I would go with the back end.

An even more confusing issue appears when you have filed an I-600A requesting approval for the adoption of more than one child but have used the approval to only adopt one. By the way, approvals are generally good for 18 months. Now you want to go back the following year and adopt another. Do you have to go through the whole INS process again? The answer is that it differs in each INS office and in each state. In North Carolina and in most INS offices all you have to do is file a brief amendment updating your home study and as long as the adoption is within the 18 months, you should be fine. However, in states such as Georgia and Florida, you have to do the whole thing all over again, from start to finish. Some INS offices don't make you go through the fingerprint routine since the FBI keeps them on file for 18 months, but then again, other INS offices do. You will find that the INS and FBI barely communicate with one another.

You may file the I-600A and complete the home study later. Your home study agency will then get the state to approve the study and that agency will then file it with the INS.

After the INS has received your I-600A, your home study and your FBI fingerprint clearance, you will, barring some home study agency brain drop or a crime against humanity on your record, receive official United States government approval that you are eligible to adopt a child. That approval arrives in your mailbox on a form known as the I-171H. At the same time, the INS will send a cable to the Moscow Embassy notifying them of this approval. The INS has started a program to replace the I-171H with another form called a 797-C. These are the same so do not worry if you get one versus the other. They are supposedly harder to forge. The Baltimore INS office, which consistently gets the highest ratings for service among adoptive parents, was in the initial pilot program. Like with all government documents, make sure you double check your I-171H for typos.

By the way your I-171H does not actually specify how many children for which you are approved. That information is located in the files at the local service office and at the Embassy which is why you should ask the Embassy to confirm that information when you email or fax the Embassy.

After you receive your I-171H you will need to verify with the US Embassy that they have received a cable (Cable 37) from the INS indicating that you are approved. You can do this through email at: *consulmo@state.gov, consularm1@state.gov, moscowconsularr@state.gov, consularm4@state.gov* or by fax at: 011-7-095-728-5247.If you send a fax or email, be sure to direct it to the "Adoption Unit." The Embassy's phone numbers are: 011-7-095-728-5058 (direct line) or 728-5000 (switchboard ask for ext: 5804). Do not call them except as a last resort and only between noon and 3 p.m. Russian time (4a.m to 7a.m EST). Email and fax are the best methods as you will then receive a paper confirmation, which you should take with you to Russia.

The reason for taking the confirmation with you is that sometimes when your facilitator calls the Embassy to set up the visa appointment, the Embassy can not locate your file. The paper confirmation will help overcome that little problem. After receiving INS approval of your adoption, the Embassy should mail you a several page letter giving some information regarding the Russian adoption experience.

After your experience with your local INS, you may be surprised to learn that the Adoption Unit at the US Embassy in Moscow has been recognized as one of most well run organizations in the United States government. Under Michelle Bond it won the highest award such an organization can receive. Eric Myers who continued the high quality of service later succeeded her. Visa assistant Anna Malkova who is well regarded has recently succeeded him.

Generally speaking, the average time from filing the I-600A to receiving your I-171H is 3 to 4 months. If you have already completed a domestic home study and just need it amended to authorize adopting internationally, then the approval time should be shorter. Of course, delays can crop up. The FBI might lose your fingerprints. The INS might have a stack of applications and the only person handling them in that office gets sick or goes on vacation. Your home study might need corrections or be delayed because of the need for a document like a certified marriage certificate from Scotland. Or you might have to deal with the Gruesome Twosome, two INS offices from hell, San Jose and Denver.

When you receive I-171H notice of approval letter, it should have box #3 checked that "Your advance processing application has been forward to the Embassy at Moscow." Beneath it should be typed "Notice of approval has been cabled to Moscow, Russia." This is done in accordance with your designation of the Embassy at Moscow at question 16 on the I600A petition. So, in other words, if you designated the Embassy at Moscow on the 600A, the cable will go there.

This is how it works, except in Illinois. In Illinois there is an additional bit of red tape. In Illinois, DCFS has to approve all foreign adoptions, and you will receive TWO I-171Hs. The second one is the one with "box 3" checked and it is only after these additional steps that your cable can be sent to Moscow as outlined.

In Illinois the additional steps appear to be that after you accept a referral you need to notify BOTH your home study social worker (through which you got your DCFS Foster Care license) AND Ms. Muriel Shaennan at DCFS in Springfield, IL. Her phone is 217-785-2692. You MUST provide her the following information after you accept a referral: Child's name (Russian and new adoptive name), country of birth, birth date of child.

After reviewing your DCFS file, she will fax INS that they can release your final I-171H. INS will send you a second updated I-171H form with box 3 checked. Then you should e-mail or fax the Moscow Embassy after you get your second I-171H to confirm receipt of your Cable.

INS Offices

The following is a list of some of the INS offices and a description of the kind of experience you can expect. The description is based on how fast you can expect to obtain your 171-H approval and how you are treated. This is not a scientific poll.

Atlanta is rated as being in the middle of the pack. Not very fast, but not bad either. Takes about 4 months for approval of I-600A.

Baltimore is in a class by itself. Terrific office. Takes about 3 months for approval.

Boston has a terrible reputation. Impossible to talk to. Yet, their time for approval is also about 4 months.

Charlotte is pretty good.

Chicago is not bad either. About 3 months. They have a pretty good reputation.

Cincinnati and Cleveland are not far behind Chicago.

Dallas is very fast and gets high marks.

Denver is next to last as giving poor service.

Detroit is getting a bad reputation for being slow.

El Paso is not very fast at all.

Ft. Smith, Ark. office is rude to people.

Jacksonville seems to be giving Baltimore a run for its money and is an outstanding office.

Los Angeles is not very good. The wait for your fingerprint date is long.

Louisville is very quick.

Memphis is pretty good. Rated higher than Atlanta. Their phone numbers are 901-344-2300 and 901-544-0264. Memphis will fingerprint you the day you turn in your I-600A if you ask.

Michigan is in the middle of the pack at about 4 months.

New Jersey is in the middle. By the way the NJ INS adoption unit phone number, is 973-645-6309. Like all INS offices they receive lots of calls from people that have no idea what they are doing so they may be rather gruff sometimes, but you will get your questions answered. Call between 2-4 PM.

New York gets pretty high marks.

New Orleans is not bad.

North Carolina will not talk to you under any circumstances.

Philadelphia was good.

Portland, Or. is dreadful. Almost dead last.

Oklahoma has poor customer service.

San Antonio has problems.

San Diego is also poor.

San Jose is dead last.

Seattle and St. Louis are pretty good.

Washington, DC is poor.

The INS field offices all have their own peculiar procedures. One reason that there is no uniformity is because the INS does not have any standard manuals outlining the current law on immigration. They claim they will have them by 2002.

For example, Denver does not like personal checks, but will only accept money orders and certified checks. They also want in the home study the size of the child's room in your home and the distance to the nearest bathroom.

Atlanta, on the other hand, will take personal checks and doesn't care about bathrooms. It will take the downloaded white form.

Baltimore will accept a copy of the I-600A downloaded onto white paper. They don't care that it is not salmon colored (orange) They will not accept a personal check but prefer separate money orders for the $460 fee and for the $50 fingerprint fee.

The DC office in Arlington VA accepts the downloaded version with one personal check including the fee and fingerprints. This office got good marks.

In the Jacksonville, Florida office they do accept the form on downloaded white paper, but they don't accept personal checks. You can combine the form fee and fingerprint fees on one money order.

One tip when dealing with the INS. If you have to go to an actual office, go as early in the morning as you can. If the doors open at 8 am, then get there no later than 7:30am. The line will grow exponentially.

I-600A Instructions

Several documents must be included with your I-600A form. You need to include proof of US citizenship and the best example is to copy the photo pages from your passport. This can be black and white copies, not color. You will need a passport to travel so you might as well use the one you have or obtain one. (This is a good time to check on whether your passport needs to be updated.) The passport must be unexpired and valid for five years. If you do not have a passport you can submit a copy of your birth certificate. If married, also submit a copy of your marriage certificate. If divorced, then they need a copy of the final decree. If the home study is not ready, explain in a cover letter that it will be provided at a later date. The $460 fee and $50 per person fingerprint fee can each be paid by regular check. (Write separate checks for these fees.) Indeed, this will give you a receipt that it was paid. You can pay by certified check, but that will not really speed the process along, as the INS must still wait for your home study and FBI fingerprint check before issuing the I-171H.

These document copies do not have to be certified, however, you will need to obtain certified copies of your birth and marriage certificates for your dossier and home study, so if you have an extra one, just send it with your I-600A. If you are adopting a second time, also include a copy of your previous I-171H. This will show them that you were approved before so they don't have to do any real checking on you. You should put in your cover letter that "Copies of documents submitted are exact photocopies of unaltered documents and I understand that I may be required to submit original documents to an Immigration or Consular officer at a later date." Sign, print your name and date it.

The form may say that the filing fee is $140. Ignore this. It is an old form. The correct filing fee is $ 460 plus fingerprinting fee. Filling out the I-600A is not difficult and should only take a few minutes.

If married, then one of you becomes the petitioner. Don't fight over it! Make sure the petitioner is a US citizen. Questions 1-9 are self-explanatory. As to question 10, regarding the name of your agency. You may not know at the time of filing the I-600A in which case just put "unknown at this time, will supplement." You can also leave it blank and just include in your cover letter that you will supplement this information later.

One result of the I-600A is a determination by the INS as to whether your child will be issued an IR3 or an IR4 visa upon entering the United States. An IR3 visa means that both parents traveled over to Russia and saw the child before the actual Court hearing. An IR4 means that only one parent saw the child and that readoption in the United States is necessary before the child can be eligible for citizenship. So the I-600A asks you at question 11 whether both parents are traveling. This will be confirmed by INS at the time that you visit the US Embassy in Moscow. The law now in Russia is that both parents must travel to adopt. In the early 1990's this was not the case, but it is now. Thus questions 11 and 12 on the I-600A should be answered in the affirmative, 14, in the negative and 15 in the affirmative. The answer to question 16 is "Moscow, Russia."

On question 13, just put down " unknown" for all three parts. You can also just take a guess at the month and year and the city in Russia you intend to visit. The INS does not hold you to these dates.

As to question 17, always put down one more than you expect and make sure you are consistent with your home study.

Always express mail the package to the INS so you can have a trace receipt of its having gotten there. You must submit it to the office that serves your location. If you live in a large urban city this is easy to determine. Otherwise ask your home study agency or your adoption agency to which office it should be submitted. This information is also located on the INS' web site.

Put on the envelope, " ATTN: I- 600A/Orphan Petition Section"

I-600

The I-600 is the "Petition to Classify Orphan as an Immediate Relative" a/k/a the blue form. You file this form with the US Embassy in Moscow when you are over there in order to obtain your child's visa. The same petitioner on the I-600A should be the petitioner on the I-600. Both parents must sign. You will need to file one for each child you are adopting. Some fill out the form before leaving the States and then fill in those blanks for which they did not have the information once they are in Russia. Others wait to complete the form in Russia. Bring an extra blank form in case you need to make a change.

Because you both had to travel to adopt the child and the child is now with you in Moscow, the form is easy to fill out. Questions 1-9 are the same as on the I-600A. You should ask your adoption agency regarding the answers to questions 16 and 17. Question 17 b and c should be answered with "no." Question 18 should be "yes" to both parts, as Russia requires both parents to travel.

Here are some other suggested answers. Question 20 should be "no" unless there is something obvious. The answer to question 21 is you, and to 22 and 23 none. Question 24 is your US address. Question 25 is Moscow. Ignore the second 25 and for 26 give your name. The answer to question 28 is Moscow, Russia.

The Embassy likes you to sign the I-600 in front of a Consular officer when you visit the Embassy for your child's visa. Do not notarize it in the States. Only notarize the I-864 in the States.

I-864

The INS began to require immigrants to file Form I-864, called the Affidavit of Support, beginning in 1997 in order to comply with the new federal law making it more difficult to bring immigrants into the United States. There is no exception for Americans adopting children overseas unless your child will be receiving an IR - 3 visa from the US. Most children from Eastern Europe receive the IR - 3, but not all. If your child will be receiving an IR - 4 visa, then you have to file this form. The difference is that an IR - 3 means that both parents saw the child before the Court hearing. By signing the Affidavit of Support a sponsor (parent) is agreeing to repay the federal government for any means-tested benefits paid to your child. Your obligation ends as soon as your child becomes a citizen. You can get the form from the INS website or call 800-870-3676. To qualify as a sponsor, you must be at least 18 years old and a U.S. citizen or a legal permanent resident. The sponsor must have a domicile in the United States or a territory or possession of the United States. The form is not difficult to fill out. Where it asks for the name of your child, use the name she will have after the adoption.

Form I-864, Affidavit of Support, should be completed and notarized before you travel. I would sign shortly before you travel, although the signature is good for 6 months. Gather copies of your last three years of filed personal federal tax returns, including schedules. Your state return is not involved, only your 1040. If you have not yet filed for the previous year, then bring the 3 years before that. If you have filed for an extension, you will need to bring a copy of that with that year's W-2s, in addition to the previous 3 years of filed returns. Make copies of all of this. The tax returns do not need to be notarized, just the signed Form. Notarize it before you leave for Russia. Apostilling is not necessary, as this is a document for the US Embassy Visa Unit, not for any Russian official. If you can't find your last three years of tax returns, you can call the IRS at 1-800-829-1040. They will likely give you a one page summary transcript of your tax return or a letter called a 1722. Both of these are acceptable to the Embassy. They take about 10 days to get and are free. If you filed electronically, then just print out the return and sign it. The I-864 serves as verification to the INS that you will be able to support your adopted child by demonstrating that your income is at least 125% of poverty guidelines. As an example, 125% of the poverty guidelines for 2000, except for Alaska and Hawaii, would require a family of four to have income of $21,312. You can find the most recent poverty guidelines at *http://www.ins.usdoj.gov/graphics/howdoi/affsupp.htm#poverty*

Be sure to bring along a notarized verification of your employment and salary. If you are basing your Affidavit on documents other than tax returns, make sure you take those. Pack all of this in your carryon, not your checked luggage.

If you rely on the income of your spouse in order to reach the minimum income requirement, your spouse must complete and sign a Form I-864A; *Contract Between Sponsor and Household Member*. If the spouse did not file jointly, but separately, then that separate tax return must also be attached to the sponsor's Affidavit along with the spouse's employment verification. If you are not using the income of your spouse, but filed a joint return, then you must include your W-2s to prove that your income alone qualifies you. The W-2s are not necessary if you filed jointly and are using both incomes to qualify. However, I would take them along if you have them, just in case. The 1722 is a substitute for your tax return so the rules regarding W-2s are the same. If you are missing your W-2s, ask your employer. By law they have to keep them for a few years. When filing the documentation with the US Embassy in Moscow, place the I-864 on top, followed by the sponsor's tax returns, evidence of employment, and then evidence of assets, if these are used to qualify.

If you are adopting more than one child, then you will need to file a second notarized I-864 accompanied by another (non-notarized) copy of your tax returns.

For information and forms see
http://www.ins.usdoj.gov/graphics/formsfee/forms/i-864.htm
or *http://www.ins.usdoj.gov/graphics/howdoi/affsupp.htm*

FBI and Fingerprints

After you have your fingerprints taken by the INS, they will travel to the INS Service Center in Nebraska. Then they will be sent to the FBI's fingerprint office in West Virginia. Once the fingerprints are logged in with the FBI, it takes them a very short time to actually run a check. Some offices are using digital fingerprinting which theoretically should speed up the process. I believe this is the case in New York. After the FBI has processed your prints they send the results back to Nebraska which sends them back to your local INS office.

The U.S. Immigration office in Lincoln, Nebraska is a regional processing office and does not deal directly with the public. They have two public phone numbers: (402) 323-7830 and (402) 437-5218.

Approximately 2 weeks after the fingerprint appointment, you can call the FBI and ask them to check whether the fingerprints have gone through. To check on your fingerprint status, phone the FBI Liaison Unit at 304-625-5590, then push 4 on the menu. Hours are from 7pm to 11pm EST. You could also try (304) 347-5769. Be aware that INS phone numbers change frequently. Voice mail is available from 7am to 11pm EST. It is easier to get through later in the evening. They are now scanning in all fingerprints they receive on cards to make searches faster.

Just tell the liaison the date and city in which you had your fingerprints done and ask if he can give you a status. If they have been approved, then you can ask him to fax a copy of the approval to your INS office. It's most helpful if you can give him your INS assigned application number so he can put that on the fax.. I believe this is called a LIN number. You can also call your local congressman's office and ask to speak to his INS liaison. His liaison can do some checking for you on your status.

Usually the FBI enters the status on Fridays. Thus, a whole week may go by before an updated status is available. Also, sometimes the FBI will tell you they can't locate your fingerprints and the next day you will receive INS approval. There is a certain amount of randomness in this process that defies understanding.

Sometimes fingerprints are rejected because your finger swirls are too light or they have damage from rough work or some other reason. One suggestion is NOT to use any hand lotion the day you are fingerprinted and if possible wash your hands right before being printed.

If they are rejected twice, the INS is likely to ask you to go to your local police and obtain a record check and a letter saying you have no record. Now most home studies require this anyway. You then give this letter to the INS. If you've lived in more than one place over the last 5 years, you'll need a letter from each jurisdiction. Just send a written request, the proper check, and a copy of your driver's license or passport for ID.

Home Study

A home study is a document created by a social worker giving a snap-shot summary of your life. This summary is based on interviews with you and from documents you provide. A home study is required by your state, the INS and Russia, so there is no getting around it. It should take about two months to complete. It must be submitted to the INS within one year from when you filed the I-600A and must not be more than 6 months old at the time of submission. The home study should be 20% screening and 80% education. Sometimes it may feel that it is the reverse. There are very few absolutes in this world, but if you can have your adoption agency also write your home study, then you should have few problems. One of the most time consuming aspects of adoption is completing the home study. If you have completed a domestic home study then all you have to do is pay a little more money and get an addendum saying you are approved for international adoption. Unlike international adoption agencies, a home study agency usually must be licensed by your state. There are some states that allow independent social workers to conduct these studies, however, you need to check with your state if this is allowed before hiring one.

When hiring a home study agency, make sure that the agency and the social worker have some experience with international adoptions. If they don't, then don't hire them. Also make sure that their state license will not need an extension any time soon. The Russians do not like expired licenses. The home study agency should tell you the cost up front; approximately how long it will take, how many visits and if the price includes post placement visits or if they are extra. They should have a working relationship with the INS and know who to talk with there. If you have a first meeting with the social worker and she makes offensive comments or you are not comfortable with her, just fire her and hire another home study agency. It's completely your decision. Your goal is just to get the document and move on. The cost is generally $1200+, but it can be less. In Utah it can cost as low as $400 and in California, as high as $2,200. Do shop around.

Home studies by independent social workers are not acceptable in all regions in Russia. Some regions want the home study on agency letterhead. In addition, there are statements of sponsorship and commitment to post placement reporting that they require come from a licensed homestudy agency. Generally, Russian home studies must be completed by a licensed social worker. The homestudy must be on agency letterhead and signed by the Executive Director (not the placement supervisor or any other person) and the agency's license must accompany the homestudy.

Russians do not really want to know about your extended family and their troubles. They do not really want to read about your entire emotional life story. They do not care about your relationship with your mother, father, brother, or Uncle. Nor do they care about the trauma caused when your childhood dog "Skippy" was run over by a submarine. So why are you asked these sorts of questions? It is certainly invasive. Just remember that it is up to you how much information you want to give beyond the basics. No one forces you to tell your entire life story. It is entirely up to you how much information you wish to disclose. The home study is just another document to check off on your list of things to do.

Now the INS in their regulations at 8 CFR 204.3 (e) requires some of these questions. The Service requires at least one personal interview of the couple and one home visit. They want the home study preparer to check your physical, mental, and emotional health. They want an assessment of your finances and whether you have a history of sexual or child abuse, substance abuse or domestic violence. You will need to disclose any history of arrest or conviction. They want a detailed description of your house or apartment. The home study must include the specific number of children you may adopt. If you are adopting a special needs child, then the home study must include a discussion about your preparation, ability and willingness to properly care for the child. Your state may also require some of the questions asked by the social worker.

A good social worker can be of great help to you. She can ask questions that relate to parenting and cause you to think things through. For example, questions dealing with disciplining your child. You and your spouse may have generally talked about it, but this question can focus you on the issue. A good social worker, who may have adopted internationally, can be a great asset.

The social worker may ask about lead paint, fire extinguishers, guns, fire alarms, child proof locks, prescription medicines, insecticides, cleaners, pets, and other potential hazards in the home. She will ask where the child will sleep and want to see the room. If you live in an older home, she may ask about updated electricity and plumbing. All of these questions are not necessarily bad questions to ask. These questions may have little to do with adopting a child, but they have a lot to do with creating a safe environment in which to parent the child.

After the home study is completed, the home study agency will obtain your state's seal of approval. Then it will be sent on to the INS by your home study agency. This is generally how it works. No doubt there are exceptions. Do not be afraid to call your home study agency and follow up as to when the study was sent to the INS. Your social worker should allow you to see a copy before she sends it, in order for you to review it for minor errors like names, birth dates and matching the number of children with the figure placed on your I-600A. You should also receive a final copy of the home study once it is signed, sealed and delivered. If the home study agency does not agree to give you a final copy, don't hire them. The reason your state must give approval to the home study is that the INS is not allowed to issue a visa to your child unless you meet state pre-adoption requirements.

Make sure you put in your home study that you wish to adopt one child more than you really mean too. As previously mentioned, it is very common for a family to adopt one child then go back the next year to adopt a second. By already having the approval in your home study for more children, you may be able to shorten the process. If you find your child has a sibling and you need to increase the number of children then have your home study amended and write a letter to the INS amending your answer to line 17. Also, make sure you add a year to your expected child's age. For example, if you want to adopt a child under 2, then put 3. The reason is that during the process of adopting that 2 1/2-year-old, he may turn 3. Thus, having some cushion on the age will mean you do not have to amend the home study and the INS approval. This has no bearing on how specific you actually tell your adoption agency. The social worker will likely want the following documents from you so begin collecting them:

1. Certified copy of your marriage license and birth certificate

2. Copy of the deed to your house or apartment lease

3. Copy of your passport and copy of your latest tax return or W-2.

4. A fingerprint clearance letter from your State or County

5. Medical form to be filled out by your doctor

6. Criminal record clearance letter

7. Some States require a child abuse clearance letter

8. Letters from friends saying that you will make great parents.

In the event you have been arrested in the past, the INS may send you a "J" letter asking you to submit original or certified copies of any court dispositions and proof of completion of court requirements. The INS is now looking for any criminal record, no matter how small. There is no logic to it. They may also ask you to supply an affidavit explaining the situation and any extenuating circumstances. If documents are not available, the INS will want the police station or court to sign a letter stating that no records exist. If you know an arrest is going to turn up, you might as well begin to collect these documents and submit them with your home study.

CHAPTER III

Russian Paperchase

Russian Adoption Law

Russians are much more organized about adoptions than the United States. All children who are eligible for adoption are placed on the Federal Ministry of Education's Central Data Bank also known as the registry. While the child is on the registry, only Russian families may adopt the child. However, once the child is listed for the required amount of time and comes off the registry, then the regional education department will ask Moscow for permission to allow a foreigner to adopt. Notwithstanding, a Russian family always has priority over a foreign one up to the time of the actual court hearing.

According to Article 126 of the Family Code of the Russian Federation, Regional Ministry officials enter data into the federal database by electronic mail or use the "Atlas" network. The child's biographical form must contain the following:

* Date of filling out the form by the children's home
* Date of entering the above data into the regional database
* Data on each of the parents and the date of issue of the document serving as the basis for placement (death certificate; parents' consent to adoption; court decision on the deprivation of parental rights, court decision stating the parents are unknown, incapable etc., certificate #24 on the absence of father)
* Data on all brothers and sisters (including half-brothers and half-sisters), with their place of residence, if possible

The original photo (or its electronic copy) of the child, taken at the time of filling out the form should be attached to the biographical form. Prior to allowing a foreign adoption, the Regional Ministry of Education must describe the efforts that were made to place the child with Russian Federation families.

Under the old laws children were only listed on the registry for 3 months and after that foreigners could adopt the child. However, in 1998 the Federal Minister of Education issued a regulation that any child who was put on the registry after July 1, 1998 must be on the registry for 4 months instead of 3. The actual timeline is 1 month for the local database, 1 month for the regional database and 3 months on the national or federal database. This law can be found in Article 122 of the Family Code of the Russian Federation.

Commonly though the local and regional database is the same so that is why it is normally just 4 months. Your agency will know whether your child is off the database and the child's status.

In addition to this change there was a change in the "abandonment" provision. A child whose mother (and father if married) have signed "relinquishment papers" will only have to wait the 4 months time on the registry before being eligible for foreign adoption. However, if no "relinquishment papers" have been signed then Russian law concerning "abandonment" says that the child must be abandoned for 6 months before adoption can be considered. In order to be deemed "abandoned", 6 months must pass from the time of the court order making the child a ward of the state without any family member appealing the decision. This is not actually the same as being on the database. An appeal period of 6 months is also the same amount of time in cases where parents' rights are "terminated" through court action because of problems with the home situation. Fortunately, this 6 months time can run concurrently with the listing on the database. At the end of 6 months the child will have the legal status of "orphan" as required by the United States for the child to be issued an immigrant visa by the US Embassy.

To summarize the registry timeline, a child must be on the registry for 4 months regardless. If the child is going under the designation of "abandoned" or " parental rights terminated" then a concurrent appeal period of 6 months must also pass.

The Regional ("Oblast") inspector for the Protection of Children's Rights is in charge of receiving and processing adoption applications. She works within the regional Ministry of Education. If your agency has a good relationship with her then she will allow your agency to work with a children's home. If your agency has a good relationship with the children's home director, then she will allow your agency to place some of "her" children. Once the child has cleared the federal data bank and your dossier documents collected, the inspector will send the application to the central federal office at the Ministry of Education in Moscow for final approval. She will send a formal letter asking that the child be removed from the Federal Data Bank and naming you as the adoptive parents. The Federal Ministry of Education will then reply with a formal letter (federal clearance letter) stating that the child has been on the registry for the required time and is now available for adoption by the named adoptive parents. After all of this, a court date can be set.

In addition to these other changes in the law that occurred in 1998, the law also required Regional Courts, rather than District or City Courts, to hear adoption cases. Back in 1992 when Russian adoptions were really first started the process was very informal and the "hearing" was nothing more than an administrative proceeding without any court involvement. Since the natural order of bureaucracy (no matter what country) is to make things more complicated without adding value, the process has progressed from administrative to a city or district court and now all the way to the regional appellate courts. The regional courts have always been where serious criminal matters were heard. Therefore, imagine the regional judges' surprise in 1998 when they found out they were to also hear adoption cases. It was a whole new area of law and there has been a learning curve.

Each Region has slightly different documents and adoption procedures that they require. Indeed, some calculate the necessary time a child must stay on the national data bank differently than others. Some regions will waive the 10-day period of appeal and some won't. There are even slight differences depending on which regional judge is responsible for your case.

One interesting aspect of Russian law is that if the father is not married to the child's mother, he has no rights towards the child. No marriage equals no parental rights. When this is the case, a "Form 4" is issued by local ZAGS (the bureau of vital statistics) which confirms the absence of marriage and thus absence of a legal father.

The Form 4 can also indicate that the mother simply gave the name of a man as the father and that she really does not know. Since she was not married to the man (whoever he was), he has no rights as father unless he establishes those rights in court.

Apostilles

The United States is a signatory to the Hague Convention on legalization of foreign public documents. By this Convention, the Russians will accept as authentic, documents that have been "apostilled."

Apostilles are state certifications by your state's Secretary of State that your notary is properly licensed. States vary as to how much they charge for apostilles. It can range from $3 per apostille (Georgia and Massachusetts) to $15 for Pennsylvania to $25 for New Jersey. In Michigan it is a $1, Ohio $5,California $27 and Indiana free. Make sure you call first in case these fees have changed. It is recommended that you use the same notary as much as possible as that will eliminate the State's need to look up different notary's licenses. California has a website that describes its procedure at *http://www.ss.ca.gov/business/notary/notary_authentication.htm*

Here is a sample of some states' addresses and fees:

VIRGINIA:
Secretary of the Commonwealth
Capitol Square
Old Finance Building
Richmond, VA 23219
Tel 804-786-2441
$10 per apostille

NEW YORK:
(New York City)

Department of State
Certification Unit
123 William Street, 19th Floor
New York, New York 10038

Hours: 9:00 a.m. to 3:30 p.m.
Phone #: (212) 417-5684
The closest subway station is Fulton on the green line.
$10 per apostille

Note that in New York State, after you have your signature notarized, the county in which he is registered as a notary must certify the notary's signature. It is only after completing that process that you then go to the Secretary of State for the Apostilles. The cost for certification of the notary's signature is $3.00 per document. When having all of this done, make sure that all of the seals are raised. Do not remove an apostille to make copies and then try to re-staple.

NEW JERSEY
State of New Jersey
Business Services Bureau—Notary Division
225 West State Street, 3rd Floor
Trenton, NJ 08608-1001
Main #: 609-292-9292

Or
State of New Jersey—Dept of Treasury
Business Services Bureau—Notary Division
PO Box 452
Trenton, NJ 08625
Ph:609-633-8258 or 609-633-8257

For New Jersey the fees are: $ 25—regular, $ 35—expedited. For expedited service, you must deliver your package by hand or use a commercial carrier like FedEx. You can't use USPS Express Mail because they don't deliver to the West State Street address. Because New Jersey has some of the highest fees in the country, there has been pressure placed on the New Jersey Legislature by adoptive parents to reduce the fee considerably. This effort should be supported. Also, it can be worth it to travel to another state, even if you have to fly, and have most of the documents notarized and apostilled in that lower cost state.

A recommendation is that you express mail your document with a return prepaid express and indicate your name, address, phone number. In your cover letter you should tell them that it is for an adoption in Russia. One way to avoid high fees is to take your documents to a nearby state that has lower fees and have them notarized and apostilled. This does not apply to state specific documents such as a birth certificate or marriage certificate. If you get into difficulty with apostilling a document, ask your agency if you can simply get a copy of the document, type that it is a correct copy on a cover page, staple the two together and have your cover page notarized and apostilled where you live. Only if you get into a real jam should you try this for official documents like marriage licenses and birth certificates. Another method of cutting costs is to determine if the region in Russia from which you are adopting will allow bundling of documents. Some will. If it does, then you must see if your Secretary of State will allow bundling. Some do not. Bundling will allow you to use just one apostille for a whole set of documents. There is a website with all of the addresses of the offices of vital records in all 50 states at *http://www.asststork.com/pages/myvitalrec.html*

A trick with state specific documents that are not located near you is to ask the clerk to send the certified document on to the state's Secretary of States' office to be apostilled. This will save time. In order to do this you need to enclose a stamped pre-addressed envelope to the state and then a second one that the state can use to send the document back to you. You will need to include all fees of course and the usual cover letters. Sometimes the state's Bureau of Vital Statistics will simply send you an apostilled version for an additional fee. South Carolina is one such state. In some states, like Georgia, the apostille process has been delegated to another office rather than the State's Secretary of State.

Like everything in life, always call ahead to make sure of the correct procedure and fee. And always double-check your notary before and after she signs the documents. Make sure the expiration of her license shown on her stamp is at least a year away. Make sure she signs using the exact name on her seal and stamp. No abbreviations are allowed.

A good tip is to open your own FedEx account. It only takes a few minutes and does not cost anything. You can do this over the phone or if you live close enough to a FedEx branch you can also do this in person. This allows the return express mail to be billed to your account, saving much time.

Dossier

What is a dossier? It is all your paperwork that you have gathered in the States. It is your home study, your birth certificate, marriage certificate, form for this, and form for that. It is all of those documents, notarized and apostilled. Your agency compiles all of this into your "dossier" and has it translated. It is sent to Russia and reviewed by the local and regional Ministry of Education departments. If the child is under 4 years of age, the Ministry of Health also must approve it. Also, the baby home director must give approval. Once approved by the Ministries it can then be submitted to the Court and the Court is under a timeline to schedule a court date. The Ministry departments may delay the process by its employees going on vacation, getting sick, or not making it a priority. They are also overworked and underpaid.

This is also true with the courts. While your agency can not control the timing of the Ministries' approval, in some Regions they may have a little more control over the setting of the Court date. Even so, a good working relationship between your agency's people and the Ministry officials can be of great importance in speeding the process along.

The dossier will likely contain some of the following documents accompanied by a certified Russian translation:

1. Your home study

2. Copy of marriage license

3. Copy of birth certificate (a quick way to get a certified copy of your birth certificate is through vitalchek at *http://www.vitalchek.com*

4. Medical report on the parents

5. Employer verification of employment

6. Proof of home ownership or proof of housing. Some Regions are happy with just a copy of your deed or lease with a notary stamp on a cover sheet saying, "this is a true and correct copy" and then an apostille. Other Regions also want a notarized and apostilled copy of your tax bill. You can get copies of anything at the county courthouse and then just have a notary on a cover sheet.

7. The facilitator should provide the Ministries with a form letter from the US Embassy stating that if the correct documents are submitted then a visa will be issued to the child. This form letter has no form number, but is on the computers at the Embassy.

8. Your I-171-H form from the INS

9. Copy of your Homestudy Agency's license

10. A post-placement agreement letter

11. Copy of your State's law on adoption

12. Some Regions ask for a letter from your pediatrician stating that he will be the child's doctor and the date of the first visit.

These documents have to be notarized and apostilled. Usually the notary statement above the notary's signature should say, " This is a true and correct copy of the original" or some variation of that. You should ask your adoption agency if there is any particular wording that they like. Of course, official documents such as birth certificates and marriage certificates will already be certified and will just need the apostille.

For some regions of Russia, a copy of the I-171H must be part of your dossier and must be apostilled. To do this, you make a copy of the 171-H and put the statement on the bottom or the back of the copy (but not on a separate page): "This is a true and accurate copy of an original." You take this copy to the notary public and have them witness YOUR signature and have it notarized. The state is then able to apostille this notary signature. If you live in New York State, you first have to have the county clerk's office verify the notary's signature and then the state will apostille the county clerk personnel's signature, and it becomes part of your dossier.

In addition, the local child welfare representatives will provide to the Court:

1. Evidence that the child was registered for the requisite amount of time on the data bank and that no Russian family has shown an interest in adopting the child. They also have to show that no family member has shown an interest as well.

2. A statement that the adoption is in the child's best interest.

3. Child's birth certificate

4. Medical report on the child

5. If child is over 10 year of age, his consent.

6. Consent of the children's home director

If you were born overseas as a United States citizen, then you can either get someone over there to obtain your certified birth certificate or you can order a certified copy of your Certification of Report of Birth (Form DS-1350) from: Correspondence Branch, Passport Services, Department of State, 1111-19th St. NW, Suite 510, Washington, DC 20522-1705. Phone number is 202-955-0308. Call them first to determine the correct procedure and fee.

If born in the United States, your birth certificate is likely located at some division or bureau of vital statistics that may be connected to the Department of Health of your birth state. They will send you a certified and apostilled birth certificate upon payment of the usual fee.

Photos for your dossier should not be just mug shots of your home or you with a zip code taped across your chest. Relax! They should reflect your lifestyle and your community. For example, you could show pictures of you at work, on vacation, doing something with friends or at church. You can include pictures of relatives even if they don't live nearby. Include the room the child will occupy even though not completed. You can include photos of your area, such as a park, recreation center, or elementary school. You can include your pets. A photo can show you doing something you enjoy, such as gardening, playing sports, or a musical instrument. Russians are not impressed with how many cars you have or how wealthy you are. They are more interested in seeing that their children will grow up in a supportive and educational environment.

Health Form

Generally, regions in Russia require a health form on each spouse to be filled out by a doctor. This is a different form than the one your home study agency wants. Most people go to their usual GP or to a doctor that is a family friend. A specialist is not normally required. The form usually needs to be notarized which can be a slight problem if the doctor does not have a notary in her office. You can either hope the doctor's office has a notary, or take a notary with you or have a notary sign after the fact, if they will do so. The health forms vary according to the region. Therefore, you should not anticipate the tests or medical review that might be required until you have signed with an agency as that agency is likely to work in only one or two regions and have the required form. Another reason not to have the medical review completed before signing with an agency is that some regions require the review within 6 months of the adoption, and therefore you may find yourself repeating the process if you do it too soon.

Don't expect your doctor or your doctor's staff to have a clue about filling out these forms. Make sure they understand that if the question is on the form, then that means your agency wants a test result or a definitive answer like "no." The words "Not tested" are not enough. You may want to fill out as much of the form as you can before giving it to the staff or have the doctor fill it out in front of you."

Usually the form requires a blood test for syphilis, HIV, and HEP. It might ask if you have TB. It also will likely have a line for the doctor to sign to the effect that she knows of no health reason that would interfere with your ability to raise a child.

The form is usually just one or two pages and is very simple. It does not ask for everything that might be wrong or that every blood test in the world be taken.

Some insurance companies might not pay for the exam or tests. If you have doubts, you might check beforehand. Alternatives that might be cheaper could be your county health clinic.

Some regions in Russia now require that the form not be any older than 3 months prior to the submission of your dossier. Other regions allow for 6 months. Because of this short timeline, you may find yourself having to go back to your doctor. Ask your agency, but sometimes simply a notarized cover sheet stating that nothing has changed will be all that is necessary. You could write up something for your doctor to type on his letterhead stating that the information documented on the physical/medical forms are still complete and accurate and that nothing has changed in your medical condition to preclude you from being parents to adopted children.

Holidays

Holidays can interfere with the process of having your dossier approved and setting up a court date and since the Moscow Embassy is closed on American holidays it can even delay the visa appointment at the Embassy. Knowing when these holidays occur can help your planning. Also, Russians, like most Europeans take a month off during the summer to vacation. Each Judge is different so you are likely to find a certain slow down occurring in obtaining court dates during the summer months. This can particularly happen in August and can extend into September. Keep this in mind if your agency tells you there is a delay in late summer. No doubt this will be the reason. Typically August is THE popular month for vacations. This is true all across Europe. Government employees in Russia get at least 5 weeks (not counting weekends) of paid vacation each year and there is a liberal holiday schedule also. Many regions have no court that month at all. You must also factor in that the U.S. Embassy's Immigrant Visa Unit is also closed on the last Monday of every month.

Listed below are the official American and Russian holidays for 2000. The days will be slightly different for 2002. Here is a web site listing all of the holidays: *http://www.usia.gov/posts/moscow.html*

January 1 Friday R/US New Year's Day	January 2 Saturday R New Year's	January 7 Friday R Orthodox Christmas	January 17 Monday US Birthday of Martin Luther King
February 21 Monday US Presidents' Day	March 8 Wednesday R International Women's Day	May 1 Monday R International Labor Day	May 2 Tuesday R Spring Day
May 9 Tuesday R Victory Day	May 29 Monday US Memorial Day	June 12 Monday R Independence Day	July 4 Tuesday US Independence Day
September 4 Monday US Labor Day	October 9 Monday US Columbus Day	Nov. 7 Friday R Revolution Day	Nov. 10(11) Friday US Veterans Day
Nov. 23 Thursday US Thanksgiving Day	Dec. 12 Tuesday R Constitution Day	Dec. 25 Friday US Christmas Day	

CHAPTER IV

The Agency Referral

Agencies

You should interview Russian adoption agencies just like interviewing for a pediatrician or a home study agency. Although you may feel intimidated, remember that they work for you. Your agency should give you references of families who have adopted and who have agreed to be references. They should (but not all do) include some families that have not had a great experience. All agencies, no matter how wonderful, will have situations that did not turn out where everyone is happy. It may have been just one of those things, or something beyond the agency's control, or the agency may have dropped the ball. But you are entitled to hear it all before making your choice. After all, this is your life and family you are talking about. Remember that you should never have to pay an agency anything but a small registration fee before reviewing their contract and set of program fees.

Most agencies have web sites where you can find a lot of information about their various programs. Here are two web sites with a list of agencies that work in Russia: *http://www.russianadoption.org/adoption_agency_list.htm* and *http://www.eeadopt.org/home/services/agency/agencies_list.htm*

One issue that is usually not very important is your geographic location to the agency. Phone, fax, mail, and e-mail work fine. Your agency does not have to be in your state for you to use them. Of course, if you feel more comfortable with actually seeing their offices and people then by all means make that a consideration. Another issue that is not too important is the actual size of the agency. A larger agency will likely have a permanent staff in Russia and everything over there will go like clockwork. However, the size of the agency has no bearing on how fast your American INS paperwork is processed and no bearing on the ultimate outcome of bringing a loving child into your family. You might think that a bigger agency means more referrals and it does; yet it also means more clients for those referrals. In the end, size of the agency's Russian operation is just not that important. Now the longer an agency has worked in Russia then the more established should be its organization and track record.

You can always do some general searches for information on an agency that you are investigating. You can search using paid services like Lexis/Nexis, *www.knowx.com* or Westlaw. These may be available at your local library.

Some questions you might ask:

1. Does the agency have an 800 number? You don't want to pay for your calls.

2. Will the agency allow you to call the children's home and speak to the doctors? This is very important since then you can get the information and answers direct. The interpretation of the answers is why you have your medical expert on the line.

3. Will the agency tell you how many other "customers" they have? You want to know where you will be in the "line" and how many children are they currently referring. This will help you figure out how long you will have to wait.

4. Will the agency give you a referral before your entire dossier is completed? This can be both good and bad. Good, because it shortens the process, but bad because it adds to your emotional stress and strain. (Of course, this assumes that the region in which your agency works allows pre-adoption information to be transmitted.)

5. What regions does the agency work with and how do these regions apply the 10-day waiver request. You would like to avoid the 10-day appeal period if you could.

6. Will the agency help you with the paperwork, or do they expect you to do it all?

7. How knowledgeable is the office staff? How long have they been with the agency? Can the person who will be assigned to your case answer questions about Russia, or do you have to wait until they get back to you?

8. When was their last Russian adoption? (If it was more than 2 months ago, then you have to wonder how well run is their program.)

9. How many referrals have been "lost"? Ask the reference families regarding the agency's "lost referral" experience. If an agency has Russian contacts that are close to the children's home director and the Ministry, there should be few "lost" referrals.

10. Do their Russian facilitators work with other US agencies or agencies in other countries? The more a facilitator works with multiple agencies, the higher the risk that your child is the subject of multiple referrals and that you could lose the child to another family. How long have they worked with this facilitator? Any problems?

11. Does the agency refer children when they are coming off the registry or that still have a way to go? You want an agency to refer children who are close to coming off the registry or are off. If they were just placed on the registry, then you run a higher risk of having the child, if an infant, adopted by a Russian family.

12. Does the agency refer mostly infants, toddlers or older children? You may find that an agency refers more from an age group other than the one in which you are interested. What is the average wait time for a boy, girl, infant? Don't let them put you off on this question. They may give the answer with a lot of caveats, but at least you will have an idea. Of course, this is also a question to ask their references.

13. Does the agency always provide a video of the child?

14. They should also give you a good explanation for where your money goes.

15. How long, and in what detail will the videotape be of the prospective child?

16. What medical records and family history will I receive?

17. Who pays for the translations?

18. Does the children's home have any objection to a doctor visiting and examining the child? Sometimes Dr. Downing, and there may be others, are able to visit a children's home if not too far from Moscow and conduct an examination of the child. It depends really on the children's home director. After all, it is her home.

19. What are the exact costs and what do the payments go to for the adoption?

20. If you give me a referral, and I do not accept, when will I receive the next referral? In other words, do I lose my place in line?

21. How many successful adoptions has your agency performed in the past year? In the age group that I am interested in?

22. If there is a facilitating agency or individual in Russia with whom you work, how long have you worked with him/her? The longer the agency has worked with a facilitator the better. You want someone who is reliable.

23. Where will I stay while in (adoption city) and in Moscow?

24. Will I travel with a group or will we travel by ourselves?

25. What support will I receive while in Moscow?, a guide and driver?,

26. What if I decide not to continue with your agency, for whatever reason, what will it cost me?

27. Who obtains the visa invitation and the visa itself?

28. Does the facilitator live in the same city as the children's home? If the agency works in Siberia, yet the facilitator lives in Moscow, and travels back and forth, then when you have a question or seek further information on a child, it may take longer to receive that information if they live thousands of miles away. Now a lot of facilitators have email access so that if they regularly travel to the outlying region they can just email you from there.

29. Does the agency require your health insurance company to sign a letter stating they will cover the adopted child? Some agencies and Regions, but not all by any means, require such a letter. If you have an individual policy versus a group policy, obtaining this letter may prove difficult.

30. In the Region in which this agency works, do you have to make two trips? (Once to meet the child in person and the second to attend court.) What support from the agency's translator/facilitator will you have at the Regional Department of Education and children's home? Who will help you file the request for a court date and for the Federal Registry clearance letter (databank release letter)? What medical review can you have i.e. photos, questioning of the home doctor, translation of medical records? How long will you have to visit and observe the child and make your decision?

31. Does the agency have rules about how long you have to be married, or the age of the child you can adopt, or do they restrict you from choosing the gender? Some agencies have such rules, most do not.

Ask about the wait from the time you submit a dossier until the time you should be receiving referrals or told to travel for your first trip. This time will vary depending on the region and the agency. But it will also vary depending on whether you are asking for a boy or girl, infant or older. Some agencies are more aggressive in tracking down birth mothers to get final signatures or fill in blanks left off of original relinquishment paperwork. Some agencies also seem quicker to get translations of documents and dossier approval by local adoption officials. Then ask the agency about the time to expect to wait for a court date after you have accepted a referral or after meeting the child on the first trip. This will vary by region and by agency, too.

Some of these questions may not matter to you. You must decide which questions are important **to you**. Other questions to ask can be found at this web site: *http://www.adopting.org/choosagn.html*

Things that some agencies do that are positive are telling clients beforehand what kind of post-placement support services they offer, telling clients that the agency will call them when they are settled in and for the client to definitely call if they have any post-adoption questions. Good agencies send information on re-adoption, applying for citizenship, and requirements for post-placement reports. For examples of bad agency behavior see Dr. Jenista's testimony at *http://eeadopt.org/home/adoptmed_hague.htm*.

As an example of how parents can differ on what is important is that some parents feel that a good agency is one that does not provide a referral until their dossier is in and deemed complete (or at least very close to being complete.) This is deemed important, as they do not want to lose a referral because the dossier is not ready. Another important factor for some parents is that they not receive a referral of a child who is not already cleared through the registry. This eliminates some of the chance for a lost referral. At the same time, other parents have no problem with having their dossier incomplete before a referral or receiving a referral, which is not yet off the registry.

Since most agencies only work in certain regions of Russia, you should find out if the regions they work in require one trip to Russia or two. One way to reduce the risk of an unpleasant surprise is to pick an agency with a track record of placing a lot of children through the specific court that you will go through. If the judge, the prosecutor, the representative of the Ministry of Education, and the social worker are comfortable working with your agency and trust the information the agency provides about you, then you probably won't have a problem. When you are picking an agency, ask how many children they have placed with the courts in the region where your referral will come from. Ask how many have been denied and why. When you are checking the agency's family references, ask how their court appearance went.

The cost of adopting varies with each agency. However, the general rule of thumb is that the adoption should cost between $12,000 and $20,000, not including an additional $4000 for traveling and staying in Russia. There should be a reduced fee for adopting a special needs child.

Adopting siblings or two children at the same time should cost you more than one, but should not be double. Adopting from Moscow may be a little more expensive than from the outlying regions.

You will eventually wonder where all the money goes that you pay. That is not an easy question. It is particularly hard since the Russian government does not really charge anything for adoptions. Some of the money goes to an agency's overhead such as office expenses, salaries, large bills for express mail to Russia, international phone calls (unless they are using email, which most are), travel expenses, advertising, licensing, insurance, and translations. The agency will also make a donation to the children's home and may pay to have Russian Ministry personnel and Judges visit the United States and see how the children are doing.

The agency pays the Russian facilitator a significant part of the funds. The facilitator is the one that maintains the relationship with the Ministry of Education, Ministry of Health, and children's home direc-tor. He files your dossier and follows the paper trail in Russia. He sets up the court date and guides you through your journey in Russia, chil-dren's home visit, and Court appearance. He answers all your questions when you are in Russia and is responsible for you.

The fee paid to the agency does not cover your out of pocket expenses while in Russia. The better agencies will give you an estimated but itemized list of expenses. You will pay all of your travel expenses including homestay visit and hotel. You will pay for your driver. Your facilitator may have another person working with him in Moscow or in the Region. You will pay for that. You will pay for a translator.

Your agency will help you with some of the paperwork (although the apostille legwork is more often than not on you) and serves as a liaison with the facilitator in Russia. It retrieves the photographs and video-tapes from Russia and sends them to you. You are responsible for hav-ing a medical review of the video and dealing with the INS.

Now in the "old days" of Russian adoptions, fees were much, much lower. It then became a victim of its own success. As more and more agencies and facilitators decided to place children from Russia, fees started to rise. There were those agencies/facilitators who went into a city and promised large amounts of money to be able to work with the homes and facilitate adoption. This caused all the other agencies working in that city to raise their fees, too, or else be unable to place children from there. So fees have gone up and up over the years. But this is not an uncommon economic spiral in many countries involved with foreign adoption and Russia is certainly not unique in this respect.

There are also exceptions. Some agencies have such good relationships that they can still work in a city even though they are not matching the higher priced agency. Indeed, in some places, if an unknown facilitator offers large amounts of cash so they can work there, officials become fearful and refuse to work with them. The general rule, if there is one, is that fees vary by region and agencies do have some flexibility depending on special needs, age of the child, or if you are adopting several children.

You may wonder if you really need an agency or if you can adopt independently. You could adopt independently if you were confident about your own ability to handle all the paperwork on the American side, and if you had a reliable Russian speaking facilitator or attorney in Russia. You must have someone in Russia who works with the Ministries and children's home director and who will translate and file your paperwork. This person must be reliable, honest and knowledgeable. It is the difficulty of finding such a person on your own which is the agency's real service to you. And no matter what stories you may have heard, there are some very good agencies out there. Final advice is to know what risks you are willing to assume and which you are not. Do not be afraid to speak candidly with your agency. The better they know you, the better they can match your referral request.

Reference Families

When interviewing reference families for an adoption agency you should ask them some of the same questions asked of the agency. This way you can compare answers. Be sure to inquire as to the year they adopted since significant procedural changes developed in 2000. Some other questions are as follows:

1. Does the agency have good contacts in Russia? Find out everything you can about an agency's contacts in Russia. Was the process in Russia smooth and quick? Any hitches? Were they able to overcome any obstacles? Do they help you through the entire adoption process? What are the arrangements for housing and travel while you are in Russia?

2. How long did the agency give you to decide on a referral?

3. What is the health and developmental condition of the children placed (with the families you talk with)? Be specific as to which children's home and age of child.

4. If a family was uncomfortable with a referral, was the agency cooperative in finding another child within a reasonable amount of time or did they try to pressure you?

5. Did the process work as the agency said it would?

6. Was the agency supportive and helpful during the process?

7. Were you informed, in advance, of all the costs involved in the adoption, including travel and incidentals?

8. What is the agency's policy about returning a portion of what you paid if the adoption doesn't work out? For example, if Russia closes or has a moratorium, you withdraw; the agency encounters problems, etc.

9. Did the agency seem to be familiar to the children's home director and other officials? (If the agency has hosted the local Judge and the director in the United States, then you can assume that they have a good working relationship.)

10. When they asked questions of the children's home director or doctor did the translator give them a verbatim translation or just a few words? Some facilitators/translators have a tendency to think they know what is best for you and will give you only the information they believe is necessary. While it may turn out that you did not need the other information, there is a trust issue involved and it should be explored with the reference families.

11. Did the family think the agency was more an advocate for the child rather than your family? A few agencies are such advocates for these children (whether for humanitarian or monetary reasons) that they forget that it is really your family's well being that comes first. This issue should be explored with the reference families.

12. What services do the adoption agency offer after the adoption? A lot of agencies feel that once you return, you are on your own. While post-adoption services are not necessary for the majority of adoptions, if you run into an issue, it would nice to know what help is available from your agency.

Referrals

The Russian law on adoptions is currently undergoing some changes. Therefore, this chapter on how the referral process works and the chapters on the video and medical review may no longer be relevant in those regions which now require the two trip process. However, because some regions continue to allow the prior procedure, and also because Kazakhstan still allows referrals, the discussion is still relevant. Also, after the Russian accreditation of American agencies is completed this year (2000), it is very possible that Russia will return to the referral process.

After choosing an agency and giving them your paperwork and your money, you then must wait for a referral of a child. Good agencies will refer you a child that is within the parameters you have set. They will also give you some time in which to decide and should not rush you. By the same token, this child is waiting for a "forever" family and a family is possibly waiting for this child, so time is of the essence.

You may wonder how an agency receives permission to refer a child. Each Region operates differently. However, if an agency has been working in an area for several years then it probably has built up relationships with the children's home director and Ministry officials. It may give a lot of humanitarian aid, or sponsor officials on trips to the United States to see how the children are doing. It may also have a great track record of adoptions so that a positive spiral is in place and they obtain more and more referrals. Some agencies work by contract with the region or state government's officials in the Health Department and the Education Department. The Health Department is over the baby hospitals and baby homes and the Education Department is over the children's homes, preschool homes, and internats (boarding schools). The agency will be assigned babies and children each month who then make the referral to their clients. A child may initially be represented by Agency A, and later be transferred by the state government to Agency B, if "A" cannot find adoptive parents in a reasonable amount of time.

A baby could be as young as 4 months old, but by the time a family considers and accepts a referral, and receives a court date, the baby is likely to be 6 months or older at time of placement. Some agencies work through a Russian facilitator who maintains the necessary contacts with the government, obtains referrals and then refers them to the agency with which he works.

The children's home director's permission to adopt is one of the required court documents. While it is a function of the state government to decide who adopts which child, the home director has some input.

The referral comes by way of a phone call from the agency saying that a video and medical summary of the child is on its way to you. They will describe the child over the phone. The video that you receive will only be a few minutes long and the medical summary will probably not be very detailed. However, if you decide to pursue this child, you should be able to get additional videos and additional medical information. The Russians do not give you much information unless you ask. But when you ask, they do seem willing to answer most medical questions that you have. Be persistent. If something doesn't sound quite right, then try to obtain the actual medical report on which the agency is basing its English translation. Sometimes when you have it translated you find other things on it.

A referral can be lost even though you have accepted the referral and accepted the child in your heart. It is a very difficult thing to have happen. Losing a referral is not a common occurrence and happens mostly with very young infants. The most common reason is that a Russian family has chosen to adopt the child. Usually this happens only in large metropolitan areas. Russian families have priority up to the date of the court hearing.

Your feelings after losing a referral are probably analogous to a miscarrriage with the loss of dreams and attachment to a child whose only manifestation might have been a short video and a photo. However, it is a loss nevertheless, and it takes the wind out of you. It takes time to regroup and feel "normal" again. Adoption is difficult, and full of hurdles, and most people who have not had anything to do with this process are totally oblivious to your pain because it's not a type that they know anything about.

In the past adoption was rarely considered by Russian families. It was frowned upon. Russians went to great lengths to hide the adoption.

They would change the birth date and birthplace of the child. That is now changing a little. Certain regions are experimenting with foster care and adoption incentives.

Other reasons for a lost referral might be where a regional judge suspends all adoptions temporarily due to problems with other adoptions. Also, a child's grandmother or other family member might visit the child, in which case the child is no longer eligible for adoption at that time. Some Courts will require that older siblings or other related family members approve of the foreign adoption and this can cause an adoption to fail. This is rare and your agency should know if this is a requirement in your region. Also, some facilitators or children's home directors might allow the child to be referred to more than one agency at a time. You might then be told that a Russian family adopted the child when the fact is that it was a family from another agency. This is unlikely to happen in the two trip process.

Families also turn down referrals. It may be the child has issues that the family does not think it can handle successfully. These issues may be medical for which the family has no insurance coverage or simply the family is not in position to deal with certain issues. Your agency should not try to pressure you. It is your decision and your marriage and your family. Instead, the agency should try to obtain another referral. Quite often what is a medical problem to one family is perfectly acceptable to another. Indeed, it is the unknown that causes the most fear.

Some families turn down a referral because they decide they want to adopt a girl rather than a boy or vice versa. Or perhaps they started out adopting two and instead decided on just one. Or the referral is of an older child or a sibling group and they want a younger child or not as many children. There are many reasons for turning down a referral that may have nothing to do with the child.

You really need to look at your family and decide what you can handle. If you are a young couple with no children, then maybe adopting a child under 3 is best. If you are a couple with 3 teenagers (let's say 13, 15 and 17), then an older child could work for you. Families wanting an older child who already have a 10 month old, 3 year old and a five year old, need to stop and think some more. Older children take a lot of work initially (new language to learn, educational delays, learning to live in a family, etc.). Dealing with all of this will take a lot of your time and energy away from your other children. You must choose the right child for your family and be realistic about what you want. Your first priority is your existing family and not an image of a child you saw on the Web late one night. There is no shame in admitting that you do not have the resources to deal with a particular issue or that you are not the right family for a specific child. Not every family is right for every child. If because of your personal schedule or personal health issues you will not be able to give the necessary attention to a certain special needs child, admit it without guilt, and choose a child that will be a better fit.

You may wonder if you have been given all the information that there is. Russian privacy laws prohibit sharing every single note in a child's full medical report the instant some adoptive family shows an interest. That doesn't happen in the United States either. If the child was a preemie, then he probably has a rather full report at the children's hospital. Just remember that this report is in Russian, is handwritten, there are no copy machines, and the children's home does not have a copy. The children's home doctor will have a summary of medical information and from that he prepares a summary and releases it to the state government, which is then released to the agency or the facilitator, who shares it with the family. The agency does not have unlimited access to the child's records or to visit the child. To visit, photograph, or videotape the child requires permission from the state government and the home director. The fact is, you will never know everything about your child's history. You just have to do as much research as you can, and then take that leap of faith. But it should be faith based on the knowledge that comes out of doing your homework first.

At some point you will have all the medical information and all the medical expert reviews you can obtain. There will come a time when you must decide whether to accept this child or not. You will still have doubts. You will not have answers to all of your questions. You will have plenty of facts about this child but not the answer to the ultimate question of "what should I do?" Yet, it is time to either take that "leap of faith" or decide against. Only you can make that decision. Just remember that when a child is born to you it comes with both good and bad. As a parent you just accept them and love them. Make the same conscious choice in your adoption and make the best of this wonderful gift of this child that you will care for and love.

In order to read the medical summary you will need to have a metric conversion table handy. To convert kilograms to pounds, multiply by 2.2:

2.8 kg x 2.2 lb/ = 6.16 lb

If the weight is in grams, convert it first to kg by moving the decimal point: 2800 gm = 2.8 kg

Length will be given in centimeters. Some conversions are as follows:
30 cm =11.81 inches
35 cm = 13.7
40 cm =15.7
50 cm =19.7
70 cm =27.5

The actual formula is to multiply the cm figure by 0.3937. Therefore 45 cm would be equal to: 45 x 0.3937 = 17.7 inches

Video

A video is important to a medical evaluation. If you read the one or two page medical form it will have the usual scary Russian medical terms on it which can be difficult for a non-international pediatrician to understand. However, any pediatrician can understand a video. Just remember that because of the video's limitations, you should use the video as just another piece of information to be placed along side all the others and not as the sole determinant. Most of the following discussion pertains to infant videos.

You should ask the agency for the approximate dates of the videos. It is important in order to evaluate the child's development. Indeed do not hesitate to ask for another video prior to accepting the referral. The videos are not very long which can make them difficult to evaluate. Further, a lot of infants are wrapped to keep them warm, so that when they are shown unclothed on the video they really are not use to moving around and may just lie there. If the child is an infant, you will want to see the child unclothed if possible. This way you can see all the fingers, toes, hands, arms and legs. Here are some of the things to look for:

How does the child respond to people in the room? Usually the child's primary caregiver will be in the room. It will be interesting if the child responds to the caregiver only. While this indicates attachment, which is good, you may need to follow up because it is even better if the child also responds to other caregivers.

Does the child move and bend her arms and legs in a normal fashion? Normal movement can indicate that cerebral palsy is not a concern. You might look to see if the muscle mass and fat on the arms and legs is approximately equal and symmetrical indicating the baby is equally coordinated and developed on both sides. Also, when the baby moves, is there any expression of discomfort?

Do her eyes follow the camera or some other toy? This indicates responsiveness and is a slight indication of the condition of her eyes. Does she track sound in the room?

Does she roll over, sit up, play with toys and move them from hand to hand? These are milestones to look for. Does she show emotions? Even crying is a good sign.

One caveat with videos is that a lot of times when you return with the child and look at the video at home, the child and the video just do not match up. The reason is that to produce the Russian video the child may have been woken from her nap and suddenly thrust into a situation with bright lights and strangers touching her and moving her around. This is likely to produce a withdrawn response and the child is simply scared and not sure of what is going on. The bright lights and attention from all these people can confuse a child. It may have been taken around mealtime, which might change how a child reacts. Sometimes the children are fed prior to their taping session because the caregivers do not want the children to cry or appear unhappy. They feel that this is not appealing to prospective adoptive parents. So that if the child seems slow, it could just be a result of the usual slowdown that occurs from eating. Also, her hair may seem sparse and red on the tape. This is from poor nutrition and will change dramatically once you have brought her home.

Also, caretakers love to offer different toys to the child. These might be toys that they take off the shelves of a large wall unit and you wonder if the kids ever get to play with them or if they are just decorations. They like to repeatedly offer toys, and not even give the child enough time to do much with the item. Another common theme in referral videos is that the child is often not verbalizing. Yet, once the camera is put away he won't quit talking. The difference is that when the video is taken the child is out of his normal environment. Often there are no other kids in the room and there are extra adults—strangers, with strange equipment. It's intimidating to be the center of attention like that.

A funny thing that could happen is that you might hear Russian being spoken in the background of the tape. You might get curious as to what is being said and have the tape translated. Don't be surprised if you find that all that is being discussed by the caretakers is their boyfriends! I have also heard of a parent whose occupational therapist looked at the tape and thought there might be a problem with the baby's tongue because he kept sticking it out during the video. When the tape was translated, the parent found that the reason the baby kept sticking his tongue out was because the caretakers were telling him in Russian to do it!!!

Sometimes the child may seem to have an ear that sticks out somewhat. The usual condition ranges from a slightly protuberant ear on one side to protuberance combined with elongation in the vertical axis and actual thinning of the ear. While you should certainly ask the medical experts about this condition, generally it is not a congenital condition, but develops in the maternity home prior to orphanage admission from infants always being positioned on the same side in their cribs. Incidence in some regions is very high, almost one in three.

Medical Review

Listed below are some of the medical specialists available to provide pre-adoption and post-adoption assessments to adoptive parents and children. This is by no means an exhaustive list. The procedure is that you mail a copy of the video (if you have one) and the medical report to the physician, and after she reviews the material, you speak with the doctor by phone. The doctor will likely call you within a few days of receiving the video and probably in the evening or at night. You should have a list of questions prepared ahead of time so the maximum amount of information is exchanged. You may wish to ask the doctor if you can record the conversation in case a spouse is unavailable or you want to keep better record of what was said. These doctors all have jobs, families and receive many videos a week, so take that into account if you pressure them to expedite a review.

Generally if you request the review of pre-adoptive medicals and videos, you should include a donation. The figure of $100 or $200 is customary, but always inquire as to the suggested donation amount. The information you receive is far more valuable.

Dr. Jerri Ann Jenista, M.D.
551 Second Street
Ann Arbor, Michigan 48103
Phone: 734-668-0419
Fax: 734-668-9492
Web site: *http://www.comeunity.com/adoption/health/jenista.html*
She is the editor of Adoption Medical News and has a long history in the international adoption medical field.

International Adoption Clinic
University of Minnesota
Dr. Dana Johnson, M.D.
420 Delaware Street SE
Minneapolis, Minnesota 55455
Phone: 612-626-2928; Fax (612) 624-8176
Donation: $150

Dr. Andrew Adesman, M.D.
Schneider Children's Hospital
Division of Developmental and Behavioral Pediatrics
269-01 76th Ave.
New Hyde Park, N.Y. 11040
Phone: 718-470-4000 Fax: 718-343-3578

Dr. Julia Bledsoe, M.D.
Pediatric Care Center
University of Washington, Roosevelt Site
4245 Roosevelt Way N.E.
Seattle, WA 98105
Phone: 206-598-3000, 3006 Fax: 206-598-3040

International Adoption Clinic
The Floating Hospital for Children at New England Medical Center
Dr. Laurie Miller, M.D.
750 Washington Street Box 286
Boston, Massachusetts 02111
Phone: 617-636-8121 Fax: 617-636-8388

Dr. Jane Ellen Aronson
Chief, Pediatric Infectious Diseases
Director, International Adoption Medical Consultation Services
200 Old Country Road—Suite 440,
Mineola, NY 11501
Phone: 516-663-4417 or 516-663-3727

Dr. Aronson can also be reached at:
151 East 62nd Street Suite 1A
New York, New York 10021
212-727-0627
orphandocutor@aol.com

The Rainbow Center for International Child Health
Adoption Health Service
11100 Euclid Avenue, Mail Stop 6038
Cleveland, OH 44106-6038

Contact: Adele, Center Coordinator
Phone: 216-844-3224

Dr. Eric Downing
Moscow, Russia
http://www.russianadoption.org or http://209.79.114.199
tel (7) (095) 799 3452 or (7) (095) 262 4079
Fax (212) 214 0873
($100 donation. Up to $650 plus expenses to visit a child)

Dr. Ira Chasnoff
Chicago, Illinois
Tel: 312-362-1940

Alla Gordina, MD
Global Pediatrics
International Adoption Medical Support Services
Tel 732-432-7777; Fax 732-432-9030
http://www.geocities.com/globalpediatrics

If you adopt in St. Petersburg and Moscow, some agencies offer the service of having your child undergo Western style medical testing at the American Medical Clinic or Filatov before you travel. Not all children's homes allow it and not all agencies offer the service. There is an additional fee involved. Also, Dr. Downing is a Canadian doctor in Moscow. If allowed by the Region, he will travel to the children's home and evaluate your prospective child.

You should try to read an article written by Dr. Jenista on "Russian Children and Medical Records" published in the July/August 1997 edition of "Adoption Medical News." It is very helpful. The phone number for back issues is 407-724-0815. It should also be in your local medical school library. Another informative article is in the November 1995 issue of "Adopted Child." Call 202-882-1794 for back issues. You should definitely read Dr. Downing's web site on medical terminology. Also, this web site has some very helpful information on what a specialist looks for in a video and in the records. *http://members.aol.com/jaron-mink/russvid.htm*

Dr. Jenista was interviewed regarding international adoption on a radio program on January 12, 2000. I strongly recommend that you listen to this program. You can access this interview by going to:

http://www.whyy.org/91FM/index.html

Then click on "Radio Times" and "Radio Times schedules", set the date to January 12, and then click on "Go get it!" Go to "Hour Two", and click on "Listen to this show".

. In general, the older the child, the easier it is for an expert to identify potential problems. Also, doctors are going to err on the side of caution since they are not able to examine the child or run any tests so expect cautious optimism at best. I would also talk to other parents who have adopted children of the same age as the referral and also from the same children's home. Do not discount other parents' experiences.

Finally, there are lots of things you and the doctors cannot see such as learning disabilities, developmental delays, speech delays, sensory integration issues, and so on. I remember a doctor who said that premature children from an institution will always have to pay some price. By that she meant that in school the child will likely be delayed in an area, you just do not know which one. Look around your neighborhood though, there are plenty of children who are physically healthy and are wonderful kids, but who have one or more of the above issues. Many of the conditions are ones you cannot see for years.

When you begin this adoption journey you have to ask yourself, "Am I prepared to deal with the unknown?" This is a question that most biological parents do not have the chance to ponder, it is just thrust upon them. Just because a child has rickets, or a cleft palate, or some other "identifiable" physical ailment doesn't mean that this child will be more of a health risk than that supposedly perfectly healthy child who comes home and has attachment issues.

Finally, there is a limit to the information that any doctor can give you, based upon a child's health records and a few pictures. You can only be prepared up to a certain point. You can guide your agency about what you think you are capable of handling, study all the medical information, read all the books, but in the end you must accept that there are no guarantees in life nor in international adoption. Sometimes, you just have to follow your intuition and your heart. A doctor's opinion is good thing to have, but it is you in the end that must make the decision.

Children's Home Medical Questions

In 1992, when Russian adoptions began, medical information barely existed. The adoptive parents may have had only a single photograph and no more than a one-page summary of medical information. The normal leap of faith that exists with any adoption was more like a long jump. By 1996 the process had become more organized. The standard (until the recent year 2000 changes) was that you received a video of the referral, plus some still shots and some medical information. Some agencies only gave you the one page medical summary and left it to you to follow up with questions to which they tried to discover the answers.

The better practice was for the agency not to wait for your obvious questions but to give you as much of the medical history as possible and to anticipate your questions. Some agencies try to fend off medical inquiries by saying that it was difficult to obtain information from the Region, children's home or facilitator. Yet, some facilitators have access to email and can give you the phone number of the children's home. You can then set up a three way phone call with your medical specialist and a translator and call the children's home doctor yourself. This is not too difficult. Both MCI and AT&T will provide a translator if you can not find one. It is very helpful to make the call to Russia with a medical professional on the line, preferably one that has dealt with international children.

Here are some of the questions that you might ask if you are able to call. They are also good ones to ask if you under the two trip process and meeting your child for the first time. You can also use these if calling Kazakhstan.

1. Current information: current head circumference, height, weight; developmental milestones appropriate for the child's age, rolling over, sitting, crawling (what can the child do); You really want to get a range of measurements over time in order to gauge the velocity of growth. Don't accept just one set of measurements taken at just one point in time.

2. Emotional development of the child (attachment evidence);

3. History of illnesses, fevers, hospitalization, surgery, etc., and outcomes.

4. What do you know about his birth parents? Their medical history and medical history of siblings. Any history of alcohol use by the birth mother? How many pregnancies?

5. What was the prenatal history (less relevant for older children)

6. Why was the child put in the orphanage?

7. Does the child have a favorite caretaker?

8. Does your child have any special friends?

9. What are the child's likes and dislikes?

10. What seems to comfort the child?

11. What kinds of foods will he eat?

12. What is the routine at the orphanage?

13. What is the child's ethnic background?

14. Does the child smile or laugh?

15. What should I know in caring for this child?

16. How is he doing health wise?

17. What do they know about the birth mother? age? number of pregnancies? Physical description? Birth father information?

18. What are the lab results for HIV, HEP, and syphilis?

19. How does the doctor think he compares to other babies his age at the orphanage?

20. Child's Apgar scores and at what minute intervals?

21. What inoculations has the child had?

22. How many children are in the home, in his sleep area, how many caregivers?

23. What toys does he play with?

24. Does he use a spoon or bottle?

25. Does he use both hands?

26. Does he pass a toy from hand to hand?

27. Will he be able to go to a normal school?

28. What is his age of development?

29. Results of any eye examination and hearing exam?

30. Result of any ultrasound of the brain?

31. What antibiotics has he been given? (Certain ones given to pre-emies may cause deafness)

32. What future help might this child need based on the doctor's experience, i.e. physical therapy, speech or developmental help?

33. Does the child have floppy muscles or stiffened limbs?

34. Has the child had any convulsions? If there is a notation in the medical record of the child being given barbiturates, you will want to know what these are for and if they are related to a seizure condition?

35. Is there anything else the doctor would like to add about the baby or give advice about? How does this child compare with other children the doctor has seen?

36. What does the orphanage need us to bring? clothes? shoes? Medicine toys?

The number of pregnancies and age of the birth mother is just one indicator of the sort of lifestyle the birth mother might lead. The older the woman and the higher the number of pregnancies then you can extrapolate that the birth mother had a lifestyle of frequent sex partners with its associative risks, possibly higher risk of alcohol, with malnutrition and poor prenatal care. Remember though that it is only an indicator and nothing more.

Older Children

Adopting older children is a great experience. Older children bring their culture, their language, and their history with them. They are interesting and fun right out of the box. Their medical reports are probably more accurate than an infants, simply because most symptoms will already have appeared and be present. The psychological issues are a little more risky. With an infant, the risk is reversed. Like everything else, you need to do your research and talk to parents who have adopted older children. If you are older, it may be that parenting an older child is better. You don't have to go through the whole diaper and baby experience, but can jump right in with children who will interact with you. You also don't have to wait 18 years until they go off the college to reclaim your life!

Some keys to assessing older children is to find out how long they have been in the children's home, did they ever live with a family, and are they attached to a particular caretaker now. These questions relate to attachment. You need to find out about siblings and where they are located. Siblings who are attached to each other are more likely to be able to attach to their new family. A good predictor of being able to attach to someone new is being attached to someone already. In addition, siblings give each other a lot of comfort and support. These are just a couple of the good reasons to consider adopting siblings if you want more than one child. Find out as much as you can about their life before she was placed in the children's home. Also, talk to other parents who have adopted older children. You will find out more from them than from any book.

If you discover that parental rights were terminated, push your facilitator and the regional officials to discover the real reasons. You may not be able to do this until you are in Russia and even so they may not open the records to you, but finding out the reasons for the termination of rights can greatly help in any post-adoptive therapy that the child may undergo. This is one reason why waiving the 10 days may not actually be a good idea with an older child. During those 10 days you will likely be able to observe your child as he really is.

Some older children may have sensory integration issues such as Central Auditory Processing Disorder. This may arise if they spent several years in the institution. This can take a toll as they may be deprived of the stimulation that comes from normal nurturing and loving. You may have to help him reclaim his right to parental love. There are professional language programs such as Fast Forward or Earobics that are available. Then there are those older children that will suffer no ill effects from institutionalization. It may be that they were in a family for awhile and had normal attachment experiences. They may not have been in the institution for very long or were a favorite of a caretaker. If you do accept a referral of an older child, send him a photo album of his forever family, future friends and pets. This will allow him to become accustom to his new life while you both wait for a court date and will give him a reason to believe that a new and happier life is just around the corner.

Older children (and younger ones as well) are likely to have siblings in other children's homes. Press your agency to discover if there are other siblings and if they are close. They may be in different homes, but travel to see each other. Adopting siblings, who are close, gives you and the children a great head start and an advantage in integrating them into your family.

There are many questions that surround adopting older children. Indeed, by the time you wade through all of the medical and family advice, you are guaranteed to be thoroughly confused. Just remember that there are plenty of stories of very happy older child adoptions. Good stories are just not news. Still, being prepared through education is the best medicine, even if painful. Gain the knowledge, file it away, and hope you never have to use it. There is an older child support list on EEadopt called PEP.

One of the risks adoptive parents take when adopting a child that comes from a background of abuse is that the child will perpetuate the abuse. Thus younger siblings may be at risk. This is one reason that when an older child is placed, it may be better for her to become the youngest in an established family. The other reason is that an oldest child has a firm sense of identity, based on birth order, and it is often traumatic to him to be displaced. Sometimes families with several children adopt a child who becomes the 3rd or successive number because the youngest children aren't affected as much by having one more older sibling. It is the first 2 children in the family who have the strongest sense of their position.

If adopting an older child, three or older, you should ask additional questions of the children's home, particularly if the child will be older than existing children in your house:

1. How does she treat the other children in the orphanage in her age group?
2. How easily is she disciplined?
3. What is her temperament like?
4. Does she show aggression?
5. What is her personality like?
6. Has she bonded with a caretaker in the home?
7. What do they know of her background?

When you are at the children's home, watch her around the other children in her group and how she plays with them and how she treats them. If she is very loving, and helpful while playing with them then she is likely to be loving and helpful to her new siblings. You do have to ask a lot of questions about their mental state and what you can get about their past and do your homework. Compare what your agency and the children's home has told you with what you actually observe.

When you travel to Russia and arrive at the children's home you will receive current medical information and be able to talk with the director and home physician. If the child was placed in the children's home because parental rights were terminated and not because the child was relinquished, then you may receive sealed court records revealing the history and basis for the termination. You may have to press to receive these records, but do so. The records will likely reveal abuse or neglect. There will always abuse or neglect or the government cannot terminate parental rights. In many ways, their system and ours is similar. The problem with being given this information when you are in Russia is that you are not given much time to change your mind and changing your mind, after all the expense and time you have put in, takes great courage.

Now don't misunderstand. Not all older children were abused and there are many, many happy "forever" families with adoptive older children, but you do have to be careful and get as much information as you can about the child's past and mental state. Before you travel you should look inside yourself and be prepared to have the courage to walk away. Do not overestimate your parenting skills. Love and good food are not cures for everything.

Infants

The general rule is that children are delayed a month of development for every 3 months in the children's home. The children tend to run on the small side as well. The reason for this is that in addition to factors such as prematurity, undernourishment and sickness, a child's development, both physical and mental, depends in large part on how much physical affection they receive. It is a common story that when the children are brought into a loving home with lots of cuddling, they suddenly grow like weeds. So it is important not to overemphasize the weight or size of a child, as the child could very well be perfectly healthy, just small. This is not to say that when the higher cognitive abilities like abstract thinking are accessed in the third or fourth grade the child might not need some extra help. But that is true with any child.

Most of the international specialists focus on the head circumference measurement, as that can be indicative of mental development. Heads grow because the brain grows, and that this mostly occurs in the first few years of life. Be aware that some of the experts are now saying that many Russian children are demolishing the medical community expectations and heads are growing when adopted after the age of 3 years. Dr. Aronson has written about what she has found in regard to head circumference in Russian children at *http://members.aol.com/jaronmink/russvid.htm.*

A small head circumference that is not proportional to the body may be a red flag as it could indicate that the brain is not growing. On the other hand, a small head circumference that is proportional may not be cause for alarm. This is an issue found mostly in infants born prematurely.

Here are some issues to investigate in regard to infants.

1) If the head circumference is proportional to her body, then the growth rate may be proportional as well. In other words, if the body is growing slowly then it would not be surprising to find that the head was likewise. If the body and head do not match then that may be a concern. Microcephaly (small head) can be caused because of genetics (parents with small heads), poor nutrition, or FAS/FAE.

2) How is the child developmentally? Is she close to her milestones after deducting for the usual institutional caused delays? Does she crawl, walk, babble and have good social interactions?

3) Was her mother young and was it a first pregnancy? There seems to be a correlation between alcoholism and a mother who is older and has had numerous pregnancies.

Small head circumference means that you need to look at the total picture in order to assess the risk.

A smaller than normal infant is always a concern, but usually they will have catch-up growth. There was a study published in the Journal of Pediatrics in June 1998.It described adolescent growth of 32 extremely premature children from birth through 12-18 years of age. All weighed less than 1000 grams at birth (<2.2lbs)

The study found that by 12-18 years of age, only 6% of the children were below the normal range for height, and these children had mothers who were short themselves. This study did not discuss the ages at which small children landed on the growth chart, but did state that 45% of all children grew faster than normal between 8 years and 12-18 years. The conclusion was that catch-up growth continues well into adolescence. Here is a web site that discusses growth and the premature infant in more detail: *http://www.comeunity.com/premature/child/growth/catchup.html*

You may also notice that some infants have their hands clenched. While it can be a sign of cerebral palsy, almost always it is not. They clench their hands because it provides stimulation and touch. If they had a lot of toys to play with, they probably wouldn't do this. It goes away after a month or so. Just give them toys to hold and massage the fingers.

You might also see some rocking back and forth by an infant or toddler. It can be mild or severe. Rocking is a pretty typical comfort behavior. They rock for comfort or when they are upset or under stress. It is probably better to just let it be. In most children it will eventually diminish and then stop.

CHAPTER V

Medical Conditions

Medical Terminology

As I mentioned in the previous "Medical Review" section, I encourage you to read both Dr. Jenista's article and Dr. Downing's Russian medical articles at his website. These articles will provide you with some background as to what the terms in the medical summary mean. Dr Gindis also has an excellent article at *http://www.j51.com/~tatyana/page10.htm* on Russian medical terminology. If you are following the two trip process, you should take at least one of these articles with you.

Russian and American medical terms coincide when they are describing actual physical features but not when they are in the subjective realm. For example, inevitably the medical summary will include the words "perinatal encephalopathy." This is a Humpty Dumpty word.

It means whatever the Russian doctor wants it to mean. It is used to describe a baby who might be equally fussy, hungry, irritable, or brain impaired. Because it means everything, it means nothing. Then there is "hyperexcitability syndrome." This term is used to describe a baby who might be crying or fussy for perfectly normal reasons. It's a nonsense word like "oligophrenia" which is translated as feeble mindedness. How can you tell a child has problems if you do not describe the objective observations. Rather than relying on these subjective terms, your medical reviewer will be looking for specific milestone developments such as does the child cry, roll over, sit up, crawl, stand, walk, play with toys, move hands and legs.

Even so, some Russian diagnoses are accurate and can not be ignored. In this chapter I would like to touch on just a few of those conditions. I also provide a brief description as to what an APGAR score means. Most doctors do not rely on the score. You will see why when you read the description. Yet it is a factor that is listed on the medical summary for infants and which always leads to further questions.

In reviewing a child's medical summary, just keep in mind the limitations of the Russian pediatric medical establishment. Their training is not western based, it's not very modern, and they generally do not have access to advanced technology such as a MRI machine If you ask how his hearing is, you will get that "he can hear sounds." You will not get a print out from an actual hearing test. They don't have that kind of machine.

Now they will take a sonogram or ultrasound at the drop of a hat. Those are routine tests that are given to all infants. Indeed, because they routinely do sonograms and ultrasounds there are a lot of false positives. Typical scenario is an ultrasound performed which was not indicated in the first place leading to a diagnosis in a patient who feels quite well. Of course, the doctor will recommend a follow up ultrasound in 6 months. Russian patients and physicians have an inordinately high regard for ultrasound studies. Sometimes they will diagnose a condition, like hepatitis, by ultrasound that would normally require a tissue specimen and a microscope. Ultrasounds are also available in Moscow without physician referral.

Another interesting aspect of Russian medicine is that a lot of prescriptions are for mixing chemicals. People will travel from store to store then go home to brew their own, such as for penicillin.

Also another good resource web site is at:
http:// *www.russianadoption.org/Adoption_Agency_List.htm* If you scroll down the site, on the right hand side you will see links to medical papers that discuss Hepatitis, FAS/FAE, parasites and post-institutional issues. Another good resource on medical issues is at:*http://www.comeunity.com/disability/index.html*

APGAR

APGAR is merely the evaluation of the baby's condition at the time of birth. A.P.G.A.R. stands for Appearance, Pulse rate, Grimace, Activity and Respiratory effort. This score enables medical personnel to identify babies that need routine care and babies who may need further assistance. The baby is evaluated and scored at one minute after birth and then again in 5 minutes. The second score is more important than the first one, as many infants may have a brief period of being "stunned" and need help initially adjusting to life. The APGAR is important to identify babies *at the time of birth* who need help and to observe whether the help that has been given has had the desired effect.

There are several examinations that are made for an APGAR score:

Heart Rate
Respiratory Effort

Muscle Tone
Reflex
Response to Stimulation
Color

The scoring is as follows
HEART RATE/PULSE: 0 points for absent heart rate, 1 point for heart rate below 100, 2 points for heart rate over 100.
RESPIRATORY EFFORT: 0 points for absent, 1 point for weak cry and hypoventilation, 2 points for good crying.
MUSCLE TONE/ACTIVITY: 0 points for limp, 1 point for some flexion of extremities, 2 points for well flexed.
REFLEX/RESPONSE TO STIMULATION/GRIMACE: 0 points for no response, 1 point for grimace, 2 points for coughs, sneezes or cries.
COLOR/APPEARANCE: 0 points for blue or pale, 1 point for body pink, extremities blue, 2 points for completely pink.

An APGAR score will typically be stated in the form of two numbers with a slash between. The first is the one minute score; the second is the 5 minute score. The scoring ranges for the APGAR are:

1. 7-10: Active, vigorous infant routine care
2. 4-6: Moderately depressed infant, requires stimulation to breathe and oxygen
3. 0-3: Severely depressed infant, immediate ventilatory assistance required

Because the APGAR score is subjective and only taken at birth, its importance after birth should not be overemphasized. It will only tell you that your child had a stressful birth or a non-stressful one.

It is just a snapshot of how the baby was one minute and five minutes after birth. Don't accept or reject a referral on that alone. Indeed, most children with developmental disabilities have excellent APGAR scores when born and most children with poor APGAR scores do well. How the child is today and what your medical reviewer says regarding the video and any conversation you have with the orphanage doctors is far more important in evaluating your child.

Fetal Alcohol Syndrome

One of the issues usually discussed in relation to intercountry adoptions is the risk of your child having Fetal Alcohol Syndrome or Fetal Alcohol Effect. In Russia, with its high rate of alcoholism, children are always at risk. However, remember that the high alcoholism rate is generally found among men. In Russian women, age is an indicator, with an older woman more likely to drink than a younger one.

Fetal Alcohol Syndrome (FAS) is always a risk in any child where the birth mother drank alcohol. Its effects vary widely. Some birth mothers can drink heavily and there can be no effect. In others, just a few glasses can cause damage. FAS occurs in every country including the United States. It is almost impossible to detect with certainty before the age of two. If you believe your referral might be affected, have one of the adoption medical specialists give you an opinion. Of course, remember that a brief video and a few still shots make any precise diagnosis of any medical condition difficult at best.

An FAS diagnosis usually is made based on impairment of growth and development plus a characteristic pattern of facial features including short eye openings (palpebral fissures), short upturned nose, low nasal bridge, flat vertical groove between upper lip and nose (philtrum), and thin upper lip and simply formed external ears. Since an infant may have some of these characteristics by just being a baby, it is very hard to make any diagnosis at a young age.

Since so many young children have developmental delays and poor growth due to neglect and malnutrition, many children will have some of the features of FAS or FAE. It is difficult to figure out when a child is delayed because of just general children's home experience or due to alcohol. Also, some children with an Asian background like Chuvash, Kazakh or Bashkir can appear to have some slight FAS facial characteristics when in fact it is just the way they may look.

A good article written by Dr. Aronson on FAS and international adoption can be found at: *http://www.russianadoption.org/fas.htm* She writes that children born to women who drank alcohol excessively during pregnancy can appear to be at increased risk for ADD with hyperactivity, fine motor impairment, and clumsiness as well as more subtle delays in motor performance and speech disorders. In the absence of physical features and abnormalities, this is called Fetal Alcohol Effects, or Alcohol Related neurodevelopmental effects. FAE is usually not apparent until children are school age. Behavioral issues will surface in pre-school. The term "Fetal Alcohol Effects (FAE)" has been used to describe conditions that are presumed to be caused by prenatal alcohol exposure but do not follow the exact configuration of the three characteristics used to identify FAS. Typically children with FAE are of normal size and have some but not all of the facial anomalies and central nervous systems (CNS) dysfunction associated with FAS. Many disabilities resulting from prenatal exposure do not show up until children are school age. Family history is important. Without the telltale facial features, identification of CNS damage as a result of prenatal alcohol exposure can be difficult.

Intervention with FAS kids should begin as early as possible and continue throughout their lives. The keys to appropriate early intervention are developing and maintaining realistic expectations, thinking long-term, learning to reframe child behaviors, and keeping an open mind about goals and strategies.

Life with a fetal alcohol child can be very difficult. Get as much knowledge as you can, and decide what you can honestly handle. The outcome cannot be guaranteed, but if your referral is suspected of having FAS/FAE, the probability of a lifelong involvement with these issues is great. You might read Ann Streissguth's book, *Fetal Alcohol Syndrome: A Guide For Families and* Communities. She gives a lot of very good, detailed information based on 25 years of research. She even includes pictures, which is helpful.

Cleft Palate/Lip

Some children have a condition called cleft palate and/or cleft lip. You will likely see at least one child in the Embassy waiting room with this condition. It is entirely treatable. A cleft lip is a separation of the two sides of the lip. The separation often includes the bones of the upper jaw and/or upper gum. A cleft palate is an opening in the roof of the mouth in which the two sides of the palate did not join together, as the unborn baby was developing. Cleft lip and cleft palate can occur on one side or on both sides. Because the lip and the palate develop separately, it is possible for the child to have a cleft lip, a cleft palate, or both cleft lip and cleft palate.

Generally surgery corrects the condition and is done in stages. It may even be outpatient. There is some postoperative pain, like with tonsils, but it is of short duration. The end result is just a small scar on the lip. Speech therapy may be necessary in some circumstances.

There is an organization called Operation Smile. They help children all over the world that are born with facial defects. Operation Smile will assist families whose insurance will not cover the entire surgery. If you have a referral of a child with a cleft palate or lip, you should contact them for more information. Their website is at: *http://www.operationsmile.org/* Another web site that contains a lot of personal information about cleft surgery is at *http://pages.ivillage.com/pp/bylerbunch/russianadoption.html*

Cerebral Palsy

Cerebral Palsy (CP) is the general term used to describe the motor impairment resulting from brain damage in a young child. The more severe the case, the earlier a diagnosis can be made. Severe cases can be diagnosed in the first few weeks or months of age. If a child is able to walk normally at 14-18 months, it is quite unlikely that the child has CP. The problem is that for most children, CP can not be diagnosed until a child is at least 18 months old. A delay in walking or a problem with limbs by a child in a Russian children's home can occur for many reasons such as malnutrition and not just because of CP.

Many of the normal developmental milestones, such as reaching for toys, sitting, and walking, are based on motor function. If these are delayed, then CP might be a reason. Indeed, your reviewing doctor will be looking for just these sorts of milestones. Yet, developmental delays are expected in these children because of the institutional environment, which makes the diagnosis difficult.

A diagnosis of cerebral palsy cannot be made on the basis of an x-ray or blood test. An APGAR score of less than 3 at the 5 minute mark is one of the few early indicators, but even this is not always so. The most meaningful review of cerebral palsy is examining the physical evidence of abnormal motor function. An abnormal motor function may be spasticity, which is the inability of a muscle to relax, or athetosis, which refers to the inability to control the movement of a muscle. Infants who at first are hypotonic wherein they are very floppy may later develop spasticity. In reviewing a videotape a doctor will be looking for normal movement of the limbs and will be concerned if floppiness or a stiff limb is indicated.

Of course, the problem is that a one minute videotape can not substitute for a physical medical exam. And an observation of delayed motor skills, which could simply be based on poor nutrition and environmental factors, is hardly an adequate basis for a CP diagnosis.

Post-Institutional Issues

Research on children adopted from Eastern European countries is just now really starting to emerge; the earliest studies (the 90-91 ones, like the Ames study) were done on kids from the terrible Romanian orphanages who came out in the first flood. You have to keep in mind that Russian, Ukrainian, Bulgarian, and Romanian institutions (to name a few) are not all the same. However, that doesn't mean you should just discard the early studies. Just that you should not automatically assume that the conclusions are equally valid in regard to your child in his particular children's home.

It is your child's particular situation and the particular children's home that is far more important in judging whether your child is at risk for post-institutional issues. First, the majority of adoptions from Russia turn out just fine. Even among older children adoptions you will find many happy families and many situations that defy the general view. Yet there are some children who will have serious psychological issues. I am not talking about developmental or speech delays. Almost all of the children have at least a mild case and it is to be expected. Rather, serious issues such as reactive attachment disorder, posttraumatic stress disorder, and sensory processing disorder is always a possibility although found in only a minority of Russian adoptions.

CHAPTER VI

Waiting and Waiting

While You Wait

You may be waiting for the day when you can travel for your first trip to Russia to choose a child. Or you may have already accepted a referral and that child is now yours. But you can't have him yet; you must wait for a court date.

Waiting for a court date can be very stressful. Usually the reason for the delay is not because your paperwork is incomplete, but because some crucial Russian piece to the puzzle is sick or on vacation. Remember the officials are very underpaid. The court date could be delayed because the Federal clearance letter (a/k/a orphan data bank letter or release letter) from the Ministry of Education in Moscow has not reached the court officials in the region. This letter states that the adoptive child has been in the Ministry's data bank for the required amount of time (three months for the Federal database). It used to be that a facilitator could simply pick up the letter in Moscow and hand carry it to the Regional Court or have it couried, but there has been a recent change and now these letters must travel by regular Russian post. Also, the Deputy Minister of Education must now sign this letter. This obviously adds to the delay. The court date can not be set until this letter is received. This change in procedure has probably more to do with the Ministry of Education taking a closer look at babies that are being adopted and not just rubber stamping the clearance letters. This procedure may continue or could change without notice.

Any delay is as frustrating for your agency and facilitator as it is for you. Your agency should be able to tell you where the kink is in the chain. Still, everything is really out of your hands, you have done all you can do and YOUR child is there and you are here. Here are some suggestions as what you can do while you wait:

If you are close to the holidays, go to the Salvation Army or some other organization and support a family with a child around the age you are adopting and give that child a gift.

Learn child CPR while you are waiting.
Gather social security and citizenship application forms
Study up on the federal adoption tax credit rules
Interview pediatricians
Begin your Hepatitis vaccine shots and any other shots you need
Begin to pack your suitcase, your child's and your donations
Check into the school system or day care centers in your area. Ask your neighbors.
Write your will so it includes your adoptive child
Discuss with spouse about parenting styles, discipline styles and which relatives get to raise the child in case you both have an accident.
Learn about your State's re-adoption requirements.

Baby proof your house. Have friends with kids come over to review. Install plug protectors, edge protectors, cabinet locks, toilet locks.

Practice with the Diaper Genie.

Diaper your dog or a furry doll for practice.

Do lots of things nice for you. It will be your last time. Go away for a long weekend with your spouse.

You should also investigate with your agency exactly which children's home your child is located. Keep pressing them until you are sure they have given you the correct information. Some agencies will just tell you the major city like Rostov-on-the-Don or Perm. Yet Rostov has 4 children's homes and its outlying towns like Novoshakhtinsk, Novocherkassk, and Shakhti also have one. Perm is the same way with at least 6 children's homes and several more in the outlying towns. With this specific information you can then post on the Internet and find someone else who has traveled to the same home and who can tell you exactly what to expect.

Study some Russian phrases

Start your child's Lifebook.

Fix up the baby's room

Buy the crib, car seat and the usual baby books. Read the books.

Post poison control and children's hospital phone numbers on the fridge

Begin thinking about what kind of adoption notices you want to send out, if any.

Write a letter to your child telling them how you are feeling while you wait for them. Give it to them when they turn 18 or some other special time.

File an application for Title IV non-recurring money if your state allows it.

Get your passport ready

Check out your county's early intervention programs if appropriate.

Ask your pediatrician for some recommended evaluators.

Clean your house like its never been cleaned before.

Take a parenting class

Find out the dates for children's consignment sales and plan to attend.

Make an effort to go out with your friends, as you will not have time later.

Take that swing dancing class you've always wanted to take.

Nest, Nest, Nest—it's your time! This waiting will be the slowest weeks of your life. Just fill your days.

Choosing a Pediatrician

Most parents choose a pediatrician based on recommendations from friends and family. Find out if the doctor has worked with international children and has any as clients. If she has not, then you can expect to have to educate the pediatrician. Indeed, if the doctor just works in a middle class community, you are likely to find that he is not knowledgeable regarding the issues faced by an international child.

Is she willing to review the referral video? Since this child might be a patient of hers soon, she should be. On the other hand, if you are not used to giving a medical conclusion based on a skimpy medical report and skimpy video, then giving such a conclusion is against a pediatrician's standard training. Also, remember that any local pediatrician review is in addition to the adoption specialists' review and not in place of it. Bringing the local pediatrician into the referral review will process allows you to lean on that doctor for advice as to what medicines you should take over to your child.

The pediatrician should allow you to make an emergency appointment as soon as you return from Russia. You should not have to wait a week to have a thorough examination and screening. You should emphasize to the doctor that the examination needs to be thorough and longer than the usual visit. If you can, you should try to make the appointment for your child before you leave for Russia.

You should raise the issue of reimmunization of your child. Even if your child has been immunized in Russia, the vaccines may have been out of date, not given the same dosage as in the States or not refrigerated. You should not accept any resistance regarding your desire to reimmunize.

Is she familiar with Hepatitis B and C in children? What about parasites such as giardia and other international medical issues? Middle class doctors do not have patients with parasites and may be resistant to testing for them. Any resistance is unacceptable.

Standard questions would be to find out if the doctor has a particular area of pediatric interest, the hours of the office, and the hospitals in which the doctor practices. Check out the waiting room, as you will likely spend quite a bit of time there over the next year. Are there things to keep the child occupied. Toys, books, fish tank, that sort of thing. Do you like the nurses and staff?

Lifebook

Some families create what is called a "Lifebook" for their child. It is an illustration of the adoption journey and can serve as the baby book they never had. The Book might include a section on the history of your life before the child such as where you grew up, lived, work, went to school, etc.

You might have a section on the adoption process itself including pictures of the agency people and the referral picture. Then a section on your child's life showing where she was born and lived and why you chose her name and what it means to you. Copies of her social security card court petition and decree and citizenship certificate could be included. Then a section on your home and fixing it up for her arrival. Pictures of her room.

A section on traveling to Russia including copies of receipts and ticket stubs. Pictures of the plane, hotel, tourist spots, homestay families. Include maps, money and brochures. You could even include a small vial of dirt or a rock from the children's home. Some families have their children's caregivers write a letter to the child which you can have her open at whatever age you see fit. This letter could be part of the book.

If there is a baby shower then you could include the invitation, photos of baby shower, and a piece of the gift paper. You could have a section regarding your return with ticket stubs, description of the travel with the child, and passport photos. If people met you at the airport then pictures of the celebration and pictures of your house when you returned. Include the adoption announcement. Include your child's own section with her favorite toy and book. Include what you found out about her immediately such as her sleep and nap patterns, favorite foods, and bathing and nighttime rituals. You may (or may not) have a medical section with information from the children's home, report from your pediatrician when you returned, hand and foot imprints, birth statistics (height and weight)

You could have a section on what was happening in Russia and the United States at the time. (This is a good reason to buy some English language newspapers while you are there.) You could include movies and songs that were playing in the United States.

The White House will also send you a welcome card for your child if you ask them. (It's a little hokey, but cute) Better yet is the flag they will fly over the Capitol the day your child is a citizen. Just ask your Congresswoman.

If you adopt an older child, then you might consider sending a copy of the "Lifebook" to her, in order for her to get used to the idea of joining your family and leaving Russia. It should be a picture book which might include actual photographs of the child, your family, your dog or cat, home, her new school, extended family, friends, the city she will live in and the places you and she will go. It might include magazine cut-outs and notes from family members. If possible, the book might include both English and Russian captions/translations. This book is particularly helpful in the two trip process as you will want to leave your child something tangible to remember you by while you both wait for a court date.

Here is a sample outline:

1. Introduction: including the child's picture and how you and your family feel about her.

2. An explanation of things to come: This portion can include a lot of magazine cutouts. Include pictures to indicate a judge will give her a new name; we'll take a train to Moscow (pictures of Russia from a tourist guide); acknowledge her feelings—understand she'll be sad to leave her friends; see a doctor; get her picture taken; take an airplane ride to the US; pictures of friends and the house.

3. An explanation of the first few weeks home and the normal routine for both weekdays and weekends. Include an explanation of her being taken to the doctor and dentist visits. Pictures of her classroom, explaining the purpose of each area; the playground; daily routine (get up, brush teeth, get dressed, drive to work/school; eat breakfast/lunch at school; come home cook dinner; a large variety of after-school/dinner activities; take a

bath; brush teeth; set out clothes for next day; say prayers; give hugs and kisses; go to sleep); our weekend routine (clean house, other chores like laundry/shopping, go to church. List potential activities and sports.

4. Spring/Summer events: pictures of friends who she will meet; pictures of family who will be visiting; magazine cutouts of the beach and pool, Fourth of July fireworks, etc.

Some families create an audio "Lifebook" for their older child. They make the tape in Russian before leaving the States or in Russia with the help of their translator. The tape explains what a hotel is and that they will fly on several large planes to get home; what a city is; that there will be lots of cars and people in the larger cities they will be stopping at on their way home; that their new mama and papa love them and it will take time for everyone to get use to being a family; all about the household pets; all about his new home and that he would have his own bed; who his new relativs would be; school; routines and house rules. This kind of tape can really help an older child understand the whirlwind adjustments to his life that he is undergoing. It can become his story.

Leaving Your Child At Home

Many families have other children at home and leave them with family members or friends while they are in Russia. You should provide the caretaker with a power of attorney to cover ordinary things as well as a specific medical power to allow for medical treatment of your child if it becomes necessary. A local hospital should be able to show you the form they use.

You should also give the caretaker your pediatrician's name and phone number, any medical conditions, medications or allergies, of your children and the name, policy number and phone number of your health insurance company. The caretaker should be given the health insurance card showing coverage for your child. The caretaker should be given a list of phone numbers of friends and relatives they can call if they have questions.

A map showing where the doctor office is located and the nearest hospital should also be given to the caretaker. Phone numbers of your local car dealer, plumber, electrician and heating and air guy should also be given. Another authorization is one to allow the caretaker to drive your car and to have it repaired.

Now in a real life saving emergency the hospital will treat your child, but it makes things go smoothly if your caretaker can show them all of this information and it is critical for non-emergency situations.

A sample form is as follows:

To whom it may concern:
As the parents of _____, we hereby author-ize_____ to approve any and all necessary medical treatment for our child.

Our child is covered by _____Insurance Company, policy number_____, phone number _____. This is a PPO(HMO). The employee member is_____.

Our child's date of birth is_____. She is allergic to - _____. Her pediatrician is _____, at_____, phone number_____. Our child's blood type is _____. Her last hospitalization was on _____for _____.

Our home address is_____. Our home phone number
is _____.
Signed (**both parents**)

Notary

A problem is explaining the trip to young children who may not
fully comprehend why you are leaving, but just know Mommy and
Daddy will be gone. You might buy a book called *Seeds of Love* and
read it to him. Other things you can do include making a map and calendar showing when you plan to leave and when you will return. Give
him stars to put on the calendar to mark out the days when you will
be home.

Some parents have audiotaped or videotaped several tapes showing
them reading stories to the kids, singing favorite poems, songs, and
rhymes and telling funny stories. They have also taken brown lunch
bags, and for each day away they have written a note on each one for
each child. Inside they placed a small toy, treat, or craft activity. Here is
an interesting web site on the issue of leaving your child behind:
http://www.adoptiontravel.com/articles/art2.htm

Employer Benefits

You may wish to use this time to investigate what adoption benefit
programs your employer may offer. One of the best is derived from the
federal Family Medical Leave Act (FMLA). As always consult with your
employer's human resources department or an attorney for specifics,
however the law is generally as follows. The FMLA applies to all:

1) Public agencies, including state, local and federal employers, schools, and

2) Private-sector employers who employ 50 or more employees in 20 or more workweeks in the current or preceding calendar year.

To be eligible for FMLA benefits, an employee must:

(1) work for a covered employer;

(2) have worked for the employer for a total of 12 months;

(3) have worked at least 1,250 hours over the previous 12 months;

The 12 months need not be consecutive. The 12 months include any time off spent on workers' compensation, military leave or court leave The 1,250 hours must be actual work hours, not including any type of leave.

A covered employer must grant an eligible employee up to a total of 12 workweeks of unpaid leave during any 12-month period for placement with the employee of a son or daughter for adoption or foster care. Leave for placement for adoption must conclude within 12 months of the placement.

Under some circumstances, employees may take FMLA leave for placement of adoption intermittently—which means taking leave in blocks of time, or by reducing their normal weekly or daily work schedule. This is in the discretion of the employer.

Before (or after) an adopted child is placed, the employee may take FMLA leave for making required arrangements for the placement—to attend counseling sessions, appear in court, consult with an attorney or submit to a physical examination. A father or mother may take FMLA leave for these reasons.

Whether the child arrives by birth or by placement, a mother or father is entitled to FMLA leave to care for the child during the first year. No medical justification is needed—the FMLA leave is guaranteed simply to care for the new child. This particular right to FMLA leave terminates on the first anniversary of the child's birth or placement.

Title IV-E

Adoptions are not inexpensive. In addition to sources of funds such as employers, state and federal adoption tax credits, the federal government also provides in all 50 states a reimbursement program called Title IV-E. This program was established to encourage the adoption of children who are otherwise considered hard to adopt. The Federal government pays 60% and the state the remainder. The state controls the program for the most part, subject to certain federal requirements.

The program was originally established for domestic adoptions. At this time, the states have applied the program unevenly to foreign adoptions. Some do and some do not. The program gives recurring funds which is means tested. More importantly, it also gives non-recurring funds up to $2000 for expense reimbursement. This part of the program is not means tested. Check with your accountant, but the $2000 should not be taxable, as it is a welfare benefit.

First check with your state's adoption services unit to see if they apply Title IV to foreign adoptions. At this time it appears that Georgia, South Carolina, Alaska, and Ohio do apply the program to Russian adoptions, but that New York, Michigan and Texas may not. Ohio's program is administered by the county Human Services Department or county Children Services Board. The initial application is usually made prior to the adoption being finalized and the $2000 reimbursement is issued after the finalization. In Ohio the application should be made in advance of travel, but after the child to be adopted is identified. In Georgia, the county DFACS office intakes the application, but the State DFACS office makes the decision. It should also be filed prior to travel.

In Alaska, the filing can be made after travel, but before any re-adoption decree. If you miss the deadline of filing before traveling to Russia, then try the Alaska method of filing before the re-adoption decree and argue that that decree is the final decree.

Remember that you are the only advocate your child has. The state adoption units normally have no idea what an international adoption is or what you have had to go through. If they reject your application, do not give up but continue to push using all of your political resources.

Assuming your state does allow Title IV-E to apply to foreign adoptions then it is necessary to file the application prior to adopting in most states. There should be no filing fee involved and the application should not be difficult. After returning from Russia your state will require some documentation explaining your child's health condition and the background of the adoption. This documentation may include a letter from your child's pediatrician and a summary from your agency regarding the adoption, and a copy of the adoption decree. Your agency's letter should include information on how your child was hard to place. This is the purpose of the Title IV program so include how long your child was on the database and available for adoption in Russia, or was with your agency or if your child was specifically referred to any Russian families who may have declined to adopt.

Generally the process for applying for the non-recurring funds follows along these lines:

Step 1 is to file the application before leaving for Russia, if you already have a referral or before leaving for the second trip in the event you are under the two trip process.

Step 2 is for your pediatrician to write up a post adoption medical report (or you can do it and have your pediatrician sign it on his letterhead). Your goal is for the State to recognize that your child has medical or special needs relating to developmental delays, medical issues, nutritional and failure to thrive issues.

You may need to give the county copies of a few receipts showing that costs greatly exceeded the $2000 non-recurring reimbursement.

Step 3 is that your county sends all of this information to the State's department which is in charge of the Title IV program. This department will evaluate the information and decide if you have proven your case. You should have administrative appeal rights.

Most counties also have an early intervention/baby's first program that provides a free evaluation of your child. Sometimes using this evaluation to substantiate your application can be helpful.

Here are some websites that may be useful:

http://www.homes4kids.org/aap50.htm
http://members.aol.com/nacac/subsidyoverview.html
http://www.fpsol.com/adoption/checklist.html#four-e
http://www.adoption.org/parents/html/iii1osa.htm

Airfares

One thing you can do while you are waiting for a court date is to check on airfares and airlines.

Most people travel to Russia on either Aeroflot or Delta. There are other airlines such as Swissair and Lufthansa. Do not fly Air France. Swissair always gets very high marks. Generally, airfares are higher from April 1 through October 1 with coach fares around $600 roundtrip in the winter and $900 in the spring and summer. However, specials are not unusual. Sometimes, due to short notice, your fare will be very high such as $1400. One problem in buying tickets is that usually you do not receive a lot of notice prior to traveling. It is rare that someone can actually buy a 21-day advance ticket. There are travel agencies that specialize in Russian travel or you can buy the ticket yourself. Check a lot of places to get a range of prices.

The debate over whether it is better to fly Aeroflot or Delta is similar to the stroller versus snugglie argument; whether you did the right thing will only be known after the fact. Delta usually has a flight that leaves at 6pm in the evening from JFK in New York and arrives in Moscow at 11:30am in the morning. The actual flight takes about10 hours. This can help with jet lag. You will also need to buy a ticket for your child. It is usually 10% of the fare and is cheaper to buy it in the States rather than in Moscow. Ask your agent about buying the child a round trip ticket originating in Moscow and when you return to the States just throw the JFK-SVO portion of the ticket away. If you do it originating from JFK, the airline may label the child a no-show and cancel the return. If you book coach, you might check on using your frequent flyer miles to upgrade to first class for your return. Unlike Aeroflot, Delta's return flights are always very crowded.

In addition to flying from JFK, Aeroflot also flies from Washington, San Francisco, Seattle and Chicago. Aeroflot usually charges just a nominal fee to change tickets. This can be important as a delay of a day or two on the return is not unusual and indeed you should give yourself a cushion of an extra day when planning your return.

Swissair sometimes has less expensive fares and fewer charges if you change tickets, but it does land in Moscow later in the afternoon. It always gets high marks for service. Swissair also will give you their lowest fare without restrictions if you tell them you are adopting from Russia. Some other airlines like British Air also have a special adoption discount.

Aeroflot flies the same Boeing type airplanes, as does Delta. A lot of people fly Aeroflot and sit in business class. It is more expensive but comfortable. May even be cheaper than Delta. If you fly business class in Aeroflot, there is a First Class lounge in the Moscow airport that is very nice. The flight attendants speak English and the service is fine. Aeroflot has been criticized for allowing smoking and drinking on its planes. Smoking used to be allowed in the last 6 seats in the back of the plane and not up front. However, Aeroflot is now taking the position that no smoking is allowed on its flights from the US. The FAA also has enacted a rule to that effect. Still, the smoking culture is very engrained in Russia and it may be a while before the practice of not smoking is universally followed. One benefit in flying Aeroflot, in addition to it usually being cheaper than Delta, is that it is less crowded going over and returning. Veteran travelers will wait until the plane levels off then immediately find an empty 3 seat row in the middle to lay down in as their bed for the night. It can be akin to musical chairs soon after takeoff. Aeroflot is probably better if you are adopting older children as they may feel more comfortable surrounded by Russian speaking passengers. The flight attendants are also willing to talk with your child.

Check the airlines' policy on changing tickets. Some allow a change with a fee and some charge no fee. The odds of having to change your return ticket by a day or two are fairly high due to the vagaries of traveling abroad and the unexpected that sometimes occurs in the adoption process. Delta used to allow you to change tickets without penalty. However, Delta has instituted a "no waivers, no favors" policy and strictly applied its penalty charges. In this regard, it is not adoption friendly. Delta has very recently introduced an "adoption discount." As with all such discounts, it may last. You must show your 171H at the ticket counter. All ticket agents do not know about it. Keep insisting. If you run into a roadblock, have the agent call the Delta Promotions desk at 800-325-7441.

Always ask anyone, whether it be an airline or hotel, if they have an adoption discount or waiver, when faced with an expensive charge. Another tip when buying a ticket is that it is usually cheaper to fly roundtrip from the same city rather than different cities. Also, taking a train which is part of the Trans-Siberian system is not a bad way to travel domestically and can be cheaper (and safer) than flying as well as give you time to recover from jet lag.

Some airlines stop over in Amsterdam. If you spend the night in Amsterdam on your return from Russia, you will need an overnight visa for the child from the immigration office in the Amsterdam airport before you go through the passport check to leave the airport. As Americans, you do not need a visa. The visa does not cost anything and will take 20-45 minutes to get. You turn in the overnight visa at the passport checking station at the airport when you fly out. Do not waste time and money getting the transit visa from the Dutch Embassy in Moscow.

Amsterdam airport has nice baby care centers with sinks, changing tables, cribs and play pens. You should definitely ask where these rooms are located, as they are clean and quiet. There is an excellent and free play area at the Zurich airport as well.

For those flying to Perm, Lufthansa has a flight on Monday and Thursday from Frankfurt that is direct to Perm. This flight allows you to skip Moscow. They also have a direct one to Nizny Novogrod. Of course, you will still have to fly out of Moscow on your return. Now this is not true if you are adopting from Vladivostok. You don't have to go out of Moscow. Magadan Airlines flies from Seattle to Vladivostok and that is the flight to take if you are going there. The roundtrip price is around $700.

If you have the time, you can also fly to some of the Scandinavian cities and spend the night, then continue with a short hop to Moscow the next day. Many people also like to stop over in Amsterdam on the return. It breaks up the trip and allows you to get about 8 hours of sleep in a hotel before making the next leg back to the States. Your child will need an overnight visa, which should be easy to get at the airport.

On your return flight, you may wish to ask for a bulkhead seat, as that will give you more room. If adopting an infant, ask for a bassinet. Returning Delta flights are usually jammed with people. If you have an infant, you will be holding her on your lap during the entire flight. If you use Delta, you may wish to consider buying a seat for your child so as to be able to lie her down. On Aeroflot, there is more room. Also, Delta no longer will allow you to walk the aisles with your child. This can be a major inconvenience.

Now flying domestically is a different story. If leaving from Moscow, you will fly out from a different airport than from the international airport you flew into. You will have to buy tickets once you reach Russia or your facilitator can. You should buy a first class ticket or business class, not coach. The domestic airlines range from terrific to frightening. A good one is TransAero.

There are four domestic airports located outside Moscow. They are fly east, west, north and south. Do not be surprised if the pilot helps with loading the baggage and if all the passengers begin to smoke and drink as soon as the plane takes off. The domestic airport's bathrooms are just a hole in the floor. Be prepared! At the domestic airport you will hear the sound of hundreds of bags having tape wrapped around them. It can be a bit startling. You first carry your bags to the weigh in where they will assess you an overweight charge. They do not seem to care that the overweight is because of donations. This is another reason the train is better. They will want to weigh your carryon as well. The domestic airports strictly enforce (as a revenue measure) the weight limits. The weight limit is around 40 kilos per person and is less than is allowed for international flights. The overweight charge is paid in rubles so be sure to have changed some money before leaving for the domestic airport. The overweight charge usual comes to about 1% of the ticket price per kilo. So if your ticket is $100, you might pay $1 per overweight kilo. One tip is that if you have already met your Moscow homestay host, then leave some items with her that you will not need until your return. This will save some space and weight.

When your flight is called you walk out on the tarmac and climb aboard the plane. If you don't speak Russian, while you are checking in, look around you. The people checking in with you will be on your flight and you will feel better and know you are on the right plane if you remember one person and look for them when you are boarding the plane. Drinking is very prevalent on the domestic planes and if you are taking one of those frightening kinds of airlines, you will start drinking too! Now there are some domestic airlines that are just fine and you will think you are back in the States. You just have to find one of those and hope it flies to your destination. When you land you will bless your driver and coordinator as you have made it! The usual arrival at a region's airport will have you stepping off the plane onto the middle of the tarmac and then crammed into a small bus that takes you to the terminal. It may remind you of flying into Dulles.

If you are flying domestically back to Moscow and VIP service is offered, take it! VIP service means that your bags are checked by people who care, that you get to stay in a relatively clean and quiet waiting room, and you get on the plane before most people. It is definitely worth the couple of extra dollars. The airport in Perm offers a great VIP service for $12, which includes breakfast.

It is difficult to get the best deal to Russia without using a travel agent. You can research the fares yourself, but a travel agent can sometimes get you special adoption rates and have the ticket changing charge waived. There some travel agencies that specialize in adoption travel to Russia such as Rainier World Travel, Inc. in Renton, WA. 1-800-432-4456, All Ways International in New York, (212) 947-0505, *http://www.awintl.com*, Federal Travel in Florida 1-800-551-8666, *http://www.adoption.com/federal*, and John Nairn at Far Horizons Travel (formerly Global Travel) in California at 1-800-574-0875. Also,

Red Star Travel in Seattle at 206-522-5995 (www.travel2russia.com). If you have confidence in an airline consolidator, you try booking through them. Some people have used Airfare Busters at 713-961-5109 or 407-391-9560. The National Council for Adoption sometimes has information about special fares and can be reached at 202-328-1200.

Here are some other airfare resources:
http://www.etn.nl/
http://www.gotorussia.net/

Visas

In order to go to Russia, you need a visa. You receive these from one of the Russian Consulates such as in San Francisco or New York or the Embassy in Washington. You will need a visa for each person over the age of 16 traveling to Russia from the United States. Visas can be either single entry or double entry, tourist or business. Single entry just means that the person will be entering Russia one time. Your agency will tell you whether the region in which you are adopting requires the parents to travel to Russia then return to the States, then go back to Russia. Most do not. However, sometimes where the ten day wait is enforced or some other kind of delay is imposed, it may be more economical to return to the United States rather than stay in Russia. In this case, a double entry visa would be preferable. Visas are $70 for a single entry and $120 for a double. This does not include what you may have to pay for an "invitation" and for expedited service. It is not unusual to pay $130 for a complete visa service.

Most families travel on business visas. They are good for up to three months. Therefore, when you apply for one you do not have to be exact as to the date of travel, just be close enough. It is very helpful to arrange the visa as soon as you have a high probability of when travel will occur.

The Consulates will normally process the visa request within 2 weeks although expedited service (for an additional fee) is available.

Some agencies will arrange for the visa and others leave it up to the families to obtain them. There are also companies that specialize in obtaining such visas and for a small fee will assist families. These are very helpful when you have only a short notice to travel.

The visa is obtained from the Consulate by enclosing an "invitation" from Russia plus the usual visa application and fee. The invitation is usually obtained from a Russian travel company or from some official source. Whoever is obtaining your visa will also obtain such an "invitation". You need to include three passport size photographs and copies of the identification pages of your passport.

If you are handling the visa yourself, and you are receiving the invitation from the Ministry of Health or Education to adopt, then you should put "adoption" down on the application as the reason for travel. If you receive an invitation to travel from a tourist agency in Russia, then you should probably write tourism as your purpose for the visit. If you are adopting in Moscow your visa invitation may have to be issued by the Ministry of Foreign Affairs. Always check first with the Russian Consulate or Embassy regarding the requirements.

If you are obtaining the visa yourself, call the Consulate or Embassy to verify the information required. There are different rules as to what's required depending on which Russian Consulate you apply through. If you apply to the Consulate in NYC, your original passport is required. If you apply to the Embassy in Washington, DC, just a plain copy of the first two pages is enough. The same for the Consulate in San Francisco. The Russian Consulate in San Francisco used to be faster at processing visa applications than the Embassy in Washington, however recently the Russians have changed their rules to standardize the process at two weeks. Expedited service is still available, but at a higher price.

Make sure you double check before you go that your visa is not about to expire. It is not good to enter Russia on an expired visa. If your visa expires before you can go, you simply obtain another letter of invitation and pay a small fee to have your visa extended by the Russian Consulate.

You will need to keep the visa in your carryon to show Russian immigration when you land in Moscow. You will also need to show it when you leave. Therefore, do not pack the visa document in your checked luggage.

You can download the form at the Consulate web site or from fax on demand at 212-693-1358 or at *http://www.avana.net/~russiah/rusvisa.htm*

The Seattle Russian Consulate has an excellent web site for Visa information and down loading of the application form. The site is: *http://www.russia.net/travel/visas.html*

The Russian Embassy is at *http://www.russianembassy.org*

Calling from Russia

You should also investigate how to call from Russia, as you are likely to want to tell someone back home your good news as well as the exact time you will be returning home.

You should be able to use all of your major phone company calling cards if you are in Moscow. Always check with your carrier prior to leaving for Russia on rates and access. In some Regions it is difficult to call the US. Unless you are on a special international plan you can expect it to cost about $3.20 a minute although some hotels like the Marriott will charge you about $8 a minute. Some of the hotels have business centers where you can buy a pre-paid card and call at a much less expensive rate. The actual calling process is not very difficult, at least from Moscow. Be aware that some hotels use pulse dialing, rather than touch-tone. This may cause difficulty when trying to reach the access number. If so, turn the phone over and see if there is a little switch to change to tone.

If you want to call from Moscow to United States using AT&T dial the local access number of 755-5042. To call from St. Petersburg dial 325-5042. You will hear an English voice prompt which will ask you for the number you are calling. Just dial the US area code and number. You will then be prompted for your calling card number and PIN. To call from outside Moscow dial 8 095 then the Moscow access code. If calling outside St. Petersburg, dial 8 812, then the St. Petersburg local access number. Since you are dialing long distance to Moscow or St. Petersburg, there will be additional charges. If calling from Yekaterinburg, Khabarovsk, Novosibirsk, Rostov-on-Don, or Samara dial 8, wait for a second dial tone then dial 10 800 110 1011.Whoever you call in America will hear an echo as you are connecting through a satellite. MCI's access number from Moscow if you are using Rostelcom is 747-3322. If using SovIntel then it is 960-2222.

A cheaper method to call is to buy a prepaid international calling card. These are available at most stores. By using one of these, you know ahead of time what the cost will be. You won't get tagged for hidden charges when you return to the States. Check with the carrier in case you need to activate it before you go.

Some carriers like AT&T and MCI also have special international plans that you can sign up for before you go. They cost $3 a month but allow you to call your home for around $.70 a minute. However, if you call some place other than your home, then very high rates apply. After you return from Russia, you can always cancel the plan and the $3 monthly charge. If your folks live within your same local calling area, you can set your home phone to call forwarding and this way dial your parents at the low rate. Just an idea.

When calling with your calling card it may be possible to save the connect fee by pushing # to end a call instead of hanging up. Then you can dial another number. Check with your carrier about this before you leave.

Since rates and programs change frequently, you should always verify the method you will use and the rate you will pay prior to leaving. You don't want any surprises on your phone bill when you return.

You can also buy an international phone card while in Russia such as a "Takso-phone" card. These cards are sold in kiosks (where newspapers and magazines are sold) and at metro stations. They come in different denominations and seemed to work almost everywhere.

Money in Russia

Russians will not accept American money that is dirty, torn, creased across the face, stamped in ink with a bank stamp, or marred in any way. The US Embassy will also not exchange any money that looks like that either. Their theory, right or wrong, is that dirty looking money is easier to forge.

It is recommended that you visit your local bank a few days before you travel and ask them for clean, brand new bills in 100s and 50s. You may also need a few 20s and 5s for tips. You need a $1 for the soda machine at the US Embassy. Emphasize that the bills need to be crisp. The bank will give you bills and allow you to proof them. Just give back the ones that don't meet your specification. Your bank should not give you any problems with this request. It is better to go in the morning and early in the week rather than late on a Friday afternoon.

By the way, it is rumored that after the United States, Russia has more $20 and $100 bills floating through its economic system than any other country.

You can wire money to Russia through Western Union. You wire dollars but receive rubles on the other end. There use to be very few ATMs in Russia and even then only in St. Petersburg and Moscow. This has changed somewhat and the number of ATMs in St Petersburg and Moscow has increased greatly. The screens have a Russian/English option. Try to use ones inside a building for safety reasons. Be discrete. Just remember that you will not have much time to go running off to an ATM. You will be on the go from the moment your feet hit Russia. The ATMs do not allow you to withdraw in dollars, but in rubles.

Neither travelers checks nor credit cards are accepted in most places in Russia. Again, St. Petersburg and Moscow seem to be the only places that accept these and even then only by the largest hotels or banks. Visa is accepted in a few stores and hotels in Moscow, however you have to be careful to review the receipt before you sign in case they add something to it. You can also obtain cash advances in rubles from hotel money exchange places using Visa with your PIN number. You have to be careful that the exchange rate used by the stores and foreign currency exchange places is one with which you agree, but nevertheless it is a relatively painless way of obtaining additional funds. Do not use a direct debit/visa card. You do not want to give anyone access to your checking account. Just use a regular visa card.

Since the Russian financial system is fickle. There may be times when you can not receive any money using a credit card advance or a wire. The best advice is to still carry American cash along with your ATM and Visa card. There has been a problem with the ATM system in Russia so do not rely solely on that means of obtaining funds.

There is no point in trying to change some money into rubles before you go. First, not only is it quite difficult to find rubles, but secondly, you really don't need any until you land at the Moscow airport. At the airport there is an exchange booth on the second floor. The rate is not the best you could get, but we are only taking about a few dollars difference. Generally Moscow has a better exchange rate than in the regions. Here is a website with the current dollar/ruble exchange:
http://finance.yahoo.com/m5?a=1&s=USD&t=RUB

Shots for Travel

Usually it is recommended to get the Hepatitis A and B shots, plus a tetanus/diphtheria and a polio booster. The Hepatitis vaccine is not cheap and you should check with your insurance company regarding coverage. Insurance companies may reimburse the vaccines if your doctor codes it for contact risk/exposure. If they deny coverage, appeal their decision and emphasize that you are adopting a child of unknown risks from a country with a high prevalence of hepatitis and that this is a small preventive cost compared with them paying to cure you. Also, tell them that the CDC recommends these shots. Push them on this. I have known Aetna/US Healthcare to first deny coverage then reverse themselves when pushed. Your regular doctor or the foreign travel office of a hospital should be able to give these shots. Your local health department may also give them. Most health departments have these vaccines available at reduced cost. Shop around in order to get the lowest price.

The Hepatitis A vaccine is two shots and the Hepatitis B is three, although you obtain the majority of the Hepatitis B benefits with the first two shots. You should talk with your doctor before receiving these shots.

See this helpful web site for additional information:
http://members.aol.com/jaronmink/immunize.htm

If you have a medical condition or are simply nervous about being sick in a foreign country, then you might investigate buying overseas medical insurance. This is available at AEA/SOS for around $55. Their phone number is 800-523-8930. They have a website at http://www.intsos.com/

Packing for Adults

1. Documents

You should be able to get both parents' clothes in one suitcase and your child's in another. Any more luggage than that, except for carryons, should be devoted to donations. If you have packed more than 2 bags for yourself, you have over packed.

The very first thing you should pack in your carryon is your documents. Do not pack these in your checked suitcase. These documents are worth more than all your clothes. You should place them in a large zipper case or in individual plastic sleeves or an expandable file folder. These can be found at an office supply store. You will need to pack your I-864, copies of your tax returns for the last three years, your 171-H, a copy of your home study, your confirmation that the US Embassy received the cable and any other documents your agency may think is important. Some agencies recommend carrying a duplicate of some or all of your dossier documents. Just ask your agency. A copy of your passport and visa should be taken. Of course your passports and Russian visas need to be accessible, as you will be showing those as soon as you land in Moscow.

Also, as part of your carryon you need your airplane tickets and lots of American cash (as well as storing it on your person). You should also put in your carryon your agency's phone number and the US Embassy's as well, in case you run into a problem at the airport when you land. One problem that could happen is that your facilitator fails to meet you at the airport. It should not happen and it probably will not, but anything is possible.

Some people put all of these documents in a three ring binder, but that can be bulky.

Here are some organizational tips for your documents.

1. Print out all the phone numbers of your contacts in Russia such as facilitator, host family, agency in the States, agency office in Moscow, US Embassy and anyone else you can think of. Give a copy to your spouse as well.

2. Timeline and instructions from your agency.

3. Plastic sleeve holding plane tickets and airline or travel agent phone numbers

4. Calling card and access number

5. Plastic sleeve holding passports (and copies of same), visas (and copies), and customs declaration forms.

6. Plastic sleeve holding copies of birth and marriage certificates if needed.

7. Plastic sleeve to hold expense receipts for adoption credit documentation

8. Plastic sleeve to hold extra pictures of your home life and photo of your child.

9. Type up tip sheets on traveling including tourist sights

10. Plastic sleeve for I-171H plus US Embassy confirmation

11. Questions to ask at the children's home and copy of all medical information on your child to use in conjunction with the questions.

12. Plastic sleeve for blue I-600.

13. Plastic sleeve for I-864 and all supporting documents.

14. Extra plastic sleeve for your child's new Russian passport and any other documents of his you have like new birth certificate, court decree etc.

15. Plastic sleeve for extra dossier and supporting documents if your agency feels it necessary.

16. Copy of map of Russia showing Moscow and the Region where the children's home is located. (Not a full size, a reduced copy)

17. Same kind of map of Moscow and of the city you are staying in, if one exists, showing tourist sites and streets.

18. Sheets of notebook paper to be used for notes

Sometimes after the court hearing, one parent unexpectedly must return to the United States. Thus you should take two executed notarized powers of attorney giving one another permission to represent the other in all adoption proceedings.

2. Clothes and Sundries

Most people go over to Russia with bags that exceed the weight limit. You just can't help it if you are taking donations over. The official luggage limits are 110 pounds per person. Delta divides it as 70 pounds for checked (2 bags) and 40 pounds for carryons (1 bag). Aeroflot is 100 pounds per person with 88 pounds for checked (2 bags) and 12 pounds for a carryon. They weigh everything together so don't worry about having the carry on a little heavy. Purses (very large purses, hint, hint) do not count. If you don't do anything to attract attention to your luggage in the States or in Moscow then the airline and customs officials would prefer a "don't tell me, I don't want to know" policy. If one of the Russian customs people does decide to get technical, the penalty is $5.00 per kilo over weight charge. This is not to say that occasionally a customs person might not decide to get technical. It happens. Just don't worry about it too much. By the way, Lufthansa reportedly never charges anything for overweight bags if you tell them they are donations to an orphanage.

Now these rules do not apply to Russian domestic flights. The Russians will charge you for overweight bags; they just won't take them off the plane. They also do not seem to care that the overweight is children's home donations. Overweight charges are simply a revenue stream.

Some Russians used plastic or duct tape to completely wrap their luggage. If you travel through the domestic airport in Moscow all you will hear is the sound of tape being wrapped around luggage. You might want to consider this, as then your luggage will look Russian rather than American, and possibly a less likely target for theft. Of course, if your luggage makes it out of JFK in one piece, you might consider that a victory in itself.

Here are some suggested tips on packing. The key is to pack light. You will not need a lot of outfits. One sweater, two pairs of pants that sort of thing. Of course, if you are not traveling outside Moscow then you might be able to get away with packing more. But it is really not necessary. One nice outfit for court is all that is needed and the other outfits can be jeans or slacks. Everything should be of the "no iron" variety. Since there is always the possibility that your luggage gets lost, pack some clothes in your carryon. Some people have used a vacuum cleaner to remove the air from the suitcase. This will reduce the size and weight of the bag.

Do not take any jewelry with you. Just a watch. This isn't a cruise. Why tempt fate.
Pack snacks like breakfast bars—your days may be long and meals delayed. Carry something to munch on.

Pack lots of small packages of Kleenex to be used in the bathrooms. Also small rolls of toilet paper for the same reason. Baby wipes work as well.

Waterless hand cleaner
Take lots of plastic bags both the zip-lock and garbage kind.
Pack washing soap packets.
European converter for your electronics
Take small ziplocks of powdered detergent (Tide) to wash clothes in sink
Take Shout wipes for fast clean up of stains, burp spots etc.
Some people take paper towels. If you do, take out the middle for easy packing.

Take a few disposable cameras. If for any reason yours quits you can still take some pictures. Also, take a spare battery for your camera. Also, take a European converter for your recharger. If you use a video camera, replace the film cassette prior to using it all up in case one of the cassettes turns out to be defective.

Keep a journal or a small tape player so you can remember all the things that happen.

Take some pens to write with and maybe a crossword book to pass the time.

Do not take a lot of books or books on tape. You simply will not have the time to use them. Take items you can leave behind.

Hot pot
Travel alarm
Small dual-voltage travel hair dryer
Adult vitamins. You will get stressed and you will get tired.
TravelSmith clothesline (if you pack light, you might need to do a little laundry)

Take a list of your medical allergies. If you are at risk for a medical emergency, you may wish to consider purchasing medical insurance and investigating what sort of medical arrangements would be available to you in Moscow. The two best medical clinics are the Filatov and the

American Medical Clinic. Both are of equal quality. If you get car sick, take some Dramamine. Car rides over Russia's roads are very bouncy. Also, take the airplane sickness bags with you when you get off the plane. They may come in handy for you or your child.

Take good photos of your home for the judge on your court date, the prosecutor and the orphanage director. They are very interested in America and interested in what will be the home life of this Russian child. Show books, maybe a piano in the photos. Bring picture post-cards of your hometown to share with host family.

Pack KaoPectate KaoLectrolyte Rehydration Solution that comes in dry packets that you mix as needed. This saves trying to take pedialyte as it would be too much liquid volume and weight.

You might take Bepto Bismal chewables to eat with each meal to coat the stomach and help prevent traveler's diarrhea and to carry artificially sweetened Kool-Aid mix to use as a rehydration fluid which can be mixed with electrolyte solutions to improve the taste.

If you are taking prescription medications with you, you may want to take a letter from your doctor describing why you need them. You will probably get away without needing it, but sometimes the customs guy can get picky.

Plastic Shoes to wear in the shower as the floors can be wet and grungy.

Comfortable shoes to walk around in.

Take a few bottles of water for the plane as well as a few for traveling in Russia. Be careful that you don't take too many, as the weight can be heavy. Bottled water is available in all urban cities and is sold by both Coca-Cola and the Russian Orthodox Church.

Take a list of useful Russian words and phrases or even a Russian/English dictionary. There is even an electronic Russian/English translator but it is a little pricey.

Jet lag medicine such as Melatonin, but consult with your doctor.

If traveling in the summer, take some bug spray as the windows have no screens. You should also take some hydrocortizone for bites and a spritzer fan to keep you cool.

If traveling in colder weather then you should have some very warm clothes in your carryons in case you deplane in extremely cold weather. It can be −25 in parts of Siberia like Magadan, and Moscow in February 1999 was no picnic. Pack really warm boots and hand and toe warmer packs. In cold weather take a nylon blouse with a high neck and collar. You can wear this under sweaters.

Take 400 film. You'll miss fewer shots due to low light. Make sure you have thick (warm) waterproof boots and very warm gloves and scarf and (preferably dark) hat. You will be glad you did. If you own fur— here is your chance to wear it or buy it. Black stretch pants (like for cross-country skiing) come in very handy with baggy black jeans over them. When it is really cold, jeans are insubstantial. Take layers. Either don't wash anything or take some soap packs and wash when you have to. Most Russians wear the same outfit everyday and so can you. The key is to take enough clothes, but not too much. Go light but warm.

If you are going to tourist sites you may want to pack a purse, as you do not have to check it when going to museums or the Bolshoi. This will allow you to have things with you. Any other kind of bag will have to be checked.

Take the usual toiletries such as a small bar of soap, toothbrushes with paste, brush/comb, shaving cream, a razor, shampoo, deodorant, hair spray/gel, alcohol wipes, antibiotic ointment, small scissors, contact lens stuff, makeup, extra pair of glasses allergy/sinus, headache stuff, prescriptions if any, Imodium, bottle opener, Swiss army knife etc, etc.

You may decide that you will listen to a portable tape or CD player. Quite frankly, you should be sleeping on the plane over and you won't have time to do any listening on the way back, and if you are on the train you should be looking out the window. On the hand, I do remember that on a 3-hour drive on a very bumpy road in the middle of nowhere I found some reggae music to be quite soothing.

Take a few books, preferably about Russia. Leave these with your translator or homestay host after you finish. They will enjoy them. News or fashion magazines also are good items to take and leave behind. Also take some playing cards and maybe a Game Boy or something small with games on it.

Take a plug for the sink, as many Russian sinks do not have them.

Duct tape is always handy. Large freezer ziplocks or some other poopy diaper container.

Laundry detergent for washing of clothes in the sink.

Maybe a fanny pack. Small alarm clock and small flashlight. The flashlight comes in handy on the plane and train so put it in your carryon.

Pack an empty film canister so you can put a little dirt in it from your child's home.

It doesn't really matter if you lock your suitcase or not. If someone at JFK or Russia wants in, it is easy to pop.

If you take a long distance calling card, make sure you bring the access number with you. (I recommend a prepaid card.)Take the number of your adoption medical specialist in America. Also take the phone numbers of your agency. Your agency will be notified by the facilitator that you have arrived in Moscow. Arrange for the agency to then phone or email your family to that effect as well.

3. Money

Your agency should not just give you a lump sum figure of how much money you should bring with you for in-country expenses. Rather, they should give you an itemized list of the estimated cost of traveling such as room and board, escort fees, interpreter, document translation fees, drivers, domestic air, domestic train, donations to orphanage, gifts to officials and host families, hotel cost, home stay cost and visas. This list will still be an estimate, however, it will give you some feel for where the money will be spent.

Take money belts for you and your spouse. Some go around the neck, waist or you can even get the leg passport/money holder. Take whatever is most comfortable and easily accessible. If you take a purse, take the kind that goes over your head and hangs across your chest. It is square and flat.

You will want to divide the money between you. If you have been instructed to give some to your facilitator, have the correct amount segregated in an envelope in your money belt. Some like the belts that go around the neck and others the ones around the waist. When you change money, be careful that you do not just open up your money belt for the world to see. There are many eyes at the Moscow airport and on the street. There are very few places in Russia where credit cards can be used. Some of the larger hotels and restaurants in Moscow do take them. It is not really worth taking them except that you can get cash advances from the money exchangers using a Visa card. Make sure you take your PIN number with you as that is necessary. Also, do not bother with traveler's checks, as they are not accepted in most of Russia. Except in St. Petersburg and Moscow, ATM machines are non existent. The ATM network in Russia is sometimes compromised. If you do plan to use an ATM machine, then set up a sub account at your bank with a separate PIN, and put in a few hundred dollars. Use this account from which to access funds while in Russia. This way no one can get the PIN and drain your entire bank account. If you plan on using a credit card in Moscow, call your credit card company beforehand. Many banks find the use of a credit card in Moscow suspicious and will put a hold on your card.

4. Electrical Adapters/Converters

Russia uses the European style of electrical outlets (two round pins a little further apart than our plugs) with 220 volt service. Assuming your equipment is 220 capable most modern rechargers are, but check) all you will need is an adapter plug. If you have a 110 volt only item, you will need a converter. Note that there are two options. Inverters and transformers. Inverters can handle high power devices (hair dryers, etc.) but should not be used more than short periods of time (NEVER overnight). These are in the $20 range and can be found at your local Radio Shack. Transformers are more expensive ($50+) and heavier, but can be used continuously, but transformers are for lower power devices (<100 watts typically). You can purchase an RCA "Foreign Voltage Adapter" kit from Radio Shack. Inside, there is a large dual wattage converter with 5 color coded plugs plus a chart indicating which plugs to use in various countries. All of this is further explained in great detail on the Eeadopt web site under travel and at this web site: *http://www.walkabouttravelgear.com/wwelect.htm#text*

Child Packing Tips

Generally your child's size will be smaller than his age. This is due to his being raised in an institution and nutritional issues. The rule of thumb is to deduct a month of development for every 3 months a child has been in an orphanage. Thus if your child is 18 months old then he will probably fit into 12 month old clothes. But every child is different so you should take a range of sizes. Be aware that as soon as your child begins to get proper food and medical attention at your house, he will likely begin sprouting like a weed. So assume that he will fit the initial size clothes for only a short time. Take clothes that you won't grieve over if they get lost, soiled or are so nasty after a week in Russia that you just throw them away. Sometimes after being with a child in close quarters with food spills, vomit, and the usual diaper action, it just isn't worth bringing his or your clothes back.

You may have heard that old rule of thumb that when buying clothes for infants and toddlers you take their age and double that for their size. For example, if your child is 12 months old. Double that to 24 months and that is the size you should look for. This rule applies to American born children. This "doubling" rule does not apply with children in Eastern Europe, especially those in institutional settings. These children usually are of a smaller stature anyway, and then add in the lack of nutrition and/or stimulation and they are just not as large as American children. One idea for Russian children that seems to work is that for every month the child is in age that is what they will weigh. For example, if the child is 16 months old, buy clothes for a 16 pound child.

If you are in Moscow or in a large city and you run out of items, you will be able to find replacements. Such items like diapers can be found in most large towns. However, it is not like going down to the corner store and will be an effort to get. Thus, try to bring most of what you will need.

For a baby:

Take several travel bottles and nipples of assorted sizes and shapes. Take 8 oz and 4 oz bottles. If you take the Playtex kind with the disposable liners, then also take a few regular Gerber bottles. Some children just will not drink out of the disposable liner type.

Also, Russian infants are used to drinking out of larger nipple holes than American bottles, so either take a pen knife to open the holes or buy some with larger holes. The Avent brand works well.

Take a few small blankets (3)
8-12 onesies, 2-4 pj's, 10 pair socks (tubes), 2-4 t-shirts

Jacket, a hat, gloves
9-12 outfits
Disposable diapers (10-12 per day, thin style)
Small plastic tablecloth to use as a changing pad
Garbage bags or large freezer Ziplocks for dirty diapers & laundry
Large diaper bag, unscented baby wipes (200-300)
Cheerios (at least half a box); goldfish

Take some small bubble bottles. They pack well, and are by far the most delightful toy you can take with you. Kids love them. Take bubbles for your child and as presents for the other children in the home.

Powdered formula: 1 can per 1 ½ days. The kids are hungry. This should be soy based, as the child may be lactose intolerant. You might even take one that is milk based as the soy is usually of the low iron variety and in some children this can also be a problem. The Russians use Kefir which I believe is from Germany. It is milk based. It tastes awful, but then so does any formula. If the child doesn't take to the soy, then just go back to the Kefir. It won't hurt for the week you are in Russia. Just use the hot water from the sink to mix the formula and shake it to eliminate "hot spots." The children are use to the Russian water so it won't bother them.

Rice cereal
Several orthodontic pacifiers with clip attachments
Anti-bacterial soap
Baby shampoo, baby wash, Baby lotion, powder, toothbrush, toothpaste, hairbrush, comb, nail clipper, thermometer
Liquid baby decongestant (baby Dimetapp)
Liquid baby acetaminophen (baby Tylenol, Motrin)
Small plastic bowls, sippy cups, spoons (plastic coating on the scoop) and 2 plastic bibs
Toys: rattle, teething rings, small stuffed animal, small blocks, keys

Don't forget that to a child anything can be a toy. They love stickers.
Small towels or cloth diapers for burping or sitting on your lap while
eating
Elimite (in case of scabies); Nix shampoo (in case of lice, but ask your
pediatrician as it may be too strong for small children)
Diaper rash ointment (Lotrimin), Baby wipes, a few band aids
Pedialyte packets, Infant Mylicon (for gas)

For a toddler:
A hat. gloves, scarf
Cheerios, Goldfish, crackers (no hard candy or peanuts because of
choking risk)
1-2 dozen sm. packs fruit snacks
4-6 containers applesauce
2-3 picture books
Toys: ball, toy cars, doll or stuffed animal, Stacking cups, baby rattle,
coloring books and a few crayons for the airplane, hand puppet
Sippy cups, bowls, spoons, forks, plastic bibs
Soothing cream for the skin if the child has a rash
Benadryl (Great for flying with kids. Make sure it is the clear kind and
not the pink colored kind. The pink dye can cause hyperactivity in some
kids. Just what you need!)
Actifed syrup-acts like Benadryl. Good for colds.
Scented diaper sacks (box of 50 purchased at Wal-Mart). Great for
"poopie" diapers at the homestay. You can also use giant freezer
ziplock bags.

Make sure you have baby food for when you find yourself traveling
with the baby and on the plane. You might not be able to find baby food
in the store when needed. It is good to have food with you in case of a
delay at mealtime. Respect your child's feeding time and don't trust that
you can get baby food when you need it.

If adopting an older child remember that the child might be developmentally younger than her age and therefore you should plan on taking toys that are for a younger child. Remember also that you are not trying to bring America to your child, but rather just bring enough to tie you both over until you can get your child back to the States.

You may wish to order an adoption medical kit from International Adoptive

Families for $75. For more information about these kits see *http://www.eeadopt.org/home/preparing/travel/travel_med/pediatric_kit.htm*

Here is another web site resource:
http://members.aol.com/jaronmink/prep.htm

Stroller or Snuglie

The discussion regarding whether it is better to take an inexpensive umbrella stroller or a snuglie is one in which there is no right answer. However, here are some thoughts:

In Russia, pedestrians do not have the right of way and the drivers drive like maniacs. Thus having a stroller can be a hazard as compared with fleeing with your life and snuglie across a street. Also, sidewalks are uneven, particularly with all the construction going on. Russia is also stroller unfriendly in that it has steps everywhere and high speed escalators in the subway.

Of course, a stroller is very nice when you are going out for a walk around the Kremlin in the spring or summer. If you child weighs 15 or more pounds, a snugglie just will not cut it. A stroller also gives a calming ride to the child. They get to sit and watch the world go by! If you are in Russia for awhile you may find that a snuglie gets to be a little tiresome as you travel around to tourist spots such as the Kremlin, Victory Park, the Zoo, TV tower, and GUM. If you take a stroller, also pack a clear plastic rain shield for the stroller. It will not only keep out the rain but also cut down on the wind blowing on the stroller.

If your child was kept on his back, he may not be used to the upright position of the snugglie. However, using a snugglie does give you two free hands and a stroller can be awkward to carry. Of course, if you find you really do need a stroller you can certainly buy an inexpensive one in Russia and use it while you are there.

There is another alternative which is an Over The Shoulder Baby Holder. You might investigate this option as well.

Children's Home Donations

Many parents try to bring donations to the home. Before packing donations for the children's home, check with your agency as to what is needed and what is the routine. Some agencies try to discourage donations and say that out of the money you paid the agency, the agency makes a cash donation to the home. You can ignore this and just do what your heart tells you. However, it may be easier and better to wait until you are there and actually find out what the home really needs and then go out and buy it right then, rather than guess. Generally, items are available in Russia, just that the children's homes do not have the money with which to buy them. You may very well find that being able to purchase fresh fruit and coloring books for the children is better than taking clothes that will not be worn. Some directors may tell you that cash is preferred so that they can buy what is needed. You need to tread carefully if cash is requested. Some homes have a special bank account for donations. You might inquire about this.

One reason an agency may try to discourage donations is that your extra duffel bag of donations ends up weighing quite a lot and is bulky for the facilitators to get in and out of cars, trains and planes. Just leave the duffel bag or suitcase with the children's home. There is no need to drag an empty suitcase back to the States. Most homes need blankets, sleepers, warm clothes, socks, and gloves. You need to take quantities of an item as they may have some 25 children in a home. Err on bringing just a few items but in quantity and in different sizes. Make sure that the medicines you bring are of a major brand, not generic and not close to expiration. The medicines should be of a normal kind with which the Russian doctors will be familiar such as Children's Tylenol, Motrin or Dimetapp. Ask your agency if the children's home doctors will accept generic drugs. Some do and some don't. Any clothing should be new and preferably with the tags still on. Used clothing, even if clean, is generally frowned upon. However, ask your agency if the home director approves of good used clothing.

Some companies will even donate items if asked. Companies like Hanes and Fruit of the Loom have sent children's clothes. Avon has donated toys, mosquito repellent and shampoo, and L'Oreal contributed bottles of children's shampoo. John O. Butler Co. and Wisdom Toothbrush Co. have sent toothbrushes and dental floss, all desperately needed in the orphanage, where many of the older children may have poor teeth. 3-M has sent bandages and Warner-Lambert, antiseptic cream, Ace bandages from Becton Dickinson & Co. and soap from Dial. Ascent Pediatrics has sent over-the-counter cold medicine and Mead Johnson vitamins, These are just a few of the companies who may be willing to donate items for you to take over.

Some suggested donations are:

Children's Tylenol, Motrin, Dimetapp
Diaper rash ointment
Multi-vitamins
Pediatric cough medicines
Neosporin ointment, antibiotic creams,
Anti-diarrhea medicine.

Toothbrushes, toothpaste, shampoo, bar soap
Bed sheets, towels, bibs, blankets,
Plastic baby bottles and nipples
Brand new children's clothing (with tags on, very important), shoes,
New children's underwear
Developmental toys are especially needed.
School and art supplies—pens, scissors, colored pencils, regular pencils, notebooks, crayons and coloring books. You can buy some of these items when you are there.
You might also take headbands or barrettes for the girls.
Leave any clothing that you brought which does not fit your child at the children's home.

Bringing a lot of toys is probably not the best use of your money. You can buy perfectly good Russian toys there if you see they have the need. Otherwise, the American toys will likely end up on a wall, unused.

Gifts

Small gifts for the people who help you are both a tradition in Russia and a nice gesture. The list should include the director of your child's home, your child's caregivers, your translator, driver, facilitator, and homestay host. Your agency should be able to give you advice on gifts and to whom they should be given. They do not have to be expensive, just of good quality. American made is preferred. Do not give gifts made in China. If they are, cut off the tags. The stores in Russia are now full of quality goods, just that no one has the money to buy them in quantity. Also, remember that the Russians you are likely to meet as part of your "Team Adoption" will be educated and sophisticated. (Our translator went to the Bolshoi twice a month!) They would really like American mementos, rather than consumables. Most Russians appreciate some-thing from your hometown.

Here are some ideas:

Calendars with American scenes are nice as well as scenic postcards.
Anything with a team logo on it such as a shirt, but no ball caps.
A kitchen towel/hotpad set.
Jewelry (coat pins, scarf clips) is always appreciated.
Coffee, makeup (especially Revlon), solar calculators
pen and pencil sets (although they may have seen lots of these), small
flashlights, post it notes
Candy, leather goods
Books in English for your translator
Pantyhose (beige, large sizes), batteries, lipsticks, gloves, scarves.
Tabasco sauce
American Indian gifts
Postcards of your city
Cutlery kitchen knives
Computer CD games and music CDs such as for movie tracks.
Cotton flat sheets
Sweatshirt (American logos are popular)
American magazines like People, Vogue, Glamour, or Redbook
Tea and coffee bags
cloth shopping bag, dark print is best
500 or 1000 piece jigsaw puzzle
large scented candle in glass jar
candy or anything else in a tin—they love the tins!
decorative playing cards
other games not language dependant

Stay away from bath gel gifts

A nice gift are small bags of M&Ms to give to the children left behind. If you bring candy, Jelly Beans, Lifesavers, and suckers are treats the children probably have never had.

For the drivers, a small amount of money (unfolded) in a money card or given in addition with a gift is always appreciated. It also doesn't take up space in your suitcase

Double check on giving pantyhose, as while that was a popular gift two years ago, there are indications, that is no longer the case. Also, some women do not use makeup, so check with your agency on that item as well. Russians do not usually make a display when receiving a gift and will open it privately. That doesn't mean that they are not happy. When they really know you, then they are very expressive and kiss and hug and even jump up and down over the smallest of gifts.

CHAPTER VII

Back in the USSR

Actually Traveling

You've gotten the great "court date phone call," or "first trip call" and are ready to travel to Russia! First thing is to check the weather in the city to which you will be traveling at *http://www.europeon-line.org/* Just type in Russia and go to the weather site. The weather is in Celsius. Moscow's weather can be found at *http://www.weather.com/weather/cities/rs_moscow.html* or at *http://meteo.infospace.ru./cities/html/index.ssi* You might also check out the American Chamber of Commerce in Russia site as it gives some travel tips at *http://www.amcham.ru/visit.htm*

Although it is rarely within your control, try to travel when your agency has another family going. Having another family to "buddy" with can make the experience much more enjoyable. You share information, resources, equipment (clocks, food, diapers), and help with each other's kids. If you have to pass the time for a few days before a court date or going home, having another family can really help to fill the hours. It can also feel safer. The best advice is to just "go with the flow." Since you are not in control of your schedule or anything else, just flow along and don't let the little things bother you.

Remember that this trip is NOT a vacation. An international adoption journey is physically tiring, emotional and exhausting work. You will be dealing with major jet lag while running from city to city and office to office. Meeting your child for the first time is very emotionally draining. You will be changing your sleep and eating patterns. Prepare for the trip as if it were a competition. Because it is. It's you against your body.

A generic schedule might look something like this:

Day 1-Leave US for Moscow
Day 2-arrive in Moscow and leave for your Region
Day 3- meet your child
Day 4-Court hearing (assume 10 days is waived)
Day-5-Get child's amended birth certificate and passport from OVIR and ZAGS.
Day 6-Travel back to Moscow
Day 7-Child's pre-visa physical
Day 8-Visa trip to US Embassy
Day 9- Return to United States

If you are in a region that follows the two trip process then this might be your schedule:

Day 1-Leave US for Moscow

Day 2-Arrive in Moscow and leave for your Region's Department of Education
Day 3- Meet with a notary if you need to file some extra documents. Visit the Department and look through the database or photo album.
Day 4-Travel to the children's home and visit with your child and the home doctor
Day 5-Tell the Department you have accepted the child and file the acceptance form, court date application and request for clearance letter.
Day 6-Return to Moscow and leave for the US

The Moscow airport, which is called Sheremtyeveo-2 after the family on whose estate it is located, has a web site containing a map showing you where everything is located such as passport control, baggage and customs. The home site address is http://www.sheremetyevo-airport.ru. If you are flying domestically you will not use this airport but rather one of the domestic airports which are located about an hour outside the city. Sheremtyeveo-2 is located about 50 minutes outside Moscow. It is 29 kilometers from Moscow.

Now it is time to pick up your bags. There are porters (sometimes wearing green vests) that charge about 50 rubles which comes to $2 or $4 a bag or sometimes a flat rate like $20. Make sure you negotiate the price before you give them your business. That is important. Having a porter can help greatly accelerate the process of moving your bags through customs, which is the next step. Even if the price is $20, this may be worth it. Those using porters seem to "glide" through customs. The custom officials sometimes ask families to open their bags upon entering the country. Usually if you are with a porter you will not be questioned and will pay no fine for overweight luggage. Also, in the back corner of the baggage claim area, there are carts for rent. You use to be able to pay for the carts in rubles or dollars, but I believe now you can only pay in rubles. At the end of 1999, the price was 50 rubles or $2. The porter in Moscow will stay with you until you find your driver.

Keep some dollars handy out of your money belt. Otherwise you have to pull them out while people are looking at you which sort of nullifies the point of keeping your money hidden.

You then drag your bags over to the red or green customs line or channel where they are placed on a small belt that takes your bags through a x-ray machine. The belt works, I'm not sure about the x-ray. Keep your eyes on your bags at all times. You give the customs guy your declaration form and he stamps it and hands it back. Do not lose this form. Make sure he stamps it. On the form you list cash, jewelry, eyeglasses, and cameras. It is recommended that you go through the "red" line, not the "green" line. The green line is for those who have nothing to declare. It used to be that you could simply breeze through the green channel, but now that most people are carrying lots of cash, you do have something to declare and should go through the longer red channel. While it is not likely, if the customs guy starts to get serious with you, just play it cool, and don't offer unnecessary information and when he stares at you just stare back right at the middle of his forehead. There are many people behind you and the customs officer will crack first as his first motivation is to process the people.

On the other side of customs are screens shielding the area from the general airport area. But you will see facilitators and friends pop their heads in and out trying to find people. Look for your facilitator or host while you wait at customs.

Once through customs you will drag your bags around the screens and into the general airport area. If you haven't made eye contact with your facilitator, look for someone holding a sign with your name on it. Your facilitator and a driver will likely meet you. Do not simply take a taxi into Moscow. This is a bad idea. Even Russians have someone meet them. There is a bus, but it is like a cattle car and has an irregular schedule and no one knows when or where it stops. If you have to arrange your own transportation, then have the Marriott pick you up. It's about $60. Or go to the Intourist desk at the Moscow airport, and pay for a taxi ride to your hotel. Even if the taxis are controlled by the Xhimky mob, hiring one through Intourist provides some safety. If you are staying in a hotel, you will likely be asked for your passport. Give it to the hotel. They will keep it for an hour or so. This is a hold over from Soviet days when all foreigners were tracked. If you plan to use the famous Moscow Metro, check out this site for a great description: *http://www.friends-partners.org/partners/skipevans/atl/russia/metro.htm*

You should keep your agency's phone number and their local contact number handy in case there is a glitch. The US Embassy number is 7-095-728-5000 (switchboard). The "7" and "095" do not need to be dialed in Moscow. The American Citizen Services Unit (telephone 7-095-728-5577) is open Monday through Thursday from 9:00 a.m. to 12:30 p.m. and 3:00 p.m. to 4:00 p.m., except on Russian and American legal holidays. In the event of an emergency, American citizens may telephone 7-095-728-5577 anytime from 9:00 a.m. to 6:00 p.m., Monday through Friday. After 6:00 p.m., call the Embassy duty officer at 7-095-728-5990.

You should try to have a local contact in Moscow as a backup. If you ask around you should be able to come up with a friend of a friend who is currently living in Moscow. Arrange to bring some coffee to him, and you will have a contact for life. If you want to meet your contact, tell people to meet you is at the fountain inside GUM or at the Tomb of the Unknown Soldier outside the Kremlin walls.

Customs Declaration Forms

All of the airlines have these forms. When you are about an hour outside Moscow you will be given one of these forms. You and your spouse should each fill one out. They simply ask you for how much money you are bringing into the country and any other valuables. It is easy to fill out. The form asks for "Purpose of Visit" and some people put "tourism" and others "adoption". It doesn't really matter. You will give the form to customs at the airport in Moscow. They will stamp it and hand it back. Make sure they do stamp it. DO NOT LOSE THIS FORM. You will need to show it to them when you make your return flight.

At times Aeroflot runs out of English forms and will only have the form in Russian. Do not panic. The form is easy and the flight attendant will certainly help you.

You may wish to obtain an extra English version of the form when flying into Russia as you will also need to fill one out when you leave. If you have trouble obtaining the customs form in English when departing Moscow, use your first one as a guide and fill out the Russian, German or French form in English.

The reason that you need the form stamped is because a new law was passed by the Duma and signed by President Yeltsin on July 5th, 1999, whereby foreigners are no longer allowed to leave the country with an undeclared amount of less than $500. Under the old regime, you were allowed not to declare hard currency brought into the country so long as you did not leave with more than $500. This was why you used to be able to breeze through the "nothing to declare" green channel at customs. That has now changed.

Filling out the form. The first line asks for your name. Second line is your citizenship. Third line is the country from which you are arriving. Fourth line is your country of destination, which is Russia. Fifth line is the purpose of the visit. Just put "adoption." Sixth line asks for number of pieces of luggage including carryons. Then you have a list of four Roman numerals asking about weapons, narcotics, antiques and rubles. Just put none for all. Roman numeral V is a blocked area. One of the lines asks for the quantity of dollars first in figures then in the second cell, in words. The other lines are for other currencies. In the line below the blocked area at Roman numeral VI, it asks for amounts of rubles, just put none. Then date it and sign it.

The form was changed in August 1999 and adds some blocks to fill in later regarding the amount of currency purchased and the amount of rubles re-exchanged.

You may think that you should not declare all of your cash. This will only get you in trouble or at the very least create an additional worry that you do not need (like buying Cuban cigars and smuggling them into the States in your child's diaper—don't!). The Russians do not really care about the dollars coming into the country. It's the dollars going out that worries them. If you are carrying more than $10,000 in cash into Russia, you will likely be asked to go to another window and fill out a blue form. I recommend splitting the money so you and your spouse are both are under this figure, but if you are over, not to worry. Just fill out this other form. The main thing is to declare what you have honestly and don't lose your form. If they ask to see your cash, just show it to them. If they ask why you have so much, say that you might be staying a few weeks and were unsure about the use of credit cards. That's close enough to almost be the truth.

If you land in Moscow without the form do not panic. When deplaning in Moscow you will find the forms right inside the door you enter in the baggage claims area. The forms are located on a shelf/table that surrounds a pillar. If you walk around the pillar you will find the forms in English at some point. While waiting for your bags to appear simply fill out the forms.

US Consulates

The United States has Consulates in St. Petersburg, Vladivostok, and Yekaterinburg but immigrant visas are only issued in Moscow. You can reach the consulate in St. Petersburg at: Ulitsa Furshtadskaya 15; tel (7-812) 275-1701; fax (7-812) 110-7022; its emergency or after hours number is (7-812) 274-8692. 7 is the country code and 812 is the area code, so you do not have to dial those if you are calling in St. Petersburg. The e-mail address is *Acs_stpete@state.gov*

You can reach the consulate in Vladivostok at: Ulitsa Pushkinskaya 32, tel (7-4232) 268-458 or 300-070; fax (7-4232) 300-091; after hours (7-4232) 471-644 and (7-4232) 287-290. The Consulate's website is at *http://www.vladivostok.com/usis/visaeng.htm*

You can reach the consulate in Yekaterinburg at: Ulitsa Gogolya 15a, 4th Floor tel (7-3432) 62-98-88 or 7-3432-564-619/91; fax (7-3432) 564-515. The Consulate's website is at *http://www.uscgyekat.ur.ru* and email can be sent to cgyekat@uscgyekat.mplik.ru.

Homestays

If you are traveling outside Moscow, I would follow the direction of your agency regarding where to stay. However, in Moscow you are likely to have some flexibility and will be able to stay in a homestay or hotel.

The homestay versus hotel debate is another one of those where there is no right or wrong. Homestays can be great. You get to actually live for a few days with a real Russian family. The cultural benefits will never be forgotten. Usually the Russian family will have at least one person that speaks some English. It could be the parent or one of the children. Homestay etiquette is that you don't wear your out door shoes inside. You take them off. Therefore, in the winter you may consider having boots or heavy shoes that are easy to put on and take off.

You will find that Russians are like everyone else. They like hot tea, although coffee is making inroads. They like sweets, think the western press doesn't understand Russian politics and do not like Gorbachev. They like to tell stories, have a party and watch soccer and hockey. The usual homestay host is very well educated and will have an advanced degree.

Usually the homestay is cheaper, although not always the case. Moscow hotels are generally closer to the Kremlin in case you want to get out and walk around. Homestays will be in the suburbs and will be difficult but not impossible to move around outside the apartment without guides.

A homestay provides you with an invaluable experience with a real Russian family. A hotel is just the usual impersonal commercial experience.

In a hotel you can walk out to McDonalds or Pizza Hut, not so in a homestay. If you stay at one of the fancy American hotels like the Radisson or Marriot, you can use your credit card. If you stay at a hotel, your facilitator will have to come get you at the hotel whereas it might be easier to coordinate travel to the Embassy and airport from the homestay.

A homestay may also provide you with baby-sitting service from the host, free or not, which may allow you to sleep, recover, and prepare for the Flight From Hell.

A hotel can offer you privacy and food choices beyond the usual heavy Russian meals. If you stay at one of the newer hotels, you will feel like you are back at home.

A homestay can offer you a taste of real Russian food. Breakfast might be bliny (thin pancakes), yogurt and tea. Lunch could be pelmeni (dumplings); a vegetable soup like borscht and salads. Supper is more soup, salads and main courses like golubtsy (stuffed cabbage) and pierogi (dumplings filled with potato or cabbage).

Finally, with adopting older children some parents believe that a hotel is best. First, if you stay with a host then the host will become involved with the child simply because the child can communicate with the host better than with you. This may not be a good thing as you will need to start bonding and teaching your child your family rules as soon as you can. For these parents, by not using a translator they force the older child to rely on them for their needs and for answers to all of their questions. This can help the bonding process. You can establish a bedtime routine, mealtime routine, bath time routine from the first day. The hotel is also a more predictable environment and allows the parent to better control events. You can focus all of your energies on the children and they on you.

Of course, some parents like the host speaking Russian to their child and letting her know what was to come such as the Embassy visit, plane ride home, your house etc.

Moscow Hotels

Moscow's hotels used to have the reputation of still being sovietized. This meant that there was no customer service, no one spoke English, and the facilities had not been upgraded since the 1950's. Since about 1996, there has been a vast building and upgrading program. New hotels have sprung up and old ones refurbished. Times have changed. Many people stay at a less expensive hotel on the way into Russia, but a more expensive one on the way out. The theory is that the added amenities are worth it when you have a child in tow.

One of the best resources is
http://www.infoservices.com/moscow/index.html
This site has maps, lists of hotels and restaurants. Other informative sites are
http://www.moscow-guide.ru/, http://www.tourintel.ru/index.html,
http://www.travlang.com/hotels,
and *http://www.geocities.com/adopting_from_russia/Moscow.html*
Wherever you stay, always ask if there is an "adoption" discount. Many times you will be pleasantly surprised. This is especially so on the slow weekend nights but not so prevalent during the business weekdays. Cribs are not normally available in the older hotels. Most families use a variation of the suitcase, drawer or pushing the double beds together trick.

Marriott has several hotels in Moscow. The Moscow Grand Marriott is very nice but expensive. Use your Marriott points if you have them. The Radisson used to be the hotel of choice for US government travelers, but the newer Marriott is now the "in" hotel and even has a government rate. President Clinton stayed there when he was in town. The staff is helpful and most speak English. It is a block from Pushkin Square. The Marriott Grand is one of the few places that take American credit cards. The phone number for the Grand Marriott is 1-800-228-9290. You can also call directly during business hours (Moscow time) and talk directly to someone in reservations. Their number is 7 095 937 0000 you might try email at grand.marriott@cnt.ru.

The rate has been quoted as $179 a night for a weekend and $199 and higher for a weekday stay. This includes breakfast. Deduct $20 if you don't want breakfast. Both of these rates are for a regular room with two double beds. This is called the Leisure Rate. As these rates are subject to change, always check before you go. If you need a nice break from Russia and a little taste of home, this may be the way to go. If you ask for the "adoption discount" and they can not find it, ask them to check under "local promotions." Sometimes during the summer busy season Marriott gets restrictive with the discount. You may need to take a letter from your agency verifying that you are traveling for an adoption.

The Moscow Grand will also arrange to pick you up at the airport for a charge. They have king-size beds, good toilets (don't knock it), free bottled water, and all the American food you can eat. They also have an indoor pool and spa so bring your bathing suit. You can communicate with them through e-mail on their web site: *www.marriott.com/marriott/MOWGR* or *http://www.marriotthotels.com/mowgr*

The Marriott has a Business Center that will allow you to have Internet access at $30 an hour. Just write offline then send it. If you are at Planet Hollywood one night, there is a cyber café below it that also provides Internet access.

Another Marriott is on Tverskaya Street (34 Tverskaya-Yamskaya) which is not as fancy as the Grand but is also very nice. It is also quiet, clean and most of the staff speaks English. A nicely furnished regular room, with one king size bed, runs about $99 a night excluding breakfast. A very large suite, with sitting room and kitchenette goes for $149 a night, which includes a huge and delicious breakfast buffet. Both Marriotts can book tickets at the Moscow Circus or Bolshoi, or confirm your plane reservations. Restaurants and the subway are close to both. You can also buy some staples at the local grocery and use the in room refrigerator to store the items. This might save you on breakfast.

The Radisson is also very nice and has a business center where you can access the Internet. The Radisson, like the Marriott, has a great health club with a big pool, a gym with weight equipment, 4 treadmills, and even aerobics classes. The Metropole Hotel is also nice, but is more expensive.

A brand new hotel is the Proton. It was built in 1998 by the Turkish government. It has been described as being like a Hampton Inn. It is not expensive, but it is not near the center of the city.

The hotel Belgrad is near the Arbat (one of Russia's great shopping districts). It is one of Moscow's older hotels, but has been somewhat refurbished. The price is also right, between $80 and $100, including breakfast. The staff speaks some English and there are plenty of restaurants and shops nearby. An Italian restaurant is across the street and a Greek one is inside the hotel. The Greek restaurant will send meals up to your room. It is cheaper than the newer hotels. It is not near the Kremlin but is near the Arbat. It is relatively clean and safe. The bathrooms are not as nice as the newer hotels. There are usually other adoptive couples staying there. You can eat breakfast in the hotel or go across the street to a McDonalds. It is a 5 block walk to the US Embassy which would be pleasant in the late spring and early fall. The babushka cleaning ladies in the hall will all talk to your baby in Russian and made sweet faces at her.. Be sure to ask for the rooms with refrigerators. They do not have cribs. It is close to two grocery stores with baby food, diapers, and formula. Do not stay at the Belgrad during the summer months of June through August as it has no air conditioning and no screens on the windows.

Back in the old Soviet days, all foreigners were put up at the Intourist hotel. The Intourist is a huge hotel located just around the corner from the Kremlin. It is very centrally located. Before 1998, the Intourist was a drab, no service former Soviet type of place. But since then a lot of money has been spent refurbishing it so now it is not bad at all. It is clean, central to tourist sites like the Kremlin, GUM, and St. Basils, near the subway station, and lots of food sites. The rooms come with a TV, phone, refrigerator and very nice bathroom. The staff is now nice and helpful. It is about $85 a night.

Another very nice and expensive hotel is the Kempinski Baltchug. It has an adoption rate. It has the usual king size bed, television, and wonderful bathroom. It is directly across the river from the Kremlin and Red Square and comes with a terrific nighttime view of both. The Kempinski is a 5 star hotel which is normally out of everyone's price range unless there is a special. Always inquire.

There is also the Swiss Diamond/Golden Ring hotel—which is located across the street from the McDonald's at the end of Old Arbat Street. This is obviously located well for shopping and is about a 30 minute walk from Red Square.

Sheraton has a hotel that is priced in the middle. It is clean and the staff professional.

Another old soviet hotel is the "Ukraina." It is located across the river from the Russian White House, which was part of Russia's recent history. It has been refurbished and has a business center where you can send and receive emails. It has large suites with lots of room but is not as convenient as the Moskva. It is priced between $100 to $150 a day. Breakfast is included. The rooms are clean and some of the suites have gigantic, high ceilings and may even include a piano. There is a gift shop and money exchange in the hotel as well. The hotel has little soaps and shampoo just like in the USA. The tubs are very deep and there is plenty of hot water (don't laugh). There are restaurants in the hotel. Food at the downstairs breakfast buffet is not bad at all. You will see the usual assortment of rolls, tea, coffee, hot and cold cereal, and sliced cheeses. You can even have a pizza delivered to your suite.

Near the "Ukraina" is a Quikmart type store within easy walking distance. It sells cheese, bread, juice, chocolate and feminine products.

Another old Soviet hotel is the "Moskva" at 2 Okhotny Ryad (095) 960-2020 Fax (095) 925-0155. This hotel is right next to the Kremlin and down the road from McDonalds. It is very convenient. It underwent renovation in 1997. In 1997 the price was $100 per night. The hotel is across from the Duma and when the legislature is in session the "ladies of the night" patrol outside. Another former Soviet hotel next to Red Square is the "Rossiya Hotel." This hotel is literally across the street from Red Square. It is very convenient plus you can get some excellent photos of Red Square from the higher floors of the hotel. It is a huge hotel. Ask to stay in one of the newly renovated rooms. It costs about $70 per night and includes a huge breakfast. There are cafes on every corner of every floor. One floor, it may be the sixth, has everything in English. Room service is good and not expensive.

If you have a large entourage with you, such as a couple of kids and maybe a relative or two, then consider staying at the new refurbished Slavyanka. It is more like a suite hotel with kitchen facilities. You can buy groceries and simply eat in. This will save on the hassle and expense of going out to eat.

Another hotel is the Hotel President. A lot of businessmen use it. The bedrooms are large, with two double beds, a desk, refrigerator and TV. The bathroom is fine and it has a large breakfast buffet. The hotel overlooks Gorky Park. There is a business center with the usual computers and fax machines. Like most hotels there is a money exchange in the building. It is expensive.

There is also a Holiday Inn in Moscow. It is about a year old and costs around $120 and includes breakfast. It is clean and nice. Some of the staff speaks English. It is about 20 minutes from Sheremtyeveo-2 and 40 minutes from Red Square. There is a free shuttle to both places.

Near the Shermetyevo II airport, about a mile away, is the Novotel. It is literally right across the parking lot from the arrival gate. It is on the other side of a major highway though, which makes walking to it difficult. The hotel has a desk inside the airport, and there is a shuttle bus. The hotel is 8 floors set around a central atrium. The Novotel is opulent downstairs and austere upstairs. There is a security officer in front of the elevators, and the elevators can only be operated by swiping a room key. A typical room has a queen size bed and a sofa, which turns into a single bed. It comes with a small refrigerator and a TV which has cable (including CNN). Bottled water was in is in your room, and replacement bottles were for sale at the bar. The bathroom has a combination bath/shower and everything is very clean. As is often found in Europe, no facecloths are provided. The staff are very pleasant and speak English. Many airline crews stay there, so the staff is multilingual. There is an excellent buffet breakfast which is included in the In the room rate. Room service is available. The Novotel has a free shuttle to Red Square leaving every other hour with the last return leaving Red Square at 11pm. Travel time each way is 45 minutes. There is a small exercise room with a small pool. There is a bar and an "American" restaurant The Novotel also offers day-rooms for about $70.00. They also have a late check-out for an additional $70. There is a small gift shop. Being right there at the airport can make it easy on your travel plans.

Remember that when you check in to any hotel, the staff will take your passport and visa for a few hours in order to register you. They will then return it. Make sure you remember that they need to return it. This is an old hold over procedure from Soviet days when all foreigners had to be registered. Eventually this procedure will disappear as has giving your key to the floor women each time you leave your room.

Moscow Restaurants

A good Mexican restaurant in Moscow is "Hola Mexico" (a/k/a Previt Mexico) near Detsky Mir. Its is located at Pushechnaya Ulitsa 7/5. The phone number is 925-8251. There used to be a Mexican restaurant called the Azteca in the Intourist Hotel. You can also order pizza from Tulio's Pizza or Deli Meals at 978-5776 or 251-3338. They also have a great variety of salads and subs. They will deliver. This may be a good alternative to expensive hotel food.

There are several McDonalds in town. If you have been incountry for a few weeks, there is nothing better. There is also a Pizza Hut, which is usually crowded. Also, a TGIF. Both of these are located not far from the Marriott Grand. Patio Pizza is also a favorite with Americans and is near Pizza Hut. There is a restaurant called Mongolian BBQ on Treveskya. It's about three blocks toward Red Square from the Marriott Grande. You can cook your own food so you know it's done right and the price is reasonable.

A subway stop from the US Embassy is an interesting Diner, the Starlight that serves great hamburgers. It is a favorite with expat business types. The story is that they brought in the Diner, lock, stock and barrel, from the United States.

Probably the best food in Russia is Georgian. Georgian food usually includes a good and somewhat spicy soup called kharcho, a warm bread called khachapuri which is stuffed with a feta type cheese, grilled meats, greens (raw) to be eaten with another type of bread, and good wine. There are two very good and reasonably priced Georgian restaurants. One is Diascuria located on a side street off of Novy Arbat. The Metro stop should be Arbat. The other is Guryia is on Komsomolski Prospekt, a ten minute walk from the Metro stop, Park Kultury.

Another good restaurant is Scandinavia located on Maly Palashevsky Pereulok near the Grand. It is a splurge place at over $50 per person. But truly outstanding fish dishes. And the place does feel Scandinavian. Another very good place is the City Grill located on Sadovaya Truimfalnaya (just a block from the Grand). Sort of an American style place with good grilled meats, salads and such, all with a semi California flair. Lots of ex pats eat there. The restaurant does have an English menu and the staff speaks some English. For reviews of all the good restaurants read the expat paper "Exile" at http://www.exile.ru

If you decide to go to a real upscale restaurant, and there are a few of those around, just be prepared to sit with the Russian Mafia.

Russian Culture

Forget all that tourist stuff, here is the real scoop on when you know you are in Russia. All Russians wear black clothing and the Russian women are dressed up all the time. The women will out fashion you, just get use to it. All of the men wear black leather type jackets.

Russians are very concerned with the dangers of sitting on cold concrete. They don't do it and they don't want us to do it. They believe it will make you very sick and cause sterility. So don't be surprised if a babushka yells at you for sitting on a concrete step. She is just looking out for your own welfare.

Every Russian is a member of the "hat police". If you are not wearing a hat then something must be wrong with you. A ball cap is not a hat and no decent Russian would wear a ball cap. Be prepared to be lectured to if your child is not wearing the proper hat.

There is a substantial difference of opinion between Russians and Americans as to the wearing of clothes. We believe that clothes should fit the temperature and that if it is warm, then you do not need layers of clothing. Russians believe that the warmer you are, the healthier you are. Thus, they will insist that your child wear layers and layers of clothes when you think just one layer will do.

Russian men do not push baby strollers or change diapers. American men know better than to say no. Still, you may get a funny look as you stroll along. Deal with it. On the other hand, women do not carry suitcases when there is a man around.

If you have a cold you should put garlic or honey up your nose. If you shake hands over a threshold you'll have bad luck. Whistle inside a building and you will lose your money. Hand shaking is a common practice, but don't shake hands over a threshold as it brings bad luck. If you give flowers, give only an odd number.

Please remember to tip the bathroom attendant a few rubles. This is basic bathroom etiquette. This is not a Russian thing, but a European thing.

Russians live in buildings with central heat. By central heat I mean the boiler in the basement is cranked up on November 1 and runs non-stop until May 30. The only way to regulate the temperature is by cracking a window. You will either get use to the hot buildings or live by a window. Those are your choices.

Russians are a communal people by culture as well as by philosophy. In restaurants Russians will not hesitate to join a table with strangers rather than dine alone. Men kiss men and show affection, women hold hands while strolling. Recreation is often arranged in groups, often with colleagues they work with. They prefer organized sports with set teams. In a collective society, everybody's business is also everyone else's.

Russians do not stand with their hands in their pockets. Do not tell a Russian that you have to go to the restroom, just excuse yourself. Do not lounge or sit on the steps of a public building. Drinks are always served with something to eat, even if only a cookie.

Now let me give you a few stereotypes, all of which have a grain of truth in them. Russians are more likely to be cautious and to value stability, security, social order, and predictability. They avoid risk. The old is preferred over the new. Russian culture is very male-chauvinistic, even though the women are more responsible. Russian women are excellent naggers. Men retreat from this by hanging around together smoking and drinking vodka late into the night. (If they had a few sports bars, you could hardly tell us apart.)

Now, Americans stand out like a sore thumb. There is not much you can do about it, even if you dress all in black. We all tend to smile and look up a lot, whereas most Russians don't smile and usually look down. Smiling is deemed to be a sign of insincerity and/or mental illness unless you are with family and friends. Smile and they'll think you're the village idiot. What is interesting is that your facilitator is probably a hybrid. He will have characteristics of old Russia but also of the new, entrepreneurial kind as well.

Russians view their laws as tools hanging in a belt. Pick it up and use it—if you like—is often the attitude. Enforcement of laws, rules, procedures is often not uniform within one region or from one area to the next.

Russians have a wicked sense of humor. Mostly it is about themselves. Here are a couple of examples.

A Russian peasant's neighbor owns a cow. The peasant owns none. The peasant finds a bottle with a genie in it. The genie says you can have one wish, would you like a cow like your neighbor? No, replies the peasant, just kill my neighbor's cow.

Stalin, Khrushchev, Brezhnev and Yeltsin were on a train. The train broke down and stopped. Stalin said shoot all the engineers. Krushchev said send them to Siberia. Brezhnev said just close the curtains and pretend like we are moving, and Yeltsin said, "I'll drink to that."

Finally, this from the St. Petersburg Times after a legislator had been arrested. "It is very sad that there are legislators in the assembly who have been arrested and put in jail," said Vladimir Belozerskikh, an independent lawmaker. But at the same time we should remember that a parliament represents the city's community, 5 percent of which are bandits and 25 percent are involved in a shadow economy. All of them would be included in the assembly in any case."

A good book to read which explains more about our cultural differences (and similarities) is Yale Richmond's *From Nyet to Da*. This book gives many more insights into Russian culture.

Safety Issues

Metropolitan Moscow has 22 million people. If you pretend you are in New York, you will do just fine in Moscow. In Moscow do not tell anyone where you are staying unless they are connected to your agency. Since you will be carrying around a lot of cash, you do not want to give anyone an invitation. Moscow is a lot like New York, except larger. The people move fast and are just as rude. A woman with a stroller is not cut any slack. Make sure you carry a piece of paper with the name and address of your homestay or hotel in case you get separated from your facilitator.

Russia has the usual begging and pickpocket scams: the girl with the fake baby asking for money; the groups of gypsy children that will crowd around you; the pickpocket behind you working with the man in front of you. These are all basic scams. Just be aware of your surroundings. If you feel trapped, create a scene. Of course, creating a scene doesn't always work. I once had a few children approach me on a Moscow street corner, so I danced around like I was doing a warpath dance. When I was done, they applauded.

Russians believe that everyone must eat, even bureaucrats. So it is possible a policeman might stop your car. Your driver will simply negotiate a fair price (fair to the policeman).

You may have heard of the Russian Mafia. They are not Siberian Sicilians. Rather they are Georgians, Chechens or even Russians. You can always tell who they are. They dress like Don Corelone, in black with wide lapels. They are the only ones who can afford a cell phone and a Mercedes. Some of them look like Odd Job from Goldfinger.

Their basic business is protection. It is simple, bloody and right out of Godfather 101. They will leave you alone. You should leave them alone. You can pretty much assume that any factory or store in Russia in any large town is paying protection money to somebody. But it is not your concern. Indeed, the big corruption is by the former Communist Party aristocracy, the nomenclatura, and not by these jokers.

Notwithstanding that Russia has a murder rate three times that of the United States, Moscow, as a whole is very safe for tourists. Personal safety is not an issue, although property theft is. You should not leave any valuables in your hotel room and all suitcases should be zipped up when you leave your hotel room. Needless to say, you should maintain American safety rules and don't go out at night by yourself or to places you don't know. An illustration of how much Moscow has changed is that there is now a public gun shop around the corner from the Kremlin that will sell you an AK-47.

During the adoptive process there is bound to be something going on in Russia that will give you pause. Just remember that your agency will not send you to Russia if there is a real safety concern. An example of a crisis is the financial collapse in August 1998. It seemed dire at the time and it did upset the normal wiring of funds. Families had to carry more cash than normal. Yet that was about the only effect the crisis had. Remember that the American press blows up every crisis in Russia as if it were the end of the world.

The NATO bombing of Belgrade was another crisis. Indeed, the Russians took a dim view of the United Sates' involvement in the bombing. Yet Russians were not upset with adoptive couples and differentiated between our government's actions and its people. In all but a few instances, the adoption process went on as before. In fact, the demonstrators outside the Embassy were actually a very small number and were outnumbered by the police. The demonstrations only lasted a few days and in all that time the Embassy's visa function went on as before. The only difference was that you went in the back door instead of the front.

Next year there will be something else and the year after that. Just keep your head and when the time comes to travel, take your cue from your agency. After all, they should be in almost daily contact with the facilitator in Russia whose job it is to keep you safe.

Shopping

It may be that you find yourself with a little time to kill. The answer is to go shopping!

If you travel near the end of the year you will have the opportunity to buy Russian holiday greeting cards. Look for New Year's cards in kiosks. They will display Father Frost, bells, winter scenes and churches.

You may also find pretty but inexpensive baptism outfits for your child. They are sold in the old Arbat as well as in other places. You can also purchase Christmas ornaments. (How you get them back to the United States without breaking them is beyond me.) There are also plenty of vendors who will want to sell you the usual Russian fur hat and St. Basil watercolor.

Many people are interested in Matryoshka dolls (sometimes called Matrioshka). A good place to buy them is in the flea market (Vernisage market) across from Moscow State University in Izmailovski Park. Also on Arbat street and in GUM. Prices vary quite a bit and are open to negotiation. Pick up the doll, turn it around and check for the quality of the lacquer job and the detail of the paint. Be sure to check if it is chipped at the center. Check the bottom to see if is signed and dated.

Lomonosov cobalt net design porcelain is sometimes a good buy. You can buy it at Gostiny Dvor in St. Petersburg and in other places around Moscow. The only way to get the pieces home is by taking them as carryon items. Lacquer furniture for children is also a common buy. You will see these in all Russian homes. Samovars are available on the Arbat as are Russian costumes.

North of Moscow are the villages Mysteria, Fedoskino and Palekh. These have the best lacquer artists. You want to buy boxes from them or find a store in Moscow which sells them. The boxes must be signed by the artist.

If you have never bargained overseas, ask a friend for the unwritten rules before you travel. Generally, you should not show the clerk that you are very interested in the item. Be prepared to walk away. Ask the price but don't look too anxious. Have a price in your head at which you are willing to buy. If you don't like the price quoted by the clerk, start walking away. Keep walking if the vendor does not reduce the price. If you want to buy several dolls or other items, demand a discount. When packing dolls for travel, be careful to avoid having the paint chip during transit. Wrap each individual unit with cloth or paper.

Moscow Tourist Sights

Before you go, read the many books now published on Moscow and its history. If you are short on time go to this web site: *http://www.lonelyplanet.com/dest/eur/mos.htm*.

In addition to the Lonely Planet and Fodor guides, there is also a pretty good travel guide by DK books at Barnes and Noble called, "Moscow". It is a DK Eyewitness book. It covers everything from where to stay, eat, shop and what to look for when picking a taxi (be very careful). It contains a survival guide with lots of practical info for traveling to Moscow and a phrase book in the back.

You can also hire a tour company. Some people have used Patriarshy Dom Tours. They can be reached at alanskaya@co.ru or try mariannashch@yahoo.com. There are also other tour companies which advertise in "Russian Life" magazine and which is available online.

In the evening many of Moscow's sights are lit beautifully with colored lights reflecting off the waters from the fountains.

Here are some of the sights you might want to catch at night:

1. The new Historical museum has lighting emphasizing the beautiful architecture.

2. There are fountains on Poklonnaya Gora with different colored lights shining on them.

3. The bridge on the Neglinnaya River is lit at night.

4. See the Church of St. Nicola.

5. Pushkin Square

During the day you might go to see Novodevichy cloister (New Convent of the Maidens). This is where much palace intrigue took place in the 1600s. Nearby is a cemetery containing all the famous Russians like Chekhov, Khrushchev and Shostakovich. The anarchist Kropotkin is also buried here. You might also see Iverskaya chapel or Petrovskiy castle.

The Kremlin, St. Basils, GUM department store and Red Square are must things to see. The Kremlin is worth a half day itself. It has a great jewelry collection in the Armory and just is a terrific place to walk around. The Kremlin has several churches on its grounds including the Archangel Cathedral and Assumption Cathedral. A row of Napoleon's cannon line the wall when you first enter the grounds. Near them is the Tsar's Bell which is huge but also very cracked. Near the bell is the huge, but not cracked Tsar's Cannon. On the outside of the Kremlin wall are many towers including the Tower of Secrets, which is the oldest, and Savior's Tower. Lenin's tomb is still on Red Square but its hours of operation are irregular. Across from the tomb is GUM, built in the 19th century and filled with hundreds of upscale stores.

If you like shopping then check out the Arbat, new and old, and the flea market across from Sparrow Hill. The Tretayakov Gallery (icons and Russian art) near Gorky Park and the Pushkin Fine Arts Museum (western art) are two of the world's best art museums. The National War Museum is also of great interest to a WWII buff.

If you arrive near a weekend, you may see lots of brides around Red Square. There is a tradition that when you get married, you have your picture taken at the Tomb of the Unknown Soldier. The Tomb is a flame and lies next to the Kremlin wall. It is part of the monument to WWII which contains markers with the names of the cities involved in the great battles. The brides also travel to Sparrow Hills near Moscow State to have their picture taken. Sparrow or Lenin Hills overlooks Moscow and the 1980 Olympic site.

You can also visit the houses of Tolstoy, Pushkin and Dostoevsky. If you hire a Russian tour guide, explain to her that you do not want every exhibit explained; only the highlights. The tour guides are trained to say something about every little thing. It will drive you crazy. Also, don't be surprised if you are told there is an additional charge to take photos in the Museums. That seems to be the general rule.

The Moscow metro is world famous and is very easy to navigate. Even so, you may want to hire a translator to teach you how to use the metro and to show you the immediate vicinity of your hotel. The metro escalators move very fast and so do the people. Just look for the big block M, they were usually blue. Walk down the steps and look for the signs that point you to the Metro (russian = metpopo). The subway is just like the subways in Rome, Florence, DC, etc. There is a bank of gates that let you enter with a subway entrance ticket or you can go to the first gate and pay the ticket person the 3 rubles. The easiest and fastest way is to find the ticket desk and give them 30 rubles (a dollar) and they will give you this white card that has a magnetic strip on it. It is good for 10 rides. You could ride the metro all day if you wanted and you would only pay for the entrance on to the subway. The card has a red arrow on it which you put into the slot on the entrance gate…wait a second or two and the card will pop out and on the back will be a print out of the date and time and a big "M" will appear on the same line. Make sure that you don't just put your card in and then walk through as you need to grab your card. Also always put your metro card back into the same spot so that you can always find it easily. If your card gets wet it won't work. The good news is that as soon as it dries out it will.

The metro is made up of 9 subway lines. Each line is colored as in D.C. When you buy your metro card you can get a 5x5 map of the line to keep in your Russian language book. It is pretty much useless to buy a English map of the Russian metro routes as all the signs down in the subway are Russian. If you have a straight shot to your destination then just follow the color coded map and make your exit. If you have to do a transfer then you will probably have to go up an escalator or down one to get to the different colored line. The great thing about their subway system is that they have a circle around the maze of crisscrossing lines. The circle is the brown line and it gets you easily from one side of *town to* the other much faster then a driver and with no pollution and no traffic jams. You should never be in a hurry to make your connection because the beauty of their metro is that every 2 minutes there is another train. Like clockwork. There are metro maps on the walls outside the metro, in the waiting area and on the subway car. A few stops have been added to the lines within the past year. Just follow the colors and the arrows. Also make sure that you know the Russian word for exit to the street so that you know how to get up to your destination. It really is easy and for $4 you can travel everywhere in Moscow. This beats the $10 an hour for a driver.

When riding the Metro, it's important to know the name of the last stop on the line, in the direction in which you are travelling. This will keep you from getting confused and going in exactly the wrong direction. If you are looking to shop, Izmailovski Park, is the name of the stop for the famous Izmailovski Park Flea Market in the ENE part of the city, where you can buy some very good Russian souvenirs.

Trains

A good article on the Trans-Siberian Railroad can be found in the June 1998 issue of the National Geographic. The railroad begins in Moscow and runs for 5,770 miles through the breadth of the country to Vladivostok. These are the best tracks and trains of the entire railroad system. In contrast, the purely local ones are very rustic in nature.

As soon as you know you know you are traveling on a train, ask your facilitator to buy you an entire first class cabin. You do not want to share. It will not cost a great deal and is worth every penny. If you take a local train the cars will not be so great. If you are on the Trans-Siberian, you will be in for a joy. The cars are similar to European trains. The cabins are small with two padded bench seats that turn into beds. There are also bunks above these so that you can actually sleep four. But why do that if you don't have to. Use the extra room to spread out. Lift up the bench seats and you will find compartments to store your bags. There will be a small table by the window. You will likely be served a boxed lunch which is not too bad. But you may want to bring your own snacks. Each car has an uniformed female conductor that is responsible for the car and who has a samovar containing hot water. The conductor will provide you with tea bags with which to use the hot water to make tea.

The train comes with a club car. If you go, leave one member behind to guard your stuff. Your facilitator may have a cabin near you so maybe he can watch your gear while you visit the club car. Do take a walk in the train from car to car. It will be a great experience. Be careful about ordering the Russian Baltika (Baltic) beer. The higher the number the more powerful the kick. A Baltic 3 is about right. If you drink a Baltic 9 you won't wake up until tomorrow.

There is a bathroom at the end of each car. It's functional and metallic. You will love the rocking and rolling of the train while you are in there. The toilet empties onto the tracks so the bathroom doors are locked 20 minutes before arriving and 20 minutes after leaving a town. There can be quite a line after leaving a town so you need to anticipate your trips. Safety is not a big issue on the Trans-Siberian. There used to be a problem on the St. Petersburg to Moscow run but that is no longer the case. Just take the usual precautions. Lock your door using the lock that is available. Some people tie a bungee cord on the door. The trains have heat but air conditioning is a little shaky. During the day most people lounge in the hallways catching some air from the open window. There is nothing more fun than sitting by the window of your cabin watching the exotic Russian landscape go by and thinking about your child. As soon as you are outside Moscow, your view will change to a forested horizon of birch trees sprinkled with wooden cabins.

Whenever the train stops during the day there are townspeople selling produce. You will also notice broken down factories that are empty and the miles upon miles of woods containing pine and birch trees. You may even see gypsies living in teepees. There is no telling what you will see. But the best benefit of a train ride after arriving in Moscow is that you can sleep in semi-comfort and get over your jet lag and be fresh for the children's home.

Here are some interesting Trans-Siberian web sites:
http://www.istar.u-net.com/ru_tsr_1.htm,
http://www.ego.net/tlogue/xsib/plan.htm
and, *http://www.e-course.com/trek/train.htm*

CHAPTER VIII

The Children's Home

The Two Trip Process

As mentioned earlier, some regions now require a two trip process. Of course, there are some regions that will still give you a referral while you are in the States and only require one trip. It all depends on the region. Under the two trip procedure, the first trip is used to identify a child and the second trip is used to complete the adoption at Court. For example, on the first trip you visit the Regional Department of Education (with your translator). The regional adoption official reviews your documents. If they are in order, she will go to the computer database or in some regions an actual photo album and give you a referral based on your parameters of age, sex, and acceptable health conditions. In some regions they will only give you one referral at a time and in others they will give you several. There is not a great deal of medical information. The official only knows if the child has something serious (cleft palate, missing a limb, etc). Otherwise they are all categorized as "healthy."

Then she will give you an authorization to visit the children's home. You then go to the children's home to meet the child or children you have preliminarily chosen. At the children's home you may have the opportunity to fax or email medical information and your observations to your medical specialist in Moscow or the US before making a final decision. Since this is not as easy as it sounds, try to set this up with your agency beforehand. Make sure you write down or tape record everything that is said to you and you should ask a lot of questions. If the child had their birth parents' rights terminated, you should investigate the reasons as thoroughly as you can. If you turn down the referral, you will be allowed to return to the Regional Department and go through their database or photo album again. This is how it is generally now being done in Moscow, Chelyabinsk, Rostov, Kirov, Komi Republic, Bryansk, and Krasnador. After accepting the referral, you will apply for a court date and request the Moscow release letter. Meanwhile you return home to the US to await notification of the court date, which should be scheduled within 10 days to 4 weeks.

If you decline all the referrals, then you return to the US and prepare to travel again to Russia, but to perhaps another region and do the whole process over. Some families have used the time before a court date to have a medical specialist in the States review the child's photo, video and medical records that they collected while on the first trip as a last check. Remember that the adoption is not final until there has been a court hearing. Some regions have gotten restrictive about taking photographs and giving you a lot of information. If you are in one of these regions, stand up for your rights. Under Russian law, they must give you adequate medical information.

There are benefits if you have to make two trips, although saving money is not one of them. The benefits are that you get to see your kid(s), meet everyone, see the town, see the orphanage, take pictures, find out exactly what to bring for the orphanage, figure out appropriate gifts for your homestay, learn a little more Russian, figure out all your connections without having a baby in tow, and make friends. You are more relaxed the second time as you are now used to the travel and can focus on the child. You also do not need to carry any of the INS documents as you will not be visiting the US Embassy on the first trip. Those documents will be needed for the second trip.

The biggest change in Russia may be this process of choosing a child while you are in Russia, without any advance information. This is somewhat of a step backward as for years the agencies have been pressured to do a better job of providing more complete medical information. Yet, this other process seems to have worked in Ukraine. It does place the burden of the medical review on your shoulders. It means that you must take with you the Russian medical definitions as described by Drs. Jenista, Aronson, or Downing and a range of appropriate height, weight, and head circumference chart points. In addition, you should take with you a few educational toys and a milestone cheat list. Just remember it will be normal for a child to be 3 or even 6 months delayed developmentally, but the toys and milestone list will allow you to fax these observations to your specialist for a better review. Be prepared. Have your list of medical questions ready, have phone and fax numbers of your Stateside doctors ready, know what you can handle and what you can not. Do not be afraid to say no.

Try to conduct your observation privately if you can or with just your translator present. Some homes crowd you with the director, caretaker and other personnel and try to hurry you. This can make the review difficult.

Again, after this Russian accreditation process of the US adoption agencies is completed, which should occur by the end of this year

(2000), it may very well be that most of the regions revert to the "old" process of allowing agencies to obtain a child's medicals and videos in advance with parents making only one trip.

Nizhny Novgorod

As an example of the two step process, here is how it has worked in the city of Nizhny Novgorod for several years. In Nizhny you travel to Russia without any referral but rather receive a referral after visiting the regional Department of Education and finding out who is off the registry given the parameters of a child for which you are searching. After accepting a referral from the Department you travel to the children's home where the child is located and you hear the medical history and background. After the child's history is read to you by the doctor (and translated by someone hired by your agency) the child is then brought in for you to meet and hold and play with. Then after spending a short time with the child you leave the home and make a decision as to whether or not to accept the child. At this point you can make phone calls to your US or Russian doctors. You may even be able to take a digital camera and have your coordinator send digital pictures to your spouse in real time, before making the decision.

If you have a power of attorney from the other spouse then only one of you needs to make the first trip. Once your child is identified, you may be able to have your coordinator take some digital pictures and email them immediately to the other spouse. You should take with you the names and numbers of experts you want to contact after receiving the referral and medical information. You should talk with them before leaving for Russia on what to look for in reviewing the medical history. If you choose not to accept the first referral you are given another referral of a child off of the registry and then follow the same procedure.

The first trip is to receive and accept a referral. Then you return after a couple of weeks when the court date is set. This has no impact on whether the 10 days is waived on the second trip. That decision is still up to the Judge.

It is not unusual for a family to accept a referral which they might not have accepted if just presented with the medical and background history back in the States. An advantage to receiving a referral while already in Russia is that you actually see and hold and interact with the child. This provides far more information than any picture, video, or medical data can. When considering a child you should hold and talk to him, play with him, see if he can respond to sound, see how social he is, see what motor skills he does and does not have, etc. Indeed, your medical specialist whom you call will likely ask more questions about how the child interacted with you and what you physically saw than anything else. Still, you do not have the same amount of time to evaluate your decision and your emotions are out there on the line.

You arrive at the Children's Home

As you enter the children's home, you will become very quiet and nervous. You will meet the home director and the home doctor. You will be taken to a waiting room, music room or perhaps a playroom. You will wait for a few minutes. It will be a moment that you will never forget. Then a caregiver will bring in an infant. The caretaker will hand him to you. The years of waiting are over.

One of the neat things that will occur is that the husband will become the center of the child's attention. A lot of children, particularly infants, have never seen a man or heard a man's voice before. They have been surrounded by women caretakers and doctors. This new creature with the whiskers will be brand new to them.

Start the cameras!

Do not be surprised if your child appears scared and is quiet. This is normal. After all, she has never met you before and there are all these people surrounding her. This may last for a few days while your child gets use to you and then suddenly he will blossom! They really do change once you get them home.

At some point, you will be told that you can now discuss your child with the children's home doctor. It is a requirement of Russian law that they tell you about your child's medical condition. This is when you pull out your written questions and start to check them off. Most of the information you may already have, yet it does no harm in asking the questions again. How much they are required to tell you is subject to interpretation. For example, a premature infant will likely have a medical record of at least 50 pages. The pages are handwritten. They may be located at the hospital and not at the home. There may be no copy machine available. You will likely be told that you can not have a copy of it even though you will pay for the copy and translation. You can always ask though. Then you might ask yourself if this is necessary as the child might be months or years beyond his birth, thus the information might not be relevant and further once the child is tested and reviewed in the States, what is the point of the old record. Just know that there likely is more information, whether it is important to know and how hard you want to push for it is your decision and whether the Russians will give it to you is theirs.

Now if your child's parents had their rights terminated, then I would push very hard to find out as much as you could. If abuse was the cause of the termination, that could have a lasting impact on your child and on your family.

If you are going to a children's home and know of another couple who is adopting from there, you might arrange to take pictures or even video that couple's child. If the other couple is waiting for a court date they might like to see their child and read or hear a description from you. I have known people to play with and give toys to another couple's child.

Sometimes the regional Ministry of Education's Children's Inspector will accompany you to the children's home. She is usually a very nice woman who is there to observe how you react to the child. She will also be present at the court hearing and tell the judge how the meeting went. She is almost always on your side.

Questions for the Doctors

After meeting with your child, you will then be allowed to meet with the children's home doctors and ask questions. Prepare your questions ahead of time, as you will be so distracted by your child and the whole emotional experience that you will forget what to ask. Generally you want to find out as much about the child's living patterns as possible. This will make it easier to transition her to your home.

Being in a foreign place is intimidating. You have the added stress of having just met your child, and you probably feel like you should not cause waves. You don't want to be the ugly American. However, in a way, by asking these questions at this time you are fighting for your child's personal history. It is your first advocate fight for your child. No one has as much interest in these questions and answers as you and your child. A lack of assertiveness will cost you the only chance you will ever have to have these many questions answered. Depending on how you feel about your facilitator/translator you may need to have a frank discussion with him beforehand. Some facilitators/translators have a tendency to think they know what is best for you and will give you only the information they believe is necessary. While it may turn out that you did not need the other information, there is a trust issue involved. You need to emphasize to the facilitator/translator that you want complete translations. No shortcuts.

Ask about your child's nap schedule and sleeping habits.. How long and when does he sleep? What is his typical schedule for a 24 hour period? What type of bed does he sleep in? by himself?

What kind of foods does she like? What do you feed her? How much? When? Does she drink milk? How is the food prepared? Does she have a favorite food? Does she have a food she dislikes or reacts badly to? What is the feeding schedule?

When and how does she go to the bathroom" Does she have a crib mate? Does she have a favorite friend? What does she spend most of her time doing? What is she good at? What is hard for her? Has she had any prior illnesses, accidents or injuries? How does she act when sick?

How does she bathe? alone? with other children? tub? shower? Is the water hot, cold, warm? How long is the bath?

What makes her happy? What toys, games or songs does she like? What does she like to do most when playing outside? What makes her angry? upset? How does she react when she has done something wrong? Or when she is tired?

What is her story? Are there any baby pictures of her that I can have or get? Where and how was she brought to the children's home? Who named her? Does she have a pet name or nickname? What do you know about her biological parents? Are there any mementos of her life that I can keep? a favorite toy? shirt?

Ask all about the time your child has spent in the children's home, how they arrived, with whom, and what they did on different milestone dates. You might try to fill in the gaps in their baby history, as these items become important to kids as they grow older.

Take pictures of the caretakers and have them write their name, and if possible a small greeting to your child to be remembered by, or something they remember special about your child. One nice touch is to take some pretty writing paper and have the caregivers write a letter to your child. You can then give it to him when he is old enough. Give any left over paper to the caregivers as a gift.

Ask to have the complete medical record on your child explained, even if you already have heard much of this when you accepted a referral. You may obtain more information regarding the child's medical conditions which you can then pass on to your pediatrician when you return home. Ask about the medical history of the parents and any siblings

Ask to see the child's play area and sleeping quarters and take pictures. This may not be allowed as they are protective of the other children, but some baby homes will give you a complete tour!

Ask what the orphanage needs such as supplies, medicine, and toys. You can always buy items in the town and give them to the baby home on your next visit.

You might gather some background information which may be of interest to your child later such as age of the facility, number of children there (average and right now), number of care givers, number of kids in their group, or in their room.

Ask where the birth parents were from if from another city. Does your child have a favorite caregiver, playmate, or toy? What treatments or tests would the orphanage doctor recommend for the child after you return home?

Some homes maintain photo histories on children and will allow you to purchase photos of your child before you met them, if you ask.

If you adopt an older child, make sure you ask the children's home what information have they told the child about you. In some cases, the child may be told that you are their biological parents and are returning to get them. This may be a symptom of the Russian idea that adoption should be kept secret. You will want to have the truth told as soon as possible, preferably before you arrive. You should ask if the child remembers her birthparents. Also, with older children you might want to know more about their mental state. Some of these questions can tip you off to attachment issues. Therefore, you might ask:

Has the child ever bonded with a caregiver in the children's home?
How does your child treat the other children in her age group? This could be important if you have other children at home.
Does she receive and give affection easily? Does she have good eye contact?
What is her temperament, and personality like? Is she easily disciplined? How is her attention span?
Is she equal in language and physical development with the other children in her home age group? Just remember they will likely all be delayed somewhat.

Some developmental red flags might be poor eye contact, socially withdrawn, self-stimulating behavior, self-injurious behavior, aggression, and hyperactivity.

If you can, observe how your child interacts with the children in the children's home. Does she play quietly by herself or join in noisily with the others? If she a chatter box with her friends? Outgoing or withdrawn?

A list of other questions can be found at:

http://eeadopt.org/home/preparing/medical/referral/post/caregiver_questions.htm

Court Questions

Below is a list of possible questions that might be asked in Court. Some Courts only want the wife to answer and some divide the questions between spouses. Not all Courts ask all of these questions. Just go with the flow. While you are responding do not be surprised if the Judge is checking your answers against your home study. The appellate courts are very methodical and meticulous. Long and complicated answers are not necessary. This is not a test. It can take from 10 minutes to an hour. Usually the Judge is there to make sure the technical requirements of the law have been carried out. He or she really just checks that the proper papers are signed and in the file. Probably 99% of all adoptions are approved. But make no mistake, the Judge is the final arbiter of the adoption.

Usually present in the courtroom is the interpreter, baby house director, a representative from the Ministry of Education (usually the Inspector), prosecutor, your facilitator, court stenographer (no tape recorder or monkey mask) and of course the Judge. It will not be unusual for the husband to be the only man in the room although Regional Judges appear to be more evenly split between the genders. All will act deferential to the Judge and stand as the Judge enters the room. You should be respectful as well. It is a formal affair, although afterwards every one will be all smiles. The courtroom is likely not to be too large, but the Judge will be seated on a raised dais in front of a huge judicial bench, containing three large chairs. But only one judge will hear your case. Lying in front of the Judge will be your dossier. Prior to any questions, the baby home director and the Ministry of Education representative are likely to give a short statement supporting your adoption.

You should dress in business attire and look the same as if you were making a court appearance in the States. This is not a time for jeans and T-shirt.

Because the Russians view the woman as the primary caregiver, most of the Court's attention will be on the wife, but this is not always the case. Also, sometimes the Judge will ask a whole series of these questions in a row which can make responding a little difficult since you don't know where to begin.

Here are some likely questions although certainly not all of them will be asked:

Do you recognize the authority of this court?

Your names, when and where born, occupation, address?

Your educational background

Describe your house, rooms, outside etc

Describe your neighborhood

Have you seen the baby/child?

Do you still want to adopt him after seeing him?

Why this age of child?

Why this child?

Are you aware of his medical record?

Are you prepared to do whatever is required for his medical needs?

What will you do if the child has unexpected medical needs?

Why are you adopting?

Why are you adopting from Russia? NEVER say you are adopting from Russia because its easier.

Why don't you adopt in the United States?

Why don't you have a biological child instead of adopting?

How will you raise him?

What are your hopes for this child?

Will adopting this child put a strain on your finances?

How will you communicate until the child learns English?

How will you teach the child about his heritage?

What religion will you raise him in?

What do your other children think about this?

What does your family think about this?

You may be asked to describe your support system-family, friends etc

Now an odd question that could pop up is one directed at who will take care of the child in case of your death. Usually families have discussed such things in general, but you might just be prepared to have a temporary answer.

You will be asked if you want the ten day waiting period waived and why. You may have even filed a petition asking for this. A good answer is that the child needs medical treatment or tests. If you use this answer, it helps if the orphanage director also tells the Judge that the child needs medical attention. You can also say that you have come a long way and that you have a small child back in the States that needs you, or older parents that depend on you, or a job which you must get back to as they have only given you a certain amount of time off.

The 10 days is the period of time within which the Judge's decision can be appealed. When the 10 days is " waived" all that is really happening is that the Judge has agreed to allow you to go forward with the process and obtain the child's new birth certificate, passport and visa while the 10 days runs contemporaneously. Technically, an appeal by the prosecutor could still occur, which is very rare.

(Asked of wife) Do you plan to continue working? How long will you take off from work?

What are your childcare plans after you return to work? (The Russians are perfectly satisfied with a response that the child will be placed in daycare.)

If you are asked how your house is paid for, simply say that you have a mortgage. Going into details of a 15 or 30 year debt schedule will violate the rule against long and complicated answers.

Do you want the child's birth date changed?

Do you want the child's birthplace changed?

Do you want the child's name changed?

Statute 135 of the Russian Family Code states that an adopted child's place and date of birth may be changed by up to three months if the child is less than a year old at the time of adoption.

If the child is older, some parents keep the child's original name or a variation of it as a middle name or a first name to connect with the Russian heritage and identity. Do not be surprised if the older child actually prefers a completely American name. If the child was placed in the baby home directly from birth, it may not matter and indeed the child's Russian name may have been given by the doctor or nurse and there may be no great familial significance. Most Russian children have formal names. The second name or patronymic name is the name of the birthfather. Most formal names have a child's or diminutive form, which are forms of affection.

There is no right or wrong answer to this question of the name. It is whatever you wish to do. If you get back to the United States and change your mind, you can always correct it when filing for readoption. Indeed, your child can always change it later as well when he reaches adulthood by filing a name change.

Now some don'ts. Don't get into a political discussion or argument with the Judge over anything. Even in America, the Judge is always right. Also, don't spring a surprise in the courtroom. No one likes surprises. Don't announce a sudden job change, marital change, medical or gender change. Finally, there is that 1% of adoptions that are turned down. Russia has over 10,000 foreign adoptions a year and at least a couple of times a year, somewhere in all of Russia, some Judge will be a hard case and simply dislike foreign adoptions.

Usually the Judge will not think crying is necessary, but crying after the decision allowing you to adopt this innocent child is not unusual. When the Judge comes back in the courtroom and announces his decision, it is a pretty special moment. If you feel like it, do it. It's your moment.

10 Day Waiver

After your Court hearing there is a 10-day period before the Adoption Decree becomes final. During this period the decree can be appealed by the prosecutor. This is very, very rare. Some say that the 10 days is a period in which you can change your mind. That may have been the case pre-1995 when the process was less judicial and more an administrative one, however, once the Judge has issued the decree, even if the 10 days is not waived, that child is yours pending the prosecutor's right to appeal. Therefore, if for some reason you change your mind during that 10 days, you will more than likely have to go through another judicial proceeding to have the adoption dissolved.

Now most Judges will waive this period and allow you to proceed with getting your child's passport, birth certificate and US visa. However, the Russians blow hot and cold about this so that sometimes it is generally waived, then sometimes an edict will be issued from Moscow and for awhile it generally won't be. Each region is different as to how they apply the waiver. Actually it is not a real waiver; just no one has come up with a better descriptive term. It really means that the appeal period proceeds contemporaneously with you going through the paperwork and taking the child back to Moscow. However, some Judges do not waive this period. You will have an indication from your agency before you travel regarding the likelihood of a waiver based on other families' experience. Just be aware that you really will not know until the Court hearing. If the Judge does not waive the period, also be aware that for some Regions it is 10 calendar days and others 10 business days.

If the 10 days is not waived, then you have some choices. You can stay in town and visit with your child, go back to the States in which case only one spouse needs to return to get the visa from the Embassy, or go off on a tourist trip. The best choice is to stay with your child, if that is allowed. You may be allowed to keep your children during that time which will allow you to bond while you wait. This will be the decision of the orphanage director and possibly the Judge. Even if you are not allowed to take her back to your homestay or hotel, you will still be able to visit and play with her every day. This is also a nice way to slowly get to know your daughter and to get a deeper appreciation of her baby home life. You can gather pictures and names of her friends and caregivers, find out more about her likes and dislikes and habits. For an older child, this is the best option.

If you have a young child at home, then you may want to send one spouse back to the States, as the separation may be hard. The worst choice to make is to go off on a tourist junket if you are allowed to see the child during the 10 days. You will lose time to bond with the child before traveling to Moscow and taking the difficult flight home. You will also lose the opportunity to gain knowledge of your child's life before she became part of your family. This is something she will eventually ask you about. Of course, if you are not allowed to see your child, then the 10 days is yours to do with as you please.

If work or family does not permit either spouse staying, then both can return to the States and pay for an escort to bring your child to the US. You do have to make sure that the region you are in does not have a requirement that a parent must personally apply for the child's passport or register the decree or anything else. You have to make sure the Russians are ok with you leaving.

Now the escort and the person who obtains your child's visa do not necessarily have to be the same person, but they can be.

Your visa representative needs to have:

1. The parents' I-600s that were filled out and signed by the parents in front of a Consular officer (unless the Visa Unit opened a file and kept those)
2. A power of attorney to act on their behalf.
3. I-864s signed by parent(s) and a photo proving that the parents have met the child.
4. Copies of the parent's passports.
5. And the usual required documents to present to the adoption unit for the child's visa. Certified Court Decree,

Amended Birth Certificate, Certified copy of old birth certificate, Child's Russian passport, medical evaluation form (pink sheet) etc

With these documents, the escort can carry the child to America provided the escort has a US visa, if Russian. The escort should also have a power of attorney from you granting them the authority to escort your child and represent you and her before immigration when deplaning in the US. You can also simply have someone handle all of this paperwork and then one of you can fly back to Moscow for a quick turnaround and travel back with the child.

After the Court Hearing

After the Court hearing you will wait for the Judge's decision. Usually this is no more than a 30-minute to an hour wait at the very most. Then you have to wait while the Judge writes up the Decree. Then you have to take the Decree to OVIR and ZAGS (Zapis Aktov Grazhdanskogo Sostoyaniya), which are the Passport office and Bureau of Vital Statistics, respectively. ZAGS prepares the new birth certificate showing you as the parents. OVIR prepares your child's new Russian passport, which she will need in order to leave Russia and enter the United States. Somewhere in the process your child will have had her passport photo taken. A lot of times this is handled by the children's home and you reimburse them for the cost. The Russian passport will have your child's name rendered phonetically in French, not English. For example, "Alexander," which appears on the birth and adoption certificate is spelled "Alexandre" on the passport.

Because ZAGS and the other departments are only open on certain days, and because you might get finished with your Court hearing late, there is always the possibility that you will be delayed in obtaining all of the these documents which will make you late in arriving in Moscow.

This is why you should have a fudge factor of at least an extra day in your itinerary.

That night your facilitator/translator will be busy translating the Decree and the other Russian documents into English for the Embassy.

Usually the day after the court hearing you will pick up your child from the children's home and return to Moscow. One issue you may wish to discuss with the home director is the question of what momentos or keepsakes you can take with you. Some parents take the clothing their child wore in the referral picture, their "baby" shoes or other clothing that is particular to their child. Of course, you should replace any items you take. Other "heritage" ideas are:

1. Baby bottle or eating utensil used in home.
2. Blankets used. Replace if taken.
3. A list of the eating/ and daily routine of your child
4. A spoonful of "earth" from outside the home. Film canisters are good to use.
5. A leaf or two from a tree outside the home.
6. Any personal items used by child.
7. Have the caretakers write a goodbye note to your child.

Add pictures of all these items to your child's life book, they are priceless.

If you are leaving your translator/facilitator behind in the region as you travel back to Moscow, then you may want to ask him to help "prepare" your child for his new life. This is especially important if the child is older (3 years and up) Have someone explain to the child in RUSSIAN, as English means nothing to him at that point, what is happening to them, and what is going to happen to them. Have them show your child photos that you brought from home of your family, pointing out his sisters, brothers, dogs, cats, house, etc. It will make the transition so much easier. Explain the trip he is about to take to Moscow and the traveling on a train or airplane. Explaining to your child what is about to happen will help him successfully leave behind the children's home and all of his friends.

CHAPTER IX

Back to Moscow

Medical Exam in Moscow

Before your child can receive a visa she must have a medical clearance. The form is known as the "pink form" although it is white, not pink. This exam is done at either the American Medical Clinic (7) 095-956-3366 or the Filatov Medical Clinic (7) 095-254-9028 or 095-423-7780. They are open on weekends. The Filatov Medical Clinic has been known to complete the exam in your hotel room when the child is sick. It is a two story building with a tree lined driveway and courtyard. It is not far from the US Embassy. The American is off a side street. Both of the clinics are very similar and offer pretty good treatment.(They also have clean bathrooms, so take the opportunity.) Both have Russian doctors who speak English and have some Western training. The exam is not thorough but rather a general look at the child. The evaluation is done for the purpose of preventing immigrants with infectious diseases from entering the country. The evaluation should last about 30 minutes. If you know your child has some illness, point that out to the doctor and obtain medicine. Review with the doctor the list of medical conditions you were given when you first received the referral. It might shed some additional light which you can then pass on to your pediatrician.

You can also ask the doctor for some medicine, if are feeling ill.

The exam at Filatov cost $95 and at the American about $100. You should submit the expense to your insurance company when you return to the States. The medical clearance form is given to the US Embassy. Ask the doctor to make you a copy so you can keep it for the child's medical records.

The United States also requires certain vaccinations prior to the issuance of an immigrant visa for an adopted child. This is not a requirement for any child under 10 years of age as long as you promise to vaccinate them when you return to the States. Since you were planning to do this anyway, this is not problem. For older children, bringing the child's record from the home so that the panel physician can certify it may satisfy vaccination requirement. Of course, even for these children, you would want to reimmunize once you are back in the States.

Vladivostok

In Vladivostok, the U.S. Consulate coordinates the issuance of the child's visa with the US Embassy in Moscow so that the parents are not required to make the 10 hour, 7 time zone trip to Moscow.

The physical is done in Vladivostok, and the parents make a trip with the child to the Consulate. A Consular officer verifies the identity of each child, signing a document prepared by the agency according to

Embassy specifications. The agency facilitator, using a power of attorney, makes the trip to Moscow while the passports are being processed. It is much less stressful and less expensive for the adopting parents. The parents then wait in Vladivostok for the facilitator's return from Moscow with the visa.

By the way, you have basically three choices of where to stay in Vladivostok. The least expensive is the Hotel Vladivostok, which has slowly been undergoing refurbishing. It is a bit rustic. It is said that along with your water you will also get your minerals. The Hotel Vladivostok does have laundry service. Also, there is a baby store (diapers, food) just down from the hotel (towards the train depot) and a grocery store across the street from the Hotel Versailles. There is another baby store north of the "Barbie" store. Take with you a cookie tin, or a sturdy Tupperware container, or something else that you can use to bring home fragile souvenirs such as tiny porcelain dolls for Christmas ornaments, which can be found at a store called Nostalgia. Nostalgia is down the hill, to the left, coming from the parking lot of the Hotel Vladivostok. It has a restaurant and a gift shop. Just keep on going down the hill to get to the post office, the main train station, and the sea terminal. Catch a tram by the statue of Lenin and go to the heart of downtown.

Moving up the hotel list is the Versailles which is more expensive. Both Vladivostok and Versailles are convenient to town. The most expensive, but also the least convenient, is the Vlad Motor Inn. It is close to American standards.

Embassy

By the time the Embassy visit arrives, you are in countdown mode. You are making the big push for the finish, knowing that the Flight From Hell is coming. You are checking things off. You've had the Court hearing, gotten the child, returned to Moscow, done the medical visit and are headed for home. Emotionally you are wearing down. Just hang in there, it will soon be over.

The Visa Unit is located at the old Embassy address at Novinskiy Bul'var 19/23 Moscow, Russia. The Embassy itself has actually moved to the new chancery building. This is the notorious building that the KGB had wiretapped from top to bottom in the 1980's. Presumably it is now been "de-bugged." The telephone number of the Visa Unit is (7)(095) 728-5058 or 5000, ext.5804. You do not have to dial the (7) if in Russia and the (095) if in Moscow. It has a good informational site at *http://www.usia.gov/posts/moscow.html*

The Embassy visit is usually no big deal. You do need to check the holiday schedule as the Embassy closes for both US and Russian holidays. There is no need to dress up for it. The Embassy personnel are very happy for you. The purpose of the Embassy visit is to obtain an immigrant visa for your child to enter the United States. Without such a visa, your child can not enter the US. Just because you have a Russian decree of adoption,which is recognized by the United States government, it does not automatically confer upon your child the right to be a citizen or the right to enter the United States. In front of the Embassy are Russian guards as well as American Marines. There will be a line of people. These are Russians. Go to the front of the line and tell them you are an American with a visa appointment. You will be let right in. The Marine guard will inspect your bags and store your camera and camcorder. You will go through the usual metal detector. It is all very ordinary. You will be directed to the waiting room which is about 15 feet wide and 60 feet or so long.

At the Embassy you will turn in your paperwork. It will probably be at Window 12 in the back. A clerk will review that you have all the necessary papers and will ask you to sign a few more forms like the Application for Immigrant Visa (Form OF-230). The Embassy clerk's initial review is just to make sure you have all of the necessary documents. You will need the child's dossier, Federal tax returns for last year and 3 years, W-2s if required, Affidavit of Support (I-864) notarized in the US, I-600 (Blue form) to be signed in front of a Consular officer, and pre-visa physical report. This is the "Pink sheet," that is actually white, obtained in Moscow from the American Medical Clinic or Filatov. You may be asked to sign a waiver of immunizations. This form is just a promise by you that when you are back home you will have your child given all of the age appropriate immunization shots. Since this is what you plan to do anyway, it is an easy promise. You will then sit back down and your papers will be reviewed in the back.

Your agency should supply you with the list of the documents you need to bring. It is important that you review all of the documents with your facilitator the day before you go to the Embassy. Insist on it. You should also bring a copy of your I-171H, Visa 37 confirmation and your home study just in case. You do not need any surprises at the Embassy. When you deliver your documents to the clerk you will pay him $335 for each child's visa. Payment may be made in cash (dollars or rubles) or travelers' checks. They do not take credit cards or personal checks. The $335 visa fee is unrelated to the $460 you may have paid when you filed your I-600A. If the paperwork is all in order, you will receive an appointment ticket to return that afternoon. If it is not in order, you will not get your child's Visa that day and will have to wait until the paperwork is fixed. In the afternoon, you and your child will go to the Embassy for your 15 - minute interview. You will need to bring with you the receipt for the $335 Visa application fee. Do not lose this receipt.

In order to get into the Embassy for your appointment, you need to be at the Arch entrance to the American Embassy a few minutes before the designated time. If you are there too early, you will just have to wait outside. Just don't be later either. Only American citizens and their adopted children are admitted to the Embassy for the interview. Agency representatives, drivers etc. must wait outside the Arch.

Parents present their interview ticket and their U.S. passports to the Embassy guards and are then escorted from the Arch to the entrance of the Spoede Building. The Embassy also wants either a driver's license or credit card, which they will hold and in return give you an identification badge. Only parents on the interview list are admitted. After passing through a security checkpoint at the entrance to the Spoede Building, you will follow the signs to the orphan visa interview waiting area, which is located behind the foyer of the building. A children's room has been established for children who are a bit bouncy.

The families will be called to one of four windows for the visa interview. The interview usually doesn't last more than 15 minutes. Parents will be asked about the adoption process, their financial status, and the health of the adopted child. They will also sign the Form 230 immigrant visa application on behalf of their child or children. This Application is submitted in the morning with your documents, but is actually signed by you at the interview, since a Consular Officer must witness it.

If the Visa is approved, the officer will sign the appropriate forms and hand the entire visa package to an Immigrant Visa Unit employee who will complete the processing of the visa and hand the sealed immigrant visa envelope to you after the interview. If there is a problem with the documents, the consular officer will discuss with you what the remaining issues are, and suggestions as to how they might be resolved.

After you receive the Visa, and unless you are just too tired, you will have this huge grin on your face, as you will have finished with all official paperwork to adopt your child. (There is some follow up paperwork back in the States, but why ruin the moment.) You then leave the Spoede Building and follow a guided path back to the Arch and Novinskiy Bulvar.

After the interview, you will be given the sealed Visa package. Do NOT open this package and do NOT pack it in your luggage. It goes in your carry-on that is with you at all times to be delivered to immigration once you have landed in the United States. Once you have received the Visa package, you or your representative may then register your child at the Ministry of Foreign Affairs, if you would rather do that in Moscow than in the States.

Leaving Moscow for Home

You will likely need to confirm your reservation a day or so before your flight. The phone number for Delta in Moscow is (095) 578-2939. If calling from Moscow, you do not need to dial (095).

Make sure you have your child's visa document package in your carryon. You will need to give this to US immigration when you land. At the Moscow airport you will need to show the Russians your Russian exit visa, your customs declaration form that you filled out when you landed, your passport, and your child's Russian passport. The airline will want to see your ticket and your child's.

You are not allowed to leave Russia with more money than when you came in. They used to give you a $500 cushion, however they have recently become very strict. So you and your spouse should divide your money before you leave and make sure you are under the amount with which you entered Russia. This should not be difficult. Just don't let one person carry all the money so that that a spouse is more than $500 over the amount she brought in. This can be troublesome if one spouse has gone home early. There is a form that you can buy for like $70 to get around this problem. A money exchanger or the US Embassy should be able to find it for you.

Get to the airport no later than 2 hours before your flight. Even earlier if you can. You will have much to do. First, go to the airline counter and pay the change of flight penalty if applicable. Do not use a credit card but pay in cash. Then go to your airline. They will want to see everyone's passports and tickets. Then go through customs and give them your customs declaration form. Then get in line to go through passport control. This is what takes the longest time to go through. They will review your passport, exit visa, and anything else they want. They may wish to look at your child's sealed US visa package, but you will get instructions from the Embassy that they should not and if they try, for you to call for a supervisor and also call the Embassy. Russian passport control is so use to adoptive parents that this is really not an issue anymore.

The passport control/border guard may ask for the Russian adoption decree. Just show it to them. All of your original Russian documents should be in your carryon in case they want to look at something.

Once you are through the passport control/border guard station you are home free. A load will come off your shoulder and you will really feel like it is finally over, you are headed for home. On the other side of the border station are duty free shops and restaurants that take rubles and dollars. You can also make phone calls from there. Usually you end up sitting on the floor by your gate with dozens of other adoptive parents, some of whom you met at the Embassy.

Now for the Flight From Hell!

Flight From Hell

Imagine being taken from the only home you know, surrounded by people you don't know, speaking a language you don't know, and then being placed in a flying machine which you may never have seen. Add to this mix that you are hungry, sleepy, not feeling well and generally cranky. This is your child. It might also be you. This is why the return flight to the United States is called the Flight From Hell. Businessmen try to avoid it all costs. On the flights are many parents and children. It can be very noisy.

You will not sleep on the plane. Therefore, it is critical that you get a very good night's sleep the night before. It may be 20 hours or so before you are able to sleep again. Through it all just keep clicking your ruby slippers and repeating "home, home, there's no place like home...."

You might take something to soothe your child on the flight like Benadryl or Dramamine. Ask your pediatrician regarding the correct dosage based on the child's weight. Test its effect in Moscow before flying as the pink kind may have the opposite effect because of the dye involved. (I recommend the clear kind.) Also, a child might have an ear infection or be congested which flying would aggravate. If you know that your child has an ear problem ask your pediatrician what you can give him to make the flight better. You can also ask the doctor at the American Medical Clinic or Filatov. Pack some Dimetapp just in case. You might give an infant something to drink while the plane takes off and lands. An older child should chew gum or also drink something to keep the ears open. Entertain them with some toys like a set of stacking cups, small cars, rattles, plastic keys, or small stuffed animals. Take some snacks. Feeding them helps.

When you land, just follow the rest of your fellow passengers to the line for US citizens at immigration. You do not have to go through the non-citizen line even though your child is a not a citizen. At JFK, there are usually about ten immigration booths so you get through it very quickly. Immigration is usually not very difficult. After they check your passports you will be directed to an immigration office where they will check your child's visa. Do not take any pictures of the INS personnel or office. This is a very bad idea and they do not like it. At immigration they will take that sealed package you received at the US Embassy in Moscow. (Remember, do not pack it in checked luggage or open it.) If you land at JFK, your whole customs and immigration experience will likely be 25 minutes tops. INS will stamp your child's Russian passport with "IR3" and give her a number. Double-check your child's passport that this is what they did. You will then be free to pick up your luggage, run it through customs and recheck it. If you are making a connecting flight, do not hesitate but go directly to the connecting gate. The reason for this is that JFK is not a small airport and getting to the other gate can take longer than you think. You do not want to spend any more time than necessary in an airport with your very tired family. You just want to get home as quickly as possible.

If you are lucky, your child's green card (which is not really green) showing her to be a Resident Alien will show up within 6 weeks to a year later with the same number as written in her passport. It really is an irrelevant document, as you do not need it to file for your child's citizenship.

When you arrive home, you will be exhausted and probably a little sick. If you can have a relative or family friend stay with you for a week while you and the child adjust, it would be better for all.

CHAPTER X

Home Sweet Home

Insurance

The Health Insurance Portability and Accountability Act of 1996 helped remedy problems with health care coverage for adopted children. The Act mandates that all employers who provide *group* health coverage for their employees must extend the same coverage to adopted children as they do other dependents. Coverage may not be restricted because of "pre-existing conditions" and must take effect at the time of a child's placement. There are some exceptions and you should check with your plan administrator.

You have a period of 30 days in which to notify your insurance company/plan administrator of the adoption. If you do not notify them within 30 days, it is as if you are adding an existing family member to the policy and there will be pre-existing conditions limitations, as per your policy's description. To be on the safe side as far as when that 30 days begins to run, notify your insurance company as soon as you return to the States. You may wish to send the notification by certified mail in addition to sending it through your company.

Bathing Russian children can be a problem when you first try it. Sometimes it is because they were only bathed in cold water, were washed with a brush or treated roughly. The soap may also have been very harsh and painful to their eyes. Also, some homes treat circulation problems with a shower of cold water. If your child shows anxiety regarding bathing, it will be a short-term problem. Here are some techniques to reduce the anxiety.

1. Make the water warm before placing the child in the tub and then get into the bath with him. Just put in a little water at first. There is no need to fill up the tub.

2. Put a few familiar toys in the tub. Not a lot, just a few. You can let him play with them from the outside first.

3. Reduce the light in the bathroom so that it is not as bright.

4. Talk or sing softly to your child in a calming voice during the entire bathing experience.

5. Hold your child during the entire bath.

6. Do little actual washing the first couple of times to try to get the child used to the environment. You might even do sponge baths for awhile.

7. Dry her in a warm towel and very gently.

8. Let the child set the pace of acclimation.. He needs to learn to trust you and the tub.

Go through this experience a couple of times and the child should lose his anxiety.

Pediatrician Visit

When you return home your child should be given a thorough medical screening. It is best if both spouses are present to help with questioning the doctor. You may find that your child is the only Eastern European child the doctor has seen. If so, then you will need to educate the doctor on the necessary tests and immunizations. You may have to be insistent. If the doctor resists, change doctors. Come to the appointment with copies of medical articles on Eastern European adopted children and their medical issues. Leave these with him so that the next family can have an informed doctor. You might give him a copy of the American Academy of Pediatrics' article on the initial medical evaluation of an adopted child. See *http://www.aap.org/policy/04037.html* and also an article from American Family Physician at *http://www.aafp.org/afp/981200ap/quarles.html*

Suggest that she consult the 1997 Red Book, *Report of the Committee on Infectious Diseases,* American Academy of Pediatrics.

Have the child checked for strabismus (eyes), giardia lamblia, anemia, rickets, salmonella, and scabies. The child should have vision and hearing tests by pediatric specialists. HIV-1 and HIV-2 should be tested by ELISA and if under 18 months of age by PCR or culture as well. Syphilis is not usually found in an infant and the Russian medical clinics treat syphilis in the population. Nevertheless, the VDRL for syphilis should be given and is another required test. Although Russian children's exposure to lead appears to be less than children in America, you might go ahead and have your child's lead levels checked just in case. Ask your pediatrician if your child can be given EMLA cream prior to having blood drawn. This cream deadens the skin area if applied an hour before and reduces the pain of the needle considerably.

Also, test for Hepatitis A, C, and include a Hepatitis B profile, to include HbsAG, anti-HBs and anti-HBc. A second Hepatitis B profile screening is recommended after the maximum incubation period of 12 weeks passes. You may want to seriously consider retesting for Hepatitis 6 months later in order to cover any incubation period. A treatment for chronic Hepatitis C has been filed with the EU and FDA. A European Union panel has recommended approval of Pegintron for the treatment of chronic hepatitis C. The FDA refused to grant priority review of the drug and has placed it on standard review, which usually takes 12 rather than 6 months.

Do not be surprised if your child has rickets. Rickets comes in two different varieties: Vitamin D deficient and vitamin D resistant. If deficient then it can be treated with sunlight, calcium and Vitamin D. If resistant, then there is a more concentrated vitamin D approach. One effect of rickets can be bowed legs. With proper treatment, the legs should straighten out within a year. Another effect of rickets can be a temporarily enlarged head. This does not always occur in all children with rickets. If you are evaluating a child with this condition though, you will need at least two photographs to rule out hydrocephaly, a front face shot and a side shot. In hydrocephaly, as fluid accumulates in the head, the head expands at the expense of the face, which gets squished and smaller. In rickets, the head gets enlarged, mostly in the forehead, but the facial features remain normal in proportion.

A stool examination should be conducted for ova and parasites. Giardia is usually treated using an awful tasting medicine called Flagyl or with Furoxone. If your child has giardia, there is a strong possibility that it has been passed on to you and you should be checked as well. Make sure your pediatrician and his lab know how to properly test for giardia. Query him on the specifics. The stool sample should be taken over three days and from different areas of the stool. Just taking one day's sample is not enough.

Also, have your child checked for lice. One cure is Nix. Be aware that Nix is not recommended for small children and there are lice that are immune. Mayonnaise and Vaseline are home remedies that also work. Some over the counter medications do not really work. Also, fingernails are better than little combs at getting out the nits. Another home remedy is olive oil. You put it in the hair, top off with a shower cap and wash out the next morning. The lice suffocate and the oil is easier to wash out than mayonnaise. Remove the dead nits in bright sunlight, with hair wet, and look at each strand of hair. This is quite tedious and time consuming but well worth the effort. Even if you think you got them all, check everyday for at least 2 weeks. Do vacuum everywhere, including your car. Wash everything in hot water that has had contact with the infected person. Boil hair brushes, combs, headbands, etc. If live lice are found, repeat the olive oil (you must have missed a nit that hatched).

There are also some rare parasites called Entamoeba Coli Cystus and Blastocytus Homoflous for which you could test if your child is not gaining weight, and eating poorly, but has no giardia type symptoms (diarrhea, very smelly stools, blood in the stool). You can also test for helicobactor pylori, which is a bacteria that lives in the thin layer of mucus that lines the stomach. The symptoms are similar to that of giardia.If your child is not growing, I would rule out the other more obvious problems before testing for this. You can also test for lead levels and for hypothyroidism which can retard growth. Interestingly, Russians have less risk for lead poisoning than do Chinese and American children.

If your child has an Asian, Rom or dark skinned background, he may have what is called a mongolian spot on the lower back. It looks like a bruise, but it is not. It is completely benign and fades over time. You may wish to point it out to your doctor and take a picture of it so that you can explain to whomever that your child was born with it. The spot's name is actually a misnomer as all children have such a spot but it just shows up more prominently in non-Caucasian children.

If you are considering reimmunizing your child (which is highly recommended), you can also have a blood titer test, which will show for which childhood diseases your child has been immunized. This test may reduce the number of shots that need to be given. The blood titer is not inexpensive though and you need to check if your insurance will cover it. Also, quite a bit of blood needs to be withdrawn which may be a problem in a child suffering from anemia. For all of these reasons, most people opt for simply reimmunizing.

Also, your pediatrician may find tattoo like marks on your child's buttocks. These are from vitamin and antibiotic shots. Also, in some children's homes, not all by any means, the children receive sedative shots to maintain quiet in the home. The Russians are very free with their needles.

Some children are unfamiliar with milk and may not like the taste. This does not necessarily indicate lactose intolerance, simply an unfamiliarity. Some families spike the milk with loads of cocoa, which usually never fails to entice a drink. Others have to resort to Pediasure. An alternative to Pediasure is Carnation Instant breakfast with a little canola oil in the bottle. Ask your pediatrician about these and other ways to increase your child's weight and overcome his malnutrition.

If your child is not responding appropriately to his new healthy environment after a few months, you may wish to have him screened at an international adoption health clinic. Ask your pediatrician or local children's hospital for the one nearest you.

Other resources can be found at:
http://members.aol.com/JAronmink/russvid.htm and
http://www.adoption-research.org/favorite.html

Scabies

Have your pediatrician check for scabies. A skin mite causes scabies. They look like small red bumps that are very itchy. The bumps typically occur on the face, head, hands or feet. Incubation period for scabies is about 2 weeks. It is extremely contagious and very hard to identify in a small and/or malnourished child. If the child's scabies were treated with corticosteroids, especially with fluorinated corticosteroids (very common in Russia) such as "Ftorocort", then the scabies may be resistant to treatment.

The usual cure is Elimite Cream. The Elimite cream is applied from head to toe and left on for 8 to 12 hours, then washed off. All bedding and clothing, including your clothes that have come in contact with the child should be washed thoroughly. If applying Elimite cream to an infant, apply it to yourself at the same time and leave it on for the night. Some infants can not take the Elimite. One suggestion is to have a dermatologist make a salve from a vaseline base with sulfur in it and then "grease" up the child for a few days. Some children will seem to have scabies but in reality have infant actopustulosis. This is a condition that is an after-effect of scabies where the scabies mites are completely gone. It is not contagious. It is an allergic reaction to the dead scabies mites that are still under the skin. Once the dead mites have disappeared, the bumps will also disappear. The usual prescription is a strong hydrocortizone cream or Benadryl and anti-itch lotions such as Aveeno anti-itch lotion, Sarna lotion, Calamine lotion. Do not use Caladryl due to its connection with Benedryl. Be careful if using these on an infant as their skin is sensitive. Secondary bacterial infection is common in prolonged scabies and if this is a case—should be treated with topical and in severe cases—with oral antibiotics. Definitely see a doctor if your child has a serious case.

Be aware that it is a common practice for the children's home to hide any outbreak from the Regional Health Department (because it does not look nice on orphanage report and does not look nice on the Health Department report). Therefore, the odds of having it treated at the children's home are not good. Indeed, the home will sometimes try to pass it off as an allergy to red dye. (Of course, many children do have an allergy to Red Dye 40, but usually the rash is temporary.)

If you are able to treat your child for scabies as soon as she leaves the children's home, then apply Elimite cream all over her body from head to toe), not leaving any area non covered. The usual rule of thumb is a 60 gram tube is for one application for average adult, or 2 applications for school-age children or 3 applications for infants. Give your child a bath in the morning. Throw away all clothes she was in on the way from the children's home to the hotel/guest house (plastic garbage bags will come handy). Change bedding and wash it in the very hot water (boiling linens is usually sufficient). Think what to do with clothing, you were wearing to visit her in the home—those are contaminated too.

Do not reapply Elimite until 2 weeks after initial treatment and try not to use steroid creams, especially those, containing fluorinated hormones ("Ftorocort", for example). When you will return home you will have to re-treat everybody, who traveled, including disinfecting the luggage (washing in hot water or dry cleaning is sufficient). Ask your family doctor to check you several times if any itching lesion will appear.

Tuberculosis

Your child may have had a BCG vaccination for TB. BCG is made from the Calmette-Guerin bacillus. Look for the small scar on the left shoulder. You may want your child to have the Mantoux/PPD with Candida control test done for TB regardless. One consideration is that if the BCG was given recently then the reaction might very well make your child sick. Also, since the BCG may cause a reaction, your doctor must be competent to recognize when the reaction is from the BCG and when it is from an underlying TB problem. Another problem is that your normal pediatrician will not know that he can test for TB where BCG was given. You will have to educate him. A skin reaction of <10 mm is usually due to the BCG. A result >10 mm should be interpreted as positive for exposure. BCG wanes, so never assume that a positive reaction is because of the vaccine.

If other children from the same home have tested positive but your child has not, then you may want to have your child retested in a year to cover any incubation period that may have been missed with the first test. If your child has a positive TB skin test (Mantoux), and a negative chest x-ray, the protocol is to treat with INH (isoniazid) as a prophylaxis for 9 months. The INH pills do have side affects such as diarrhea. If you can get your pediatrician to agree, then have your pharmacist crush the pills and mix them in jam. That should stop the diarrhea. Some pediatricians may not want to mix it with food, as the INH tends to bond with the food and not be completely absorbed. Some parents have switched to liquid INH and mixed it with a little water and then given it as a nighttime bottle.

Here are websites with helpful information on TB:
http://members.aol.com/jaronmink/tb2.htm
or *http://orphandoctor.com/monthly.htm*

Children's Dental Care

If you adopt an older child, you may face dental issues as soon as you return. One of your first stops should be to a dentist. Be aware that some of the children:

1. Have never had fluoridated water
2. Have rarely had milk
3. Have never taken vitamins
4. Were weaned from milk to sweetened tea
5. Drank sugary tea several times a day
6. Never saw a dentist in Russia, or did so only to have a tooth pulled
7. Never brushed their teeth before arriving in the children's home

The consequence is that the children may suffer from porous teeth as they do not have enough calcium in the diet to support good bone growth. They may also have weak tooth enamel and lots of cavities or even gum disease. They may have had delayed development of adult teeth. Once the immediate work is completed, the good news is that after fluoride treatments, the establishment of good teeth brushing habits, vitamins, good diets, lots of calcium, and regular checkups, their teeth are remarkably improved.

If a lot of dental work is needed, yet your insurance will not cover it, consider having your child seen at a school of dentistry. They sometimes will provide free dental care as a teaching tool.

Not all children will have these problems. In some of the homes they do brush their teeth, but the problem is common enough that a dentist visit should be on your list.

Hepatitis

When you return from the United States it is recommended that your child be screened for Hepatitis A, B, and C. Until recently there were only limited treatments for Hepatitis B and C. At this time most treatments for chronic hepatitis involves the patient taking Interferon, which is rather expensive at $300 every 10 days. There are new drugs in the pipeline such as Pegintron and for Hepatitis B one called adefovir dipivoxil which is made by Gilead Sciences. If your child does test positive he should see a hepatologist as soon as possible and if you have not been vaccinated, you should be tested as well.

Hepatitis A is usually transmitted by drinking water or eating food that has been contaminated with fecal matter containing the virus. Symptoms only develop after the time when you are most infectious. It may cause flu-like symptoms such as fatigue, fever, poor appetite or nausea. Hepatitis A usually resolves itself in a few weeks and does not cause permanent liver damage.

Parasites

Giardiasis is a disease caused by the intestinal parasite, giardia lamblia. It is very common worldwide. You can get even get it from hiking in the back woods in America where it is found in streams contaminated with animal feces.

It is also common in children from institutions. Symptoms include those you would associate with gastrointestinal discomfort: diarrhea; cramps, bloating and gas; smelly stools; weakness, and weight loss. These are similar for helicobactor pylori. Sometimes the disease exists even though no symptoms appear. Testing is usually done by detecting antigens—immunological "signature" of the parasite—in the stool samples (preferably 3 samples, collected on 3 separate days).Relapses are common, especially in a immunocompromised host and newly adopted children are considered temporarily immunocompromised.

As a result of the disease your child's development will be delayed. He is also at risk of passing it on to other children and family members. It is very important that your pediatrician test for giardia.

The most common cure is a medicine called Flagyl. It tastes just awful. But it is absolutely necessary in order to get rid of the disease. Retesting is necessary after the cure has run its course. The cure will also cause the beneficial bacteria to die off which means that for sometime after taking the medicine your child may be sensitive to some foods. Be sure to ask your doctor about this post-cure problem.

There is another parasite called dientamoeba fragillis. If your child is having chronic diarrhea and it is not giardia, then have a test for this one as well as. You will also find that although a whole range of parasites were tested for the first time, that a second set of stool samples may reveal the little buggers. It is not unusual for parasites to get missed in a stool sample. If the stool sample is taken from a diaper, try to place cellophane inside so the stool does not come in contact with the diaper.

Treating giardia type symptoms that do not respond to the usual treatments can be very frustrating. You do not know if you should continue with further Flagyl or Furoxone, do a biopsy of GI tract for other pathogens (like helicobactor pylori), look for presence of secondary infection, or test for lactose intolerance. All of these things can cause the same symptoms as giardia thereby masking the results of Flagyl treatment (since results of stool samples are often unreliable). It can be hard to tell sometimes if the Flagyl treatment was successful in eradicating giardia if the loose stools remain as these might be caused by other pathogens or the result of antibiotic treatment or food allergies.

Even after the infection is cleared you should be on the look out for consequences of the disease. For example, a child may suffer, post-giardia, from malabsorbtion and may need to be treated with an enzyme preparation (Ku-Zime, etc). Fat free, especially a milk-free diet can sometimes only add to the problem. Lack of fat—the building material for the intestinal wall, can predispose to delayed healing of the intestinal covering.

Subsequent to giardia treatment, the child may suffer from disbacteriosis, which is an imbalance of intestinal bacteria, which helps to digest food in the colon and an overgrowth of pathological flora, secondary to either intestinal disease or antibacterial treatment or both. If the child is taking an antibiotic you may want to ask your doctor about bacterial preparations together with any course of antibiotics. You can buy acidophilus or lactobacilli in any health food store and probably pharmacies. To a lesser degree, yogurt and other sour milk products such as buttermilk, cheese, and sour cream can also help.

Interestingly, it has been seen that in recently adopted children overeating can cause diarrhea, just because their bodies can not digest such amount of food. That condition is very common among adopted toddlers. Be sure not to limit their access to food, but provide them with easily digestible, high in fiber, healthy snacks such as bananas, applesauce, and bread.

There is also toddlers diarrhea caused by many factors, but mostly by apple juice. Sugars in apple juice are known to cause abnormal fermentation in the intestines and to predispose to diarrhea even in the absence of conditions. Toddlers diarrhea frequently is "treated" simply by normalizing their diet and especially their fat intake. One of the most frequent causes of constipation in pediatrics is excessive consumption of milk.

Useful web sites:
http://members.aol.com/jaronmink/giardias.htm
http://www.mc.vanderbilt.edu/peds/pidl/gi/giardia.htm

Post Adoption Education Issues

If you adopt an older child, one of your first questions upon returning to the United States, in addition to a medical evaluation, may be about education. Some of the children will pick up English at an incredible rate and within months be practically fluent. Others may have difficulties due to developmental delays and need help. There is a debate on whether it is better to put a Russian child immediately in school or hold him out until he is more culturally integrated. It all depends on the child. Some children respond very well to the stimulation of being in a school. Others may feel overwhelmed if they are not acquiring English fast enough.

Some basic questions are:

How quickly should I put him in school after coming home?
Should I place him in his age appropriate grade or his appropriate developmental one?
   Should I keep him out and just do home tutoring for a few months?
How do I handle ESL (English as a second language)?
How should I handle objections of school officials?

A consideration in starting an older child in school is that they will likely make new friends quickly. These friends help in social and language development in a way no one else can. It helps them feel like they do belong here. Don't be surprised if they have a slight accent. It will be part of their exotic charm.

Most school districts provide ESL classes. These may meet from one to two times a week. Many ESL classes will have bilingual children where the home language is different than English. Their progress may be different than your child's although the ESL teacher may not recognize the reasons. Your child has a lot more on his plate than these children. He is trying to integrate into a new family where he must learn the family routine, family customs, how to handle new siblings and parents, trust and attachment issues, etc. The other children are not juggling all of these other issues and therefore your child's progress should not be compared to theirs. Another issue with ESL classes is that they are focused on Spanish speakers. This may mean that your child is better off with a private tutor or just learning at home.

Some older children have trouble "hearing" the difference between similar sounds "b" and "d" and "p" for instance. They may know the letter but not fully register the sounds of each letter. This may cause you to privately tutor him in this area using one of the private programs that are available. Some older children also may need help in learning English grammar and writing. It all depends on the child and whether he had any schooling before adoption. If he did have such schooling, then learning English may be easier. Dr. Boris Gindis has a very informative article on the web entitled " Language-Related Issues for International Adoptees and Adoptive Families." I highly recommend it. You can read it at *http://j51.com/~tatyana/language.htm* Dr Gindis also has a paper on schooling the international adoptee (IA) at *http://www.j51.com/~tatyana/page10.htm*

All parents of older children are urged to have thorough assessments done on the child in the language of the child's country of origin to pinpoint present and future learning difficulties. Testing her as soon as she comes into the country will clarify what kind of difficulty she is having, how serious it is, and what kinds of therapy will be most effective in her treatment. Testing will also show any discrepancies in IQ vs. performance skills. If there are any discrepancies present in her base language, the assumption will be made that these discrepancies will also exist in the same subjects in English. This prevents your future kids from falling into "ESL Limbo."

"ESL Limbo" occurs as soon as your child loses her base language (often within a matter of a few months). The school personnel will start the "just wait until she has more English" litany. That wait can interfere with your child's ability to obtain services for the REAL issues of actual learning disabilities. This can inhibit you from seeking speech therapy for your child long before it is actually verified that there is a problem. Testing soon after arrival is just another way to save yourself possible problems in the future. It is no different from re-inoculating your kids or checking for parasites or testing for HIV, Hep B and C, and TB. If you're lucky, your children will never need services from the school system, and you can use the tests as a base-line and file them away in your records.

Some children may need a school's special education services. Special education falls under the acronym of IDEA (Individuals with Disabilities Education Act) which is a federal law. Each State has its own special education regulations. Each State also has some kind of parent training education center. There is an organization that has state specific information called the National Parent Network for Disabilities (NPND). One recent change in IDEA is that the use of "developmental delay" now includes ages 3-9 whereas it was previously only for 3-5.

Getting " help" for your child obviously begins with a determination by an evaluation team that your child is "delayed". The outcome of such an evaluation should be an Individualized Education Plan (IEP)

Make sure that the child study team allows you to share your insights into the child's strengths, weaknesses and overall development. Evaluations should be non-discriminatory which includes being done in the child's native language if necessary. This is tricky because after a few months the children are between Russian and English so it's hard to know which language to choose. Also, the written evaluation should reflect the child's strengths, not just weaknesses. The most important component of the resulting IEP should be goals and objectives. Also, the IEP must show strategies to deal with behavior problems. Remember that you are your child's only advocate. He has no one else. Don't let the school put him in a class or assign him a designation that you don't feel is appropriate.

If your child is about to enter elementary school you may find that a planned introduction is a great icebreaker. With the approval and assistance of the class teacher (and your child, of course) you might introduce their new classmate and show a bit of your Russian videotape. You can explain about Russia and give a brief version of your child's adoption and the obstacles he is facing such as a new country, new friends, new family and new language. A class exercise using a map of the world and letting the students find their city then your child's might be helpful. Then you might give out little flags or something indicating Russia. This exercise can be an icebreaker and the children will actually compete to help your child assimilate.

If you want your child to retain as much Russian as possible or feel that hearing Russian will help the child integrate in the family better, you may want to consider buying a satellite dish and subscribing to Russian programming. The Russian programming comes from a different satellite than the one that carries all the US stations. It is a bit hard to aim at from the West Coast as it is barely over the eastern horizon, but it is not impossible to get a clear line of sight. For people on the East Coast this will not be a problem as the "bird" will be higher in the sky, but if you live on the West Coast, make sure you can see the eastern horizon from your roof or wherever your dish will go.

Some families buy a few Russian language videos and tapes. These are easily bought in Russia or from catalogs or websites. They have found that their child sometimes needs to hear his native language in the beginning and this can help with transition issues. They have also hired Russian speaking babysitters or teenagers to come over and play with their child, which also helps during the transition period. Finally, a Russian speaking therapist can ask your child how she is coping and allow her to fully express her feelings. These are just a few ideas of things that can help your older child make the transition into your family and to a new language.

Finally, it is important to realize that these children have significant learned survival skills, which they come with, and which must be unlearned for school success. It is not unlike de-programming.

Attachment and Transition Issues

After the initial physical medical issues are taken care of, one of the most important psychological issues is "attachment." Attachment means bonding between a child and a parent. It happens very early with an infant and the more delayed the process the more difficult it can become. That being said, it is not impossible to have attachment at any age and if the child attached to caregivers at the children's home, or spent some time in a family setting, or is bonded with a sibling, then the groundwork has been laid.

Initial bonding by a child is not so unusual. Yet this bond can sometimes be an "insecure bond" and it may be longer before the attachment is deep and permanent. After all, you are a stranger to this child and he to you. The attachment process is something on which you should focus and work hard to nurture. Some signs of "insecure attachment" are that the child continues to be withdrawn or stiff or will show affection indiscriminately to strangers or just simply go off with anyone.

If it is possible to stay at home for awhile, this will help the bonding process. Also, try to limit social situations so that your child and your family spend as much time together as possible without outside distractions. If you can say some words in Russian so that your child can communicate basic needs and wants, that is also helpful.

Another idea that people have also used is to engage in deliberate holding, hugging and touching as much as possible. Some call this Holding Time (Dr. Welch) or baby time. You should try to make eye contact and talk softly to him. Let him follow you around the house or climb into your arms whenever he feels a need. You might let him take a bath with you or spend time massaging his skin with lotion in order to promote close contact. You have to recreate that early attachment time that was missed. You may even have to teach your child how to give hugs.

You will know you've succeeded when he loves to cuddle, seeks consolation from you when hurt, and is eager to see Mom and Dad when you return from the store or work. If he wants only you when other adults are around and his eye contact is good, then you should take this as a measure of success.

It is also perfectly normal to have other transition issues with an older child. First, and foremost, is the fear and helplessness she might feel about being transitioned from everything and everyone she knew into an entirely new and different environment. This is culture shock to an extreme degree. All her underpinnings are gone, and it will take time and lots of patience on your part to wait for her new foundation to be built and for her to become part of your family.

Second, don't underestimate the language frustration she might go through. Even if you speak perfect Russian, she's hearing English all around her that she doesn't understand. Americans who travel to foreign countries feel the same thing. It's very disconcerting, especially if you are a verbal processor. She has all sorts of thoughts and feelings that she isn't able to express right now. The frustration of that is sometimes overwhelming. That is why an older child's transition anxiety is greatly reduced if there is someone she can speak with who knows Russian.

Besides which, when you just return from Russia you are extremely tired. You've all had a very hard trip and will need to emotionally and physically recuperate. Be sure to eat well and get plenty of sleep. Transition work is HARD work and requires more sleep than normal. You are also extremely concerned about your new child's wellbeing and peace of mind, but there are some rough spots she may have to work through on her own. Think about cutting down on stimulation and visits with friends and extended family for awhile. Try to keep things real simple. Set a routine and stick with it. Some older children fit in to a new family like a hand in a glove, but many need extra work. Provide comfort, calm, and quiet as well as some space and distance for all of you when she seems overwhelmed.

Also, part of the normal bonding process of a child into a new family is called "reparenting". It means that the child, no matter how old, will regress to a former developmental level in order to be "reparented" by the new family. This is an unconscious/subconscious effort to find his or her proper place in the fabric of the family. In many children, reparenting means rolling back to very young and immature levels because they have missed so many of the normal developmental milestones. For them, it's a double load to carry. For children who have spent entire lives within an institutional setting, they struggle with the lack of knowledge about normal family interactions.

Transitioning an older child can take lots of time, but things do get better. The temper-tantrum/frustration stage of transition is very common for older kids. With improved English language skills this too passes.

There are books on this subject and medical experts who specialize in this field. One such book is *Facilitating Developmental Attachment: The Road to Emotional Recovery and Behavioral Change in Foster and Adopted Children* by Daniel A. Hughes.

Other behavior to prepare for and which may or may not manifest itself is anger and grieving. Many things cause anger. Your child may have anger at his birth family for giving him up or for a lousy home life. He may be angry and grieving at leaving the only life (and friends) he has known. He may have anger and frustration at initially being unable to communicate in English or Russian with anyone. The symptoms will be tantrums, hitting, and crying. If they go on too long, seek professional help.

Now many older children just breeze right through these stages without missing a beat. But if you aware of the possibility, then you can be prepared to help your child and that is what parenting is all about.

You may find that alcohol was a factor in your older child being placed in the children's home. The parents' rights may have been terminated because of alcohol abuse. If this situation exists, you may wish to consider limiting alcohol in your home, as it may be a concern to your child.

Some parents also find that older children need to be transitioned to proper hygiene. Toilet paper may have only been used once a day. Nor are they are used to flushing it. You may not be able to get the point across to use it every time (for girls) so you might concentrate instead on daily baths with complete clothing changes.

They will not have taken baths frequently, nor changed clothing as often as we do. Oral hygiene will not be up to American standards, either. Get some cute toothbrushes and flavored toothpaste. Get special kid shampoo and that foaming soap in a can. Try cute towels and wash clothes or sponges, etc.

Consider taking them swimming a few times a week and having fewer baths at home. They'll probably have to have a quick shower before getting in the pool.

They may not be used to sleeping in pajamas. They don't have top sheets, just a duvet with a cover. Try having them sleep in oversize T-shirts. There will be many, many little differences that you will see. A thousand little things will amaze them, from how to buckle a seat belt to how to use a single lever faucet.

Institutionalized children have had less experience in making choices than children raised in a family. They do not know about food choices, clothing choices, activity choices, etc. Don't overwhelm them by presenting them with what to them are difficult choices. Be careful not to overdo anything. Reduce the amount of stimuli to which they are subjected. You have to be very careful taking kids out in public who do not speak English and could not ask a stranger for help. You need to be sure they will stay with you and not run off before you do so.

With toddlers you may find that he needs and wants to be treated like a baby. This can be wonderful if you thought you might miss out on his "baby time." He may also want to stay in a crib longer than other children. He may consider it his private or safe place and enjoy "his crib." There is no urgency to moving a child to a bed. He'll get there before he goes off to college.

They won't know how to get in and out of a car, and not to ding other car's doors. So park far out in the lot away from others. They won't know how to cross our streets.

Suggested food to try at first: hot dogs and other cured meats, meatloaf, chicken, fish, vegetable soup, yogurt, white cheeses, oatmeal and other cooked cereals, fruits, crackers, breads. They will not probably have ever eaten lettuce, peanut butter, cold cereal, colored cheese, broccoli, sweet corn, or steak.

Again, these are just general comments. Your child may have none of these issues. Children are very much like snowflakes.

CHAPTER XI

Almost Done

Social Security Card and Green Card

Applying for your child's social security card is the easiest thing you can do. You should try to do it as soon after you return and have had a chance to settle down. You must go personally to the social security office. If you are in an urban area there will be several to choose from. Take all of your originals with you. You can fill out the form before you go or fill it out at the office while you wait. It's a short form so it won't take you but a minute to do. It is Form SS-5. You can call Social Security at 1-800-772-1213 and they might send it to you. You can also download the form from their web site at http://www.ssa.gov/online/ss-5.html

Most social security personnel do not know that your IR - 3 child is automatically a US citizen, nor do they care. Do not try to argue the law to these people. It is like talking to an orange. You can try a supervisor, but the odds are against you. If they do give you any trouble about anything, an alternative is to find another office where the IQ is above room temperature or wait until the person you spoke with is not there.

If you can wait until you have received your child's citizenship certificate, then do so. Amazingly, the Social Security Office will actually honor an American Passport and allow your child to be entered on their computers as a US citizen. However, if you do not have the US Passport then they will want to see your child's green card. The odds of having such a card within a month or two of returning are astronomical so do not worry if you don't have it. If you do not have the US Passport, show them her Russian passport with the IR - 3 number stamped inside. This proves that she is an authorized resident alien. Show them her Russian decree and the English translation. They will make a copy of both and tell you that they have Russian translators who will verify the translation. (Yeah, right!) They will give you back all originals once they have used their trusty copy machine.

Show them her amended birth certificate with translation. They will also want some identification as to who you are. A passport or driver's license will suffice.

The terrific thing is that you will receive the social security card within 2 weeks to a month later. That is pretty efficient in my book. The social security number will allow you to file your tax return and claim all child deductions and credits. You can do all that without the number, but it just makes life easier.

Now be sure to return to the Social Security office once your child has her citizenship certificate or US Passport. The reason is that you need to change the designation in their computers from "alien" to "citizen." It makes a difference as to available benefits. If they make an error on the spelling of the name or anything else, it is easy to change. Just takes another trip and filling out the same form again.

The form itself is easy. First put in the full name of your child. Ignore the part about "full name at birth if other than above." This does not apply. At paragraph 3 check the box for "Legal Alien Allowed to Work." If you don't believe it, just look at the IR3 stamp in her Russian passport. At paragraph 6, just put down whatever the information is shown on the amended birth certificate. If you have changed the date and place of birth, then use those. The answer to paragraph 10 is "no."

A word about the famous "Green Card." It's not green. The INS will automatically send it to you after your return. The card will have on it your child's picture and the IR3 number. It usually arrives at your house between two months to a year after you return. You should place it in your safety deposit box and take it out again to give back to the INS at the citizenship interview. As you can see, there is not a great deal of point to the card if you apply for citizenship fairly soon after returning home. You will need it though, if you are planning to take your child out of the country before he becomes a citizen. In order to be able to leave and return, your child will need his Green Card and another document from the INS.

Sometimes the INS loses your child's visa paperwork that you gave them in the sealed envelope at the point of entry (JFK, etc.) and will ask you to resubmit on a Form I-89. You need to do this in order to get the "Green Card." Form I-89 is a form that is "not for public distribution". In order to complete this form, you will need to go to the INS office in person.

Tax Considerations

This is not meant to be tax advice, and you should consult your accountant, but here are some reminders. When you return you should obtain your child's social security number as soon as possible. It should not take more than a month to receive it. With this number, and barring a few exceptions, you may be able to receive the following benefits: dependent deduction, child tax credit, and adoption tax credit.

The Adoption Tax Credit is a wonderful gift from your government. It is also more complicated than it looks. In general it provides a tax credit (worth far more than a deduction) up to $10000 per international adoption. It also has provisions relating to employer provided assistance. To take the credit you need to fill out and follow Form 8839 when you file your tax return. You should carefully read IRS Publication 968. Both of these can be downloaded from the IRS website at *http://www.irs.ustreas.gov* or you can call 1-800-TAX- FORM. The publication is located at *http://www.irs.ustreas.gov/plain/forms_pubs/pubs/p96801.htm*

Additional information can be found at the JCICS website: *http://www.jcics.org/tax.html*

Families have no problem having enough expenses to take the credit. That is not the problem. The problem comes in interpreting the AGI limitations, Alternative Minimum Tax and carry forward rules. These are too complicated to discuss here. However, generally you must have less than $150,000 AGI to be entitled to the full credit. Between $150,000 and $190,000 there are limitations and over $190,000 you can not take the credit.

Also, do not forget to check into any state credits for which you may be eligible. For example, Missouri gives a $10,000 credit for special needs adoption, including international adoption.

Citizenship Application

If your child does not qualify for citizenship under the Child Citizenship Act, then your child only becomes a citizen of the United States upon the issuance of a Certificate of Citizenship. Until then she is a Resident Alien. She can hold both American and Russian citizenships. Dual citizenship is not a problem. After you file for the social security number, file for the child's citizenship. There is no point in waiting. Do not wait for her "green" card. The "green" card is not necessary (and its not green).

To apply, you fill out and file form N-643, Application for Certificate of Citizenship on behalf of an Adopted Child. The filing fee is $145. If 4 months passes since you filed and the INS has not cashed your check or sent you a receipt, then that is bad. You will need to re-file the whole thing as the INS has lost the application. You may be able to find out the status of the application by calling 800-375-5283, but it won't be easy.

Some offices are quick to issue the Certificate, but most take a year to 2 years. Usually you will receive a notice and receipt that they have received your Application. Then about a year later, you will receive an appointment notice giving you the date and time for the interview. Do not lose this notice, as you will have to show it to the INS as confirmation of your appointment. Other than these two pieces of paper, you will receive no other contact from the INS. On the date of the interview, you may take your child and meet with an overworked INS person. If your child is under age 14, you do not actually have to take him with you, although most do. The INS person will ask you a few questions and then hand you the Certificate of Citizenship to sign. He will also ask you take an oath that the answers on the application are true. Proofread the Certificate carefully. It is not unusual for it to have typos. It is far easier to change the Certificate right then, rather than afterwards. **Do not leave the room before proofreading the certificate.**

Now the INS will type your child's name exactly as your translator in the Russian Court Decree translated it. Therefore, you must make sure that your translator has done it correctly. The best time to do this is prior to your Embassy visit in Moscow. If your translator has made a mistake, he can correct it on the decree and then sign a statement at the bottom that he made a mistake and write the correct name. One kind of mistake is placing a "K" rather than a "C" for Catherine. But really it can be any sort of typo. If you return to the States and there is an error, then the re-adoption Court Order will cure it. The INS will go by the re-adoption Court Order in that case and not by the Court Decree.

Some offices have a ceremony, but this is rare. Usually for children it is more of an administrative process. The certificate may say at the bottom that it is against the law to make copies of it. The law has now changed and you can and should make copies.

If you get tired of waiting, call your Congressman. They are good for that sort of thing.

One very neat idea is to have your Congressman send you the flag that flew over the Capitol the day your child becomes a citizen. The cost is around $10. They run these flags up and down all day long every 5 minutes. You can also order a small flag set on a stand showing your child's heritage with flags of the US and Russia. These can be obtained from Gates Flag Co. at 1-800-US-1776.

Actually filing the N-643 can be a troublesome process. The requirements state that the three photos must be identical, unglazed and taken within 30 days of the date of filing the citizenship application. Their regulations further state that the photos are to be in natural color and taken without a hat. The dimensions of the face should be about 1 inch from the top of the hair to the chin. The face should be a frontal view with the entire right ear visible. The photograph must be on thin paper with a light background.

Most places that take passport photos can not accommodate these requirements because their photos are on glazed paper. If you find that you can not get anyone to follow the requirements, then go ahead and file regular passport photos. The INS is fairly reasonable when it comes to filing for a child's citizenship and will likely ignore the technical defect. There are few offices that will not waive this requirement.

Do not send any originals with your application. Just send copies. Bring the originals with you to the interview. Mail the application by certified or express mail so you have a record that it was received.

Since you will likely not yet have the "green" card or Alien Registration Card when you file your application, just put in the IR# number which was stamped in your child's Russian passport. That is all they want anyway. Include a copy of the amended birth certificate and final adoption decree, both the Russian and English translations, and a copy of the photo page from your passport, and a copy of your marriage certificate. Bring all originals with you to the interview. By the time you have your interview you will likely have the "green" card. Since you will have to turn it in to the interviewer, make a copy of it for your child's Lifebook.

The INS would like a statement from a Russian translator that he is competent to translate and that the translation of the Amended Birth Certificate and the Final Adoption Decree is accurate. Take this statement to Russia with you. Either have your Russian translator type and sign this statement on the English versions of these two documents or have a separate statement. The separate statement should say something to the effect " My name is _____, and I am a resident of _____, Russia. I accompanied the_____ when they adopted _____. I certify that I am competent to translate in both Russian and English and that the English translations of the Amended Birth Certificate and Final Adoption Decree are correct and accurate." Then have him sign and date it. If your translator does not give you such a statement, then just have someone in the States who is fluent in Russian sign one.

By the way, if you land in Hawaii from Russia (or from China, Korea) then on certain days of the week you can hand them your I-600 packet and your N-643 for citizenship and get citizenship right then for your child. This only makes sense since everything in your packet is the same stuff you have to file with N-643. This is the only port of entry that lets you do this. If you are landing in Hawaii, I would recommend asking the Honolulu office about this procedure.

Children who arrive in the United States on an IR - 3 visa acquire US citizenship automatically upon admission to the United States pursuant to the Child Citizenship Act. Children with IR - 4 visas have to wait until they are re-adopted before they qualify under the Act."

Re-Adoption

Although the federal government and most states recognize your child's adoption, a few states like Iowa, make you file for a re-adoption before they will recognize the adoption. This process is also called domestication of adoption. Here is a web site containing a full review of all 50 States' requirements in regard to re-adoption: *http://www.calib.com/naic/resources/forsum.htm*

Actually there are some good reasons for filing for re-adoption in any state. When your child has to show some school authority or employer his birth certificate it is better to use derivative documents like a states' Certificate of Foreign Birth than original Russian certificate. If you have to pull out the original amended Russian birth certificate or Decree from the safety deposit box, you will be fearful of losing it and you will have to deal with the Russian translation issue. It is far better to be able to use the Re-adoption Decree and the State's birth certificate for this purpose. Furthermore, if you lose the original birth certificate, it is practically impossible to get a replacement. Further, there will be no question whatsoever of inheritance rights and if you ever move to another state that does not recognize the adoption then you have a state adoption decree that the other state must recognize.

The downside to re-adoption is that it may cost money. In some states it is a very simple process and you can do it yourself. In others, it is so complicated that you have to hire an attorney. Check with your county's adoption clerk, court clerk, or probate clerk as to the procedure. Another problem is that some clerks will ask you for your Russian originals. Do not give them to her, but instead insist on speaking to a supervisor. Most courts will allow you to file copies and the Judge will simply compare them with the originals in the courtroom.

Passport

The last piece of paper in this whole journey is applying for your child's passport. The benefit of doing this is that then you no longer have to use his original Certificate of Citizenship to prove he is an American citizen but can use a derivative document like his passport.

You can download the application at
http://travel.state.gov/download_applications.html

The application requires two photographs, a $40 fee and proof of US Citizenship. The problem is that some (but not all) passport offices require that you send in the original Certificate of Citizenship. Check with your passport or post office to see if you must send in the original or if a copy will do. It will be very hard for you to actually send the original considering what it took to get it, but if required you must simply hold your breath and enclose it with your application. The great news is that you will get it back! If you wish to make sure the Certificate of Citizenship is not folded when it is returned; you should attach a note stating the request. Another good idea is to place the Certificate in a clear plastic sheet protector and staple it shut. This way they can see it without opening it.

If you file with a post office and the child is under 14, then you usually submit two personal checks, one for $25 to "Passport Services" and the other for $15 to "USPS" (the post office). It takes about 6 weeks to receive the child's passport if you do not pay for expedited service.

Once you have obtained a child's passport you can use that as identity and proof of citizenship for such things as school, job and future passports. It is also easier to replace if lost. Obtaining a passport soon after obtaining citizenship is important as you can then safely put away the Certificate of Citizenship forever. It will also help a great deal if you plan to take your child out of the country.

Post Placements and Registration

The Russians require a certain number of post-placement reports after you return from Russia. They want to see that their children are being taken care of and are in good shape. It is a very reasonable request. Your agency will tell you how many reports you need and coordinate the filing of the reports. Usually your agency will ask you to fill out a form and write a letter describing how the child is doing. Photographs usually accompany the report. Your agency then translates everything and sends it on to the Regional Ministry of Education. The post placement report is included in your fee to the agency. If the agency does not file these reports in a timely fashion, the Ministry will not be happy with them or you. So it is important for them, as well as for you and future Russian adoptive families, that they be timely filed. Indeed, at one time referrals in the Chuvash region, and in particular with orphanages in Cheboksary were placed on hold because the post-placement reports had not been coming in.

The actual number required has varied over the years and indeed can vary depending on the Region. Generally, you will need to file one at 6 months and at a year, then one in each of the following two years. There is an indication that some regions are requiring more reports. Again, your agency will know.

The cost to you will likely be the cost of apostilling the form and the cost of an actual post placement visit by a social worker, if that is required.

The post placement form may ask you what you have done to help maintain the child's connection to Russian culture. The funny thing is that it may actual mean more to you than to your child. It may come as a surprise but a lot of the children do not really want to celebrate an annual "Gotcha Day." Nor do they want to see the initial video that was sent to you or really discuss their Russian past. Their attitude is that they are American now and they want to be treated that way. Each child is different, but just make sure that any "heritage connection" you try to make is one the child wants, and not just you.

Russia, like Ukraine, now requires that you register your child with the Russian Embassy in Washington, D.C. or with one of the Russian Consulates when you return. You can actually do it in Moscow if you want, but it may be cheaper to do it in the US. Registration at an Embassy or Consulate is a normal procedure for citizens living in a foreign country. The US even encourages its own citizens to do it. Since the Russians feel like these children are still Russian citizens until they are 18 years old, the registration requirement is just part of that. The registration form is one page and you must submit it to the Russian Embassy or to a Consulate with the child's Russian Passport, a copy of the parents passports, a copy of the adoption certificate, two passport photos of the child and $57. Always first call to verify the requirements. The Russian Embassy is at *http://www.russianembassy.org/*

If you send a self enclosed stamped envelope they will send the child's passport back. The form asks for the child's name and street address. Of course, the Russians already have this information from your dossier and from the Russian passport application so it is really just duplicative information.

Rude Comments

After you return to the States you may be faced with rude comments from friends, family, and strangers about adopting a child from Russia. Here are some suggested replies:

Question: Which one of you is adopted?
Answer by the child: We were all adopted by one another.

Question: How much did it cost?
Response: You look them in the eyes for several seconds then respond, "Oh (long pause) Why do you ask? or "Why do you want to know? and just look at them, not responding to their question. Of course, if they say they are interested in adopting, then you can actually give them information.

Comment: What a good samaritan you are for helping this poor orphan.
Response: I feel very blessed to finally be a parent. Parenthood is a lot more than a good deed. It is a lifelong commitment to love.

Or
Response: Actually, we're the lucky ones. We have a beautiful son/daughter who has added so much more to our lives than we could ever hope to give him/her.

Comment: What were her birthparents like?

Response: I consider that to be her personal information, so I don't discuss it. (Usually people apologize.)

Question: Why Russia-why not the US?"
Response: Why do you think a child in one nation is more or less important than another. Every loving adoption is a success.

After Thoughts

Having a child that comes from a children's home environment is a walk into the unknown. But then that is the way it is with all children. You never really know what their personality will be like or how they will be when they reach adulthood.

In one sense though, you have a head start. Like a child who comes from a family with a history of an hereditary disease, you know that your child may be at risk for certain issues. Because you are aware of the possibility, you are more in tune to your child and more likely to get help if such a situation occurs.

You will be more sensitive to your child's development and take action if it is necessary. The action may be to hire a tutor one summer to help them with a subject, or to get medical help if that is the issue. You will be more tolerant, more accepting, and more knowledgeable. Enjoy the journey!

I will leave you with a story I once read about a beachcomber who was observed picking starfish off the sand and throwing them in the water before they dried out and died. The beach was littered with thousands of starfish so the observer told the beachcomber that his actions made no real difference. At that moment the beachcomber picked up a starfish and tossed him in the water to safety and replied, " it made a difference to him."

All children have the right to be loved, to be nurtured and to reach for a dream. A chance is all they ask.

CHAPTER XII

Lagniappe

Frequently Asked Questions

What if my child wants to find his Russian birth parents?

The Russians are not too keen on the American idea of open adoption. Indeed, the Russians have strict privacy laws regarding keeping the adoption proceedings sealed. Of course when your child is older, he may wish to visit his birth city or perhaps even find his birth relatives. This is only natural. By the way, neither your child's birth parents nor siblings gain any special access to an American visa simply because your child was adopted by you. As far as the INS is concerned, the connection is broken once you've adopted. The Russians treat adoption like we did many decades ago. Russian women often feign pregnancy and adoptions are handled in utmost secrecy and privacy. Physical looks are carefully matched and the child may never be told he/she is adopted.

Should I have my son circumcised?

There is no medical reason to circumcise a child, and for this reason most health insurance plans will not pay for it. Instead, it is a cultural decision. You do have to be sure to clean the area more thoroughly during a bath. Most European men are not circumcised and in the States it currently runs about 60/40 in favor. One consideration is that the child will be under general anesthesia and will experience about a week of discomfort. Sometimes there is a problem with changing the diaper and then dealing with a bloody scab. If you're going to have a circumcision performed, do it in a hospital with a reputable pediatric urologist. There is a very informative policy statement on the American Academy of Pediatrics website. The web address is: *http://www.aap.org/policy/re9850.html*

I've heard it is difficult to get information from Russians?

Russians, like a lot of Europeans, have difficulty at first with the American style of frank and blunt questioning. While we perceive it as the most efficient method of obtaining information, they may perceive as being rude. They will often not respond to direct questions if they do not know you. You may have to ask several times to get an answer to a question and may have to ask it a different way each time. Be polite but persistent. Once a friendly and personable relationship is established, then they are more likely to respond with a lot more information. Just don't be surprised if they are reserved and not as forthcoming at first. It's the European way.

Must both Spouses travel to Russia?

Yes, both parents must attend the Court hearing. At least one spouse must appear at the Embassy to apply for the child's visa, unless a representative has a power of attorney.

What do I do if my spouse must leave early and return to the States?

Your agency will know the rules. Generally, if a spouse has to leave after the Court hearing to return to the States, then the leaving spouse must sign a completed (no blanks or incompletes) I-600 form and give you a Power of Attorney authorizing you to act in his place. The Embassy needs proof the absent parent has met the child, such as a photo of them together. The remaining parent cannot sign the I-600 for the leaving spouse; the Power of Attorney does not extend to the signing of the I-600 petition. Always call the Embassy before you leave Moscow to make sure they do not want anything else. Sometimes they have asked to see airplane tickets.

What do I do if I have no crib in Russia?

Here are some ideas if you find yourself in need of a crib. Push your twin beds together and put the child between you. Put the baby in an empty suitcase with a blanket. Pull an empty drawer out, put a blanket it in then the baby. Put the baby on a blanket on the floor and surround her with suitcases so she can't go anywhere.

I've heard Moscow is different than the Regions?

If you have ever worked in a federal agency you will notice that rules that apply outside Washington, do not apply at headquarters. So it is if you are adopting from Moscow. Everything in Moscow seems to be a little different. One of the new requirements is a letter from your mortgage company stating your loan amount, how much you have paid, and the balance. They also seem to want a medical review on you that is not any older than three months (Vladivostok is the same). Also, generally Moscow does not waive the 10 days. Moscow seems to make up new little rules as they go along. The other Regions seem to stick with a list. You agency should be on top of any changes, just be aware that Moscow is different than the Regions.

Where can I get a good map of Russia?

If you can find a February, 1976 National Geographic, it contains a map that details how different nationalities populate the former Soviet Union. Michelin, of course, has wonderfully detailed maps, which can be found in any large bookstore. There are also maps you can download from the web. See these web sites:

http://www.aimnet.com/~ksyrah/ekskurs/maps.html#Russia
http://www.intersource.com/~iar/rmap.shtml
http://www.luvdakidzadopt.org/maps.htm
http://plasma.nationalgeographic.com/mapmachine/

Where can I obtain Internet access in Moscow?

There is a cyber café in the post office next to the Intourist Hotel on Tverskaya Street. Some of the larger post offices have them. The computer may be set up for Cyrillic, but you should be able to switch it to English fonts. Test your computer at home as to how to switch between languages. It should not be difficult. Another cyber café is located below Planet Hollywood.

Most new hotels and refurbished hotels have business centers where you can access the Internet for between $7.50 and $9 per 15 minutes. It may pay to write offline first. If you want access from your homestay or older hotel, read the information on this web site first: *http://home.earthlink.net/~kfafox/Internet/*

Should I learn Russian?

You do not have to learn any Russian for your adoption. It will go just as well if you do not know any of the language. However, it is like traveling in any foreign country, knowing the native language broadens the experience. Also, it is not all that difficult. A couple of months of listening to tapes in a car while you are commuting to work will give you enough pidgin tourist Russian to get by. A background in the Greek language is certainly helpful as the two are based on a similar alphabet.

Now if you are adopting an older child or even one as young as 4, you should consider learning some basic Russian, just to help with the bonding process and to make the trip less stressful. Even infants under 1 can recognize when you speak a few Russian words to them. You can use the Pimsleur audiocassettes, which are expensive or *Childspeak: 99 Ways to Speak to Your Child in Russian* which is available from the Adoption Center of Washington at 1-800-452-3878. It's an audio language tape and booklet with Russian pronunciations. It helps you learn how to greet your child, has words and phrases for eating, sleeping, soothing, and playing. It is phonetically based. The cost is $29.95 plus $4.00 shipping and handling (price includes donation). Some have also used *Russian In Three Months* (with Cassette), Nicholas J. Brown, Michael Jenner (less than $30). Also, parents have used Baron's 2-cassette and book kit *Getting By in Russian* for $20.These may also be available at your local library. There is also Russian-English Dictionary by Kenneth Katzner. Also, a language book by Teresa Kelleher. This book gives English-equivalent pronunciations that are quite good. The tape is easy to follow and well-paced. The book and tape are $42.95. The book is "A Language and Parenting Guide" of 67 pages. The book includes 20 pages of phrases you will need in each of your adoption travel and adjustment situations. Also included are travel tips, bonding stages and expectations, enhancing bonding and parenting pointers. To contact Teresa: Adopttlc@aol.com or Tender Loving Communications, P.O. Box 90 Taylor, AZ 85939-0090.

I highly recommend taking a set of the adoptive traveler cards which can be purchased for $15 at this web site: *http://www.roanoke.infi.net/~bcrawf/rusvocab.htm* There are online translators of varying ability. One is at: **http://www.translate.ru/**

There are language lists on the Eeadopt web site at: *http://eeadopt.com/home/heritage/russia/index.html and http://eeadopt.com/home/heritage/russia/language.htm*

Will my being Jewish be a problem?

There is a pattern of anti-Semitism that runs through Russia's history and exists today. The largest groups of émigrés to Israel are those from Russia. Nevertheless, there does not appear to be any anti-Semitism in the adoption process.

I've heard you can adopt from former Soviet Republics?

There are former Soviet Republics that are open to adoption. They periodically open and close as they revise their adoption laws. Some of these countries do allow for adoptions of children who are younger than the Russian children. Some examples of countries that allow adoptions are the Baltic countries, Ukraine, Georgia, Belarus and Kazakhstan. The adoption law in Kazakhstan was signed in December 1998.

Since the law on foreign adoptions is relatively new, expect some revisions to occur as the process develops. It is probably safe to say that there are fewer agencies working in these countries. As always, research carefully the agency or facilitator you hire. I have included a description of the Ukrainian and Kazakhstan process in the last chapter.

How safe is the water?

Russian public water can cause problems with American stomachs. Russians generally think their water is just fine, but it all depends on what you are used to. To avoid any difficulties, you should only drink bottled water while in Russia. This is widely available. Both Coca-Cola and the Russian Orthodox Church sell water. Saint Springs or Vera are good brands. Even seltzer water is better than taking a chance with a faucet. Of course, it is hard to tell when a bottle has gas in it or not. The only way you can reliably tell is to squeeze the bottle. A bottle with gas is almost solid when you squeeze it. A bottle without gas dents in quite a bit.

You might drink bottled water but brush your teeth with seltzer. You can always boil water using a small hot plate. If you plan to stay a few weeks, then take a water distiller or pump. They will cost around $165 from Magellans. Anything costing under $100 probably won't really help you get rid of the giardia organisms and heavy metals although some swear by filter bottles at ww.safewateranywhere.com. Iodine tablets also work. If you drink the public water, the odds are you will make it home without Stalin's Revenge. However, pack some antibiotics just in case.

Can I Choose a Child from a Photolist?

Agencies used to post photos of adoptable children on the Internet. However, the Russian Ministry frowns on doing that. Indeed, when you are at a Children's Home the Russians will not want you to intentionally take pictures of other children. This is not to say that you can not find such a photolisting, just that it is no longer common practice.

If I am disabled, can I adopt?

If the husband has a disability, there appears to be no restriction. If the wife has a disability, the Russians may require some demonstration that the disability does not affect the wife's parenting ability. The discrimination is based on the idea that the wife is the primary caregiver. In truth, there really have not been enough cases upon which to say whether the Russians really require this extra proof as a routine. There have been adoptions where the wife was in a wheelchair or had recovered from cancer so a disability is certainly no automatic bar. If there is any question about a past medical problem, some agencies have the adoptive parent obtain a doctor's letter that states the person is in good health and has normal life expectancy.

What happens to the children after age 16?

Children generally leave the home after the age of 16. In some places it is 18. Their time is up and they must move out into the world. They move out without any money or much in the way of possessions. The boys, if they are really lucky, have been taught a trade. This is probably a minority. A lot of the boys are conscripted into the army. In the Russian military, conscripts are treated very harshly. After the army, their life is on the streets. For the girls the prognosis is equally grim. Prostitution and begging are not uncommon. This description does not cover every child, but it occurs often enough. Some statistics show that one third of the children become homeless, a fifth criminals and ten percent commit suicide.

Should I take a car seat?

Russians do not use car seats. Nor do they use seat belts. After you put your luggage and yourselves in the car there is simply no room. Add in another family and there really isn't any room. Normally you just hold your child on your lap. Now don't forget that whoever picks you up at the airport when you return to the States should have a car seat. But since your child has never been in one, expect some crying.

What affect has Y2K had on Russian Adoptions?

At first, the Russians announced that they were just going to see what goes wrong before fixing it. However, there was a small effort made to anticipate problems. Since Aeroflot has to meet US standards to fly into the United States, there isn't any problem taking Aeroflot to Moscow. Nothing happened in Russia when January 2000 rolled in. Electricity and heating were not affected. The US Embassy in Moscow was closed from December 23 to the end of January because they wanted to see what would happen. Nothing did. One saving grace was that Russia is not really as dependent on computers to run things as the States. It is more of an analog society. It may be less efficient, but at least it will get them through the millenium.

Do I send out baby announcements?

When you return from Russia, you may want to send out an adoption announcement similar to a birth announcement. Some people buy cards from a store on which they place their child's photo. On the front you might write "Please help us welcome (or are thrilled to announce, or placed in our loving arms) the newest addition to our family." Then her name, birth date (birth city) and adoption date. There are lots of variations, which are limited only by your imagination.

What is Sensory Integration Disorder (Dysfunction)?

Sensory Integration Disorder is another form of difficult behavior. It refers to problems a child may have with the tactile and auditory senses. The child may exhibit difficulty with hearing, touching, sound or sight. A child may be overly sensitive to noise (hypersensitive) or not react normally to things that should hurt (hyposensitive). One form of therapy that has had a mixed review is Auditory Integration Training (AIT). Another is the Tomatis Listening Method. In rare cases some children may even problems accepting solid foods as the issue might be a severe oral aversion, which means they do not like food in the mouth. The EEadopt website has some good information at *http://eeadopt.org/home/parenting/development/sensory_integration/index.html*

How can I give money to the children's home?

Some homes have a special bank account to receive humanitarian aid. This account is most likely to be held at SBERBANK, which is Russia's largest savings bank and perhaps the only solvent one. It is government controlled. You might be able to wire money to the children's home account although the fee is likely to be high. However, before doing so, see if the home director wants a wire and double check that it is indeed the account of the children's home to which you are sending the funds. The bank's SWIFT address should have the full name of the home and its address. SBERBANK should also give you a receipt. Whether the money is actually used for the children is another story. A better alternative is for someone to hand deliver rubles to the children's home director. Insist on a receipt. Sometimes adoptive parents even go with the home director and let her pick things out with them that the children need. Now that is fun!

How can I change my I-600A to Russia?

Try to change countries before you receive the I-171H. You can do so by simply mailing in a letter to your local INS amending the I-600A. If you have already received the I-171H, then you must file form I-824 (Application for Action on an Approved Application or Petition) at a cost of $120.00 to have your approval sent from your old country to the US Embassy in Moscow. The INS will send a Visas 37 cable to the old and the newly designated posts. In the cable to the old post it will say, "Pursuant to the petitioner's request, the Visas 37 cable previously sent to your post/office in this matter is hereby invalidated. The approval is being transferred to the other post/office addressed in this telegram. Please forward the approved advanced processing application to that destination." After awhile you should email the adoption unit in Moscow and ask them if they have received your file. When you file your I-824 to change countries, make sure you tell them in a cover sheet that it is for an adoption. If INS knows it is for an adoption they will process within 30 days, otherwise it will sit for months on a desk.

Be aware that if you want approval to adopt in two countries rather than simply transferring approval, it is likely to cost you another $405 and a second I-600A. Just you won't have to be fingerprinted again. Also, some people have actually received their I-171H approval even though they left line 16 blank on their I-600A. In that case all they did was to send or fax a letter to the INS telling them which country they wanted the approval sent to. No additional fee was required.

How do I notify the INS if I change Agencies?

Have your new agency write a letter on their letterhead stating they are now your agency for all adoption proceedings. Then write a cover letter to the INS enclosing the letter from your agency and informing the INS to make the change in their files. Enclose a copy of your I-171H with your cover letter.

Are my children Russian or American?

Your children are Russian. If they receive a citizenship certificate from the United States, then they are also American. They can travel under either passport. Some of the Russian passports will show that they expire in 5 or 10 years. Even if you do not renew their Russian passport, your child still has the right to claim Russian citizenship, as long as the Russian government allows him to. Most countries have an artificial cutoff at 18 when your child is supposed to declare his citizenship. This is usually artificial, as most countries (such as France) will allow you to submit documentation later to prove and reclaim your dual citizenship. Now the State Department's official position is that they do not recognize the other citizenship, however, this is completely irrelevant since it is only your relationship with the other country that is at issue.

How do I adopt if I live overseas?

The INS regulations at 8 CFR 204.3 cover this. You can find them at *http://www.access.gpo.gov/nara/cfr/waisidx_99/8cfr204_99.html* Your I-600A can be filed with the INS office in the country you reside. You can have your home study prepared by anyone that is licensed or authorized by the foreign country's adoption authorities to conduct home studies under the laws of the foreign country. There is an indication that if you are fingerprinted at a United States Embassy or consulate then you do not need to be fingerprinted by the INS and are exempt from the $25 fingerprint fee. You would then file your completed fingerprint card when you file your I-600A. See the regulations for further details. If you live overseas and adopt there, then if the child is with you for two years you may be able to file a Family Petition, Form I-130, rather than go the I-600 orphan route. You should check with an immigration attorney to see if this is available to you.

How long is my I-171H good for?

Just to review the time lines again. You have one year within which to file your home study after filing your I-600A. The home study or the most recent update must not be any older than six months at the time you submit it to the INS. Once you receive your approved advanced processing (the I-171H), the I-600 must be filed within 18 months of the date of such advanced approval. Now if you do adopt, it may be possible to use that very same I-171H to adopt again within that 18 months. Whether you can or not depends on your local INS office and your state's home study requirements. Some states will allow you to simply send in a two-page update and you are off to Russia again. Other states require a completely new home study. Some INS offices are satisfied with using your old FBI fingerprints to run a check on you. The FBI actually keeps them on their system a little longer than 18 months. Other INS offices make you do the whole fingerprint ordeal over again. It really all depends. The first step is to check with the US Embassy in Moscow by fax or email and ask them if you are approved for more children than you have already adopted and if your file is still open. If it is, then find out from your home study agency what the rules are about updating the home study. Even if your file is not open, some INS offices will allow you to piggyback on your old I-171H and using the home study update, amend your I-171H. You just have to check.

Should I adopt one child or two at a time?

There are pros and cons. The Pros are that you get all this adoption stuff over with at one time. You don't have to go through the whole thing again. Especially if you are older and want to complete your family quickly. You also save money. Normally agencies only charge a third or quarter more for an additional child plus you get an additional Adoption Tax Credit and Title IV reimbursement check. The children stimulate and play with each other. They grow up as best friends. They will always be there for each other. Displacement issues may be nonexistent. Somehow, two babies together are even cuter than one and you will find yourself an instant celebrity and everyone will want to come over and play with your babies. You've given one more child a home. They also realize that they are not the only adopted Russian child in the family and can take comfort in the similar experience of their sibling.

Now the Cons. It's hard to travel home from Russia with two children. Sometimes they both want to be fed, cuddled and played with at the same time!. It takes lots of paraphernalia (diaper bag, carseats, stroller) to go anywhere. You spend a fortune on formula and diapers. If you adopt unrelated children in which one is older, it could add stress in the home which could negatively affect the older child. You also are able to give one child your full attention which he may need in order to happily integrate into your family.

Is there adoption financial assistance?

The National Adoption Foundation in Danbury, CT can provide such assistance. The National Adoption Foundation Loan Program offers unsecured loans and home equity line of credit loans of up to $25,000 to adopting parents. The annual percentage rate (APR) is usu-ally very competitive compared to other unsecured loans. NAF can be contacted at (203) 791-3811 for loan applications. Also, you can call 800-448-7061 to apply for a loan over the phone. Usually, you will hear something within a week. The loans are usually below credit card rates. The loans are funded by MBNA America of Wilmington, DE. There is some confusion as MBNA claims they really do not offer a special adop-tion rate. The number for MBNA is (800) 626-2760. Credit unions may also offer a special adoption loan program. NAF also offers grants that are not based on income. Call them for that information as well.

There is also a foundation called "A Child Waits Foundation" at *http://www.achildwaits.org.* A Child Waits is a non-profit charitable foundation which provides loans to parents needing funds to complete their adoption. There is also the DOMOI Foundation, which promotes international adoptions and may provide loans. Its address is The DOMOI Foundation (Shayna Billings, Ex. Dir.), 1915 Polk Court, Mountain View, CA 94040 (650) 969-1980.

Some families have also received donations from fundraisers held by their church.

At what age are children not allowed to be adopted?

The current US law does not permit children 16 or over from being adopted. There is an exception if you have adopted a younger sibling and the older sibling is between 16 and 18. This exception may not be available if other siblings have been adopted by another family.

How does the Russian naming system work?

In Russia, the child is given a patronymic name. The term patronymic refers to a naming system that incorporates the name of the father into the name of the child. In Russia, the patronymic is used as a second given name (a middle name, if you will), with the suffix "ich", "vich" or "ovich" (for boys) and "ovna" or "evna" (for girls) being added to the father's given name. So, if your child's patronymic (middle) name is Vladimirovich, that means that his birth father's name is Vladimir.

Why is my child's head shaved in the video?

Some Russians believe that shaving children's heads makes their hair grow faster. (This appears to be based more on myth than reality.) It could also have to do with lice control in the children's home or in a minority of cases emotional problems of children which would cause hair twisting, etc.

What is PAD?

PAD is post adoption depression. It is very similar to post pregnancy depression and for the same reasons. It is not uncommon. Probably more than 50% of adoptive mothers get some sort of situational depression. You cry and are depressed and you don't know why because you are so happy. You cry because parenting is so hard and you want things back the way they used to be. Yet you are so in love with your new children you wouldn't change a thing. Eventually everyone gradually adjusts to the changes in the family and in time as the stress disappears, the depression will too. If it becomes too serious, then you may want to get help from a professional.

Physicians and the mental health community expect new birth mothers to go through a transition period after the birth of a child. Many articles about the birth mother experience attribute the depression to hormonal changes. Others relate it to the stress of being a new parent (which probably triggers hormonal changes). Just know that post-adoption stress is real—and it can lead to post-adoption depression. Factors that can effect the depression is your support system and your goal of trying to be "Super-Mom" or the "Perfect Parent." If you have a good support system of family and friends so you can catch a break every now and then and go off by yourself or with your spouse, that will help you. Do not feel "guilty" for doing something for you for a change. If you pressure yourself so you feel you must be the perfect mom (just like a bio mom), this can trigger the depression. Also, it can be very difficult at first transitioning from working full time to suddenly being at home full-time and away from daily contact with adults. You have to plan for you to get a required dose of "adult reality" on a regular basis.

Even fathers can feel depression. The nighttime feedings, loss of independence to come and go as you please, and the demands on personal time all have an impact. This depression is not the same as unhappiness. You can feel overwhelmed with your new child, but that does not mean that you do not love your child or believe that this child is not right for your family. Just accept that it is normal to feel down after the trip to Russia and to permit yourself to have these feelings and to recognize that they are perfectly alright.

Why do Russian women have so many abortions?

On average, a Russian woman will have 7 abortions during her lifetime. Some have many more. The "pill" is not readily available in Russia. Where it is available, the cost is prohibitive. Nor is there much education on other forms of contraception such as condoms or IUDs. Therefore, abortion has been and will likely continue to be, the contraceptive of choice.

Is there a problem if I have a hyphenated name?

The only problem is if your passport is in your maiden name. It is recommended in general, not just in adoption, to change your passport if your name changes. Whatever is your passport name is what you travel under. You really do not want to have inconsistent documents. Simplify your life and your adoption. You can find information on passports at http://travel.state.gov/passport_services.html and for expedited service at http://travel.state.gov/passport_expedite.html.

Have there been studies on how adoptive children from Russia are doing?

Since the large numbers of Russian adoptions is a fairly recent phenomenon, it has really been too soon for any long term studies to have been completed. Most of the currently published books and studies are based on the early Romanian adoptions. However, you can not simply say that all children's homes are alike no matter where located. Certain issues **may** have a commonality, yet each child's story is by its very nature an individualized event with its own peculiar history. Know that history and you will know that child. So much is dependent on such factors as whether your child was abused, or neglected, in a good children's home or a bad one, his age, had loving caregivers or not, and length of stay in the home, that it is hard to compare your child with a study.

If you read a study, check its relevance by first checking for the country of origin of the study group, then for the age of the children and finally for whether it is a self selective group. For example, a specialist that treats attachment may say that all Eastern European children have an attachment issue because that is the only population of children that she sees.

A summary of some of the studies can be found in Dr. Boris Gindis' articles in the Communique (a professional journal for school psychologists) at: *http://bgcenter.com/communique-article.htm* You can also read some in the "Pediatric Annals" issue on international adoption in Volume 29, Number 4, April 2000. Back issues can be ordered at 856-848-1000.

How many ethnic groups are there in Russia?

There are hundreds. Here are some sites with lots of information. *http://src-h.slav.hokudai.ac.jp/eng/Russia/minority-e.html*, Red Book of Peoples of Soviet Empire at *http://julia.eki.ee/books/redbook/introduction.shtml* and Peoples of Siberia at *http://www.nmnh.si.edu/arctic/features/croads/siberia.html*

Can I breastfeed my adoptive child?

If you're a guy, this could be difficult. Otherwise, the best overall source of information about adoptive breastfeeding is the book *Breastfeeding the Adopted Baby* by Debra Stewart Peterson. The La Leche League sells this book in its catalogue, but it is also available through other sources. This book is fairly short (140 pages), but it is packed with information. You probably should contact your local La Leche League for additional information and check out their web site. You need not have ever been pregnant in order to breastfeed

What is the Intercountry Adoption Act of 2000?

It is a bill that will impose rules on intercountry adoptions by countries which have ratified the Hague Treaty. Russia and Ukraine have not ratified the Treaty at this time. The purpose is to regulate and clean up some of the bad agency practices. The bill has been reported out of the House International Relations Committee. Originally this bill had some very troublesome provisions which have been removed in its current version. Now there are:

*NO provisions allowing international adoptions to be "vacated" by foreign courts after the child has come home to his her family;

*NO provisions requiring that a child eligible to be adopted by foreigners wait 12 months before placement; and

*NO provisions prohibiting adoptions by single persons.

This bill recognizes that most agencies operate ethically and competently, but that some do not. There is a recognition that parents adopting abroad should have somewhere to turn to voice their complaints when they are aggrieved. On the downside the bill establishes a new federal oversight authority, which may add additional complexity and regulations to the process. The bill may be changed as it goes to a vote. The complete text of the current version of the bill may be accessed by going to the web site of the House International Relations Committee at *http://www.house.gov/international_relations/*.

How can I travel with my adopted child if she is not yet a US citizen?

If you are planning to travel to a European country with a child who only has a Russian passport and US green card, then you will likely need to obtain a visa for your child. Most western European countries do not require this of Americans, but they do of Russians, and until your child becomes a US citizen, she is completely Russian. Visas can be obtained in advance from Embassies or consulates. It can be expensive and time consuming if you are planning to visit several countries.

How do adoptions in Bulgaria work?

Expenses and time to adopt are similar to the Russian experience, although methodology is a little different. The entire adoption process is 8 to 10 months. This time frame starts after your Dossier has been completed, sealed three times (State, US, Bulgarian Embassy), translated and arrives in Bulgaria. This can all be happening while you are waiting for INS approval.

You must make two trips. One trip to visit and accept a child and then a second trip some 6 months later to take your child home. Each trip takes about a week to complete. Only one parent needs to go. You do not need your INS I-171H before making the first trip. You just need a completed dossier. Some people find it very hard to meet their child and then return months later. But updated photos and videos are provided and you can send gifts. Many Bulgarian orphanages are in better shape than orphanages in other areas of EE. Each region has slightly different rules but generally childless couples or single women can adopt a child age 12 months or older. Children aren't available for adoption until they are one. Adopting unrelated children is not easy to do. Unlike Russia, no court appearance is necessary, as the adoption is final before the second trip. Expenses for hotels, meals, and taxis are less than in the big Russian cities. Many agencies have a Bulgarian program and the EEAC web site has a Bulgarian list.

The conditions in the orphanages seem to be a mixed, as in other countries. There doesn't seem to be much malnutrition, and the kids are generally physically healthy. FAS/FAE is less common. But deprivation can and does exist, with conditions in orphanages varying greatly. The children available to foreigners are mostly Roma (Gypsy). Bulgarians tend to adopt ethnic Bulgarian children. The Roma children are beautiful with their lovely complexion, dark hair and big dark eyes.

What is the risk of adopting from Chernobyl?

Very short-lived iodine isotopes that disappeared within months of the Chernobyl accident did cause an increase in thyroid cancer risk in children living near Chernobyl. However, studies have shown that there is no known medical reason for a child born after 1986 to be at increased risk for thyroid cancer because of the Chernobyl accident.

The estimated risk is greatest for children born between 1983-86. According to reports at an international conference in 1996, children in the heavily contaminated Gomel, Belarus region have something less than a 1% chance of developing thyroid cancer over 70 years. Most of the so-called contaminated regions have a rate much smaller than this. For children born after 1986, the risk of thyroid cancer is nearly the same as for children born in the West.

Can I adopt from Moldova?

Moldova allows foreign adoptions. It is a small former soviet republic. There are three options regarding travel in Moldova. You can spend 3-4 weeks in country and complete everything in one trip. You may also fly over for court (3-5 days) and return to pick up your child (7-10 days). The third option is to fly over for court (3-5 days) and have your child escorted home. Only one parent has to travel. Singles and older parents may also adopt. See these web sites for more information: *http://usis.iatp.md/adoption1.htm* and *http://usis.kappa.ro/Consular-Section/Adoptions.html*

Can I adopt from Poland?

Poland allows foreign adoptions. Since the birth rate in Poland is not very high, fewer newborns are available. In Poland, foreign adoptions represent 10-15 percent of all adoptions. Every year only 50 percent of children awaiting adoption are placed in Polish and foreign families. Domestic adoptions take priority over foreign adoptions. Priority goes to Polish residents or to people of Polish ancestry. Their regulations provide that the mother cannot be more than 40 years older than the child. Most Polish couples are interested in adopting babies. Older children, even if completely healthy, are less likely to find a new family, thus a foreign family has a better chance at adopting if they want an older child. In Poland the National Adoption Center (KOA) has all the information on the child. Prospective adoptive parents receive full information about the health of the child and as much information as the KOA can collect on the genetic family.

Adoptions can probably be arranged at a much lower cost than the typical U.S. adoption agency rate if you use a Polish attorney to handle all the paperwork. There is a good web site called "FAQ about Adopting in Poland" that can be found at *http://www.polish.org/en/frames/faq_main.html* which gives a lot of detailed information on what is needed for adopting in Poland as well as a list of agencies helping expedite Polish adoptions. The US Embassy also has a good review at *http://www.usaemb.pl/Consular/iv_adopt.htm#1* There is also a pretty good article published in June 1999 in the Warsaw Voice on Polish adoptions which can be accessed at *http://www.warsawvoice.com.pl/v555/society.html*

Can I adopt from Belarus?

Belarus used to have a moratorium on foreign adoptions but reopened the program in 1999. The Belarus process is very similar to that in Russia before Russia's recent changes, just some extra forms and steps. They do not have a 10 day waiting period.

What is Failure to Thrive (FTT)?

This is a nonsense label that American doctors sometimes give to a child. It is not a diagnosis. All it means is that your child is significantly below the average in height or weight. The real diagnosis could be a parasite problem, a GI problem, thyroid or human growth hormone problem, prematurity, or genetics i.e. the biological parents were on the small side. It could even be that the child was so long in the institution that the psychosocial dwarfism condition that is usually cured through catch-up growth can not be completely overcome. Since the FTT label doesn't actually help parents or doctors analyze the issue, it is as much a useless word as the Russians' perinatal encephalopathy.

Is there a problem bringing donated medicines into Russia?

If it is just over the counter items like vitamins and Tylenol, then usually there is not any issue at customs. However, if you are bringing in prescription medicines then you might want to do the following:

1. Pack medications separately from your luggage and mark it clearly"humanitarian aid". Pack it in such way, that you will be able to open and close it easily—or at least have additional packing tape to secure your package after customs.

2. Have a disclaimer ready (preferably in Russian) with the names of medications, expiration dates and were those medications are going (detski dom, dom rebenka, etc.) It has to be stated that all medications were given to you as a donation—that can help you to avoid customs fees. If you can have an actual letter (fax is enough) from your orphanage with the request for those medications—it will help a lot.

3. Be calm, cool and collected during customs control. If they want to detain the medicines or charge customs fees, try to convince

them that this is a very small shipment, not intended for sale and that you did not pay anything for those medications.

Can I go for a jog in Russia?

You will not see many Russian runners. It has not caught on yet. However, you can still run if you take some precautions. In Moscow, try to run early in the morning. Otherwise, the traffic, lights and congestion make it no fun. Use your street smarts, be careful, don't get lost, dress in muted colors, stay away from drunk Russians and you should be fine. Always carry copies of your passport and visa, enough money for cab fare and a note written in Russian that could be given to a cab driver to take you back to where you are staying and the number to the US Consulate or Embassy. The streets often have many of the same landmarks and it is very easy to get disoriented. There are no street signs, for one thing. Addresses and street names are written on buildings. Many buildings are alike and identical buildings can appear in clusters or strips all over the place. In Moscow one of the best places to run is along the Moscow River. Another good choice is around a park. The idea is to find a route with little cross traffic.

If staying in Moscow, Yekaterinburg or Vladivostok, call the Regional Security Officer (RSO) at the US Consulate or Embassy and get his opinion as to where is a safe place to run. Monitoring the safety and security for Americans is his job.

If you are staying at one of the nice hotels in Moscow that has a gym, the better policy is to work out there rather than take any chances. Some just run up and down the stairs in the hotel.

If I adopt a toddler, will he be potty trained?

Not likely. Remember that potty time in a children's home is a group thing at a specific time. They are all in the potty room sitting on their pots, which in some homes are these orange plastic pots. There may have been a lot of crying, although in some homes the children use them like race cars scooting along while sitting on them!

Some children are even afraid of bathrooms for the first couple of weeks you have them home. They may be frightened about sitting so high off the ground, as they are used to these little bucket type things. If you are adopting a toddler, bring some diapers just in case. Do not bring Pull-Ups. Look at it this way, if he really is potty trained what a pleasant surprise. Just don't count on it. With all of the confusion, difference in foods he will be receiving on the trip home, and being pulled out of the only environment he's ever known and being dragged from one place to another (airports, embassy, hotels, etc.), there are bound to be a lot of accidents.

Descriptions of Children's Homes

To give you an idea of what some of the children's homes look like here are some descriptions. Homes in Glazov, Izshevsk and Votkinsk are described in the Sept/Oct 1999 issue, Vol 32, No. 5. of "Adoptive Families." It is very interesting. You can order the issue from Adoptive Families of America in St. Paul, Minnesota at 1-800-372-3300.

Rostov Region

Our daughter was adopted from the Rostov Region of Russia in June of '97. Most of the buildings in the area were tired looking, mostly brick. We turned down what looked like an alley, which was the entrance to a dirt compound the orphanage was built around. There were a couple big trees and lots of weeds and piles of junk. No playground equipment...just a bunch of kids running around in their underwear because it was so hot. The compound side of the orphanage was white stucco walls with dull green trim (green was the color of choice for all the buildings it seems). Inside we were led down a hall (another shade of green) past a kitchen and through what was our child's play/eat/sleep area. One end of it had small tables and chairs where they ate their meals of mostly soup for the entire time we were there…and on the other end the wall was covered with a huge outdoor mural. There was a couch and a desk that separated the beds from the table area…and the beds were nothing but mattresses on the floor. There was one small nightstand. Through a set of tall double doors we were led to the "waiting room," which faced the street with a wall of windows, covered with lace curtains. There were tables, couches, and a TV and piano. The floor was a wood parquet pattern which must have been beautiful in its time. The facilities were clean, if sparsely furnished and worn with time. We saw two toys in the place but there may have been more—-we were only allowed in these two rooms. One was a ragged bear and a doll missing its nose.

Komi Republic, Syktyvkar Region

When we adopted our son in December of '97 his orphanage was a stark contrast. Again we were only allowed in the playroom where we were introduced to him. There was another playroom for younger children where they dressed him when we were ready to leave. The director's office had huge built in shelves stocked with dolls and toys of all kinds that didn't look like they had been used much. This region of Russia operates in the black because of natural resources. It was dark outside about 18-20 hours of each day and the ground was covered with a deep layer of snow and it was very cold, minus 40 degrees. There was a nice playground outside equipped with a sandbox and things like that (you could only see the outlines of them in the snow though). The rooms we were allowed in inside were well equipped with mats and bars and balance beans and all kinds of sensory stimulating activities. The walls were painted with beautiful murals of cartoon characters, fairies, flowers and the like. When they got our son ready to leave, the room they dressed him in had a huge built in playpen and the kind of equipment one would see in most daycare centers here in the states.

Krasnodar Territory

In the city of Novorossiysk which is located some 2,000 miles south of Moscow on the Black Sea.

Baby Home

The Baby Home was a two-story building that looked very old and decrepit from the outside. There were rusty-looking grates on the windows, chipped and broken stone stairs and railings, and peeling paint all over. The outside yard was overgrown and the "playground" looked unsafe for children. It had 2 or 3 climbing things made of splintered wood and a few other rusty pieces of equipment.

Upon entering the Baby Home, the inside felt very gloomy—almost spooky. The place was cool, dark and damp, and the entry door led into a poorly lit corridor that had 4 locked doors off of it. One led to the director's office; one led to the first children's group facility. One led to a stairway and another led to a corridor that went to other sections that housed other groups of kids and staff.

Inside one group's section the look and feel improved. We entered a large 20' x 20' recreation-type room which had hardwood floors, most of which was covered with a red tapestry rug. The ceilings were very high. There were several dark wood display cases with glass fronts and they contained a myriad of toys. The windowsills were covered with dolls and stuffed animals and there were white lace curtains on the very tall windows. There were several playpens full of toys. On one side of the room there was living room-type furniture—a sofa, two chairs, a table and lamp. Caregivers often sat and held, read to, and played with the children here. Another section of the room had little tables and chairs for the kids to sit at, along with doll beds and high chairs, and a few of those walking/seats for those babies beginning to move around. There was a desk and a television set in this room, too. In the back section of the room were a freestanding divider and another sofa and table. It looked like the place the caregivers might sleep.

There was a back door that led to the kids' sleeping room—approximately 12' x 15'—that was very dark, even with sunlight coming through the tall windows on the side wall. The room was a pale green with a few storybook characters painted on the walls.

There was a print carpet on the floor and the only furniture in the room were the dozen or so toddler beds lined up on the two sides of the room. Each had matching blankets and pillows, and there was a tiny chair at the end of each bed. The remaining wall had a built-in closet-type structure with a dozen narrow cubbies with hooks for clothing.

A second door off of the main room led to the eating and kitchen facility. This room had three small tables with four chairs at each in one section, and a counter, sink and stove with overhead cabinets in the other section. It was a very tiny food preparation area. Everything was very rundown but very clean. A dozen bibs were hanging below the cabinets. The last room in this group's facility was a tiny anteroom (maybe 6' x 8') off the kitchen that contained a single large, deep sink, wall hooks with towels, and cubby shelves containing the kids' potty seats.

When we arrived at the scheduled time, the main room was brightly lit, fresh smelling, and the kids were all tidy, and busy at play. On days when we arrived unannounced, it was a lot darker—most lights were off or curtains drawn, and the place didn't feel as fresh or cheery at all.

As for the care the children received, it appeared to be excellent. The caregivers were all very warm, affectionate women who clearly had established loving relationships with the children. The kids were held, played with, attended to when they cried or sought assistance, and kept very tidy and clean. One group had 9 or 10 kids and there were three caregivers on duty at all times, working shifts that consisted of 3 days on for 24 hours and 3 days off for 24 hours. They lived there, ate there, and slept there on their assigned workdays. There were about 80 kids in this Baby Home.

I was there for mealtime, naptime, potty-time, and playtime and was impressed with it all. Certainly everything was regimented—like clock-work—and the kids followed the routine like little robots. Meals were well balanced and sizable and the kids appeared to be well nourished. All the same, it was a sad place to be—a day-to-day existence of limited and repeated activity, limited and shared toys and clothing, and nothing to be excited or enthusiastic about. Most of the kids were not eligible for adoption because of visits or inquiries from family members as little as one time per year.

The staff had become very attached to my child in the months they had cared for her. Outside the orphanage in the entry courtyard, each of her caregivers, including the orphanage doctor and director, held her and spoke with her individually, ending their goodbye with a teary hug and kiss on each cheek.

Children's Home

The children's home was also old and decrepit looking from the out-side, and very similar inside. My time there was limited. I did have access to the main recreation room, the corridors and sitting areas between the group living quarters, and the director's office. As with the Baby Home, the inside was very dark and gloomy most of the time, with a few brightly-lit rooms where visitors were present or expected. The walls all had storybook characters similar to the children's section of a public library, but appearing in dimly lit foyers and corridors they were a bit eerie. The facility did appear to be very clean. The atmosphere here was very different than in the Baby Home. The director was much more business-like and did not seem to have any emotional attachment to the children. The few caregivers I met were very brusque and seemed to run the place in a "colder", more military manner. After their departure from the orphanage (and subsequent to their return to the U.S.) some older children indicated that there were some tough disciplinarians among them and beatings were not uncommon.

The children seemed to have some degree of independence, coming and going in and out of rooms on their own. But they, too, were on a very regimented schedule of meals, playtime, and sleep.

Republic of Mari-El
In the city of Yoshkar-Ola which is a 17-hour train ride east of Moscow

Baby Home

The facility was new, modern, bright, and well equipped both inside and out.

In addition to the group living spaces, which consisted of recreation rooms, eating rooms, sleeping rooms and bathrooms, the facility also housed an infirmary, a chapel, and even a swimming pool—all of which were used regularly. There were also small classroom-type rooms where speech therapy and other individual care were given.

The kids ate at the little tables in their little chairs, with their plastic bibs tucked under their big bowls of food. They collectively and uniformly would wash their hands, sit on the pots, and go sleep at naptime. The children received loving care from the Baby Home staff. My child was always being showered with hugs and kisses, cuddled and rocked to reassure her that everything would be fine. She received a lot of love and attention from these caregivers. The departure from this Baby Home was emotional for everyone involved. One of the caregivers had access to email and she asked for my email address to stay in touch. Upon my return, we began weekly online correspondence and I have sent photos and letters to the staff to keep them up to date on my child's new life.

We even had a visit in our home from one of her caregivers that was traveling in this area!

Perm Region

In the city of Solikamsk which is located three hours north of Perm. Perm is 800 miles east of Moscow near the Ural Mountains.

Baby Home

We adopted our son in 1997 from Solikamsk. The home was a two story concrete rectangular building on a dirt street. It was painted and not worn looking. The front door was made of very heavy wood in contrast to the painted concrete building. The home was very clean although not well lit. We were led into a large room on the first floor containing a mural of forest scenes and a piano. There were many toys on a cabinet against one wall. We were not sure if these were for show or if the children played with them. The room seemed to double as both the music room and the visitor's reception area. The room was about 30 feet long by 15 feet wide and had a set of windows along one side overlooking the road below and the forested land outside the town. The home director was a doctor and there were about 5 caregivers for 40 children. The children seemed to be from infant to age 4. The children had drawn pictures and these lined the wall as you went up the stairs.

On the second floor were little cots in neat rows against the wall. It was like a barracks type dorm room. It was very clean and tidy. No blankets just sheets as they kept the home warm. The cots were all made up. We saw a small play area next to the infant crib room. The play area was clean but only had a few toys in it. The crib room had old wooden cribs against the walls on either side. There were 4 on each side. There were no bumper pads or much in the way of toys. One room had a large playpen, but with no toys in it.

On the first floor we saw a small square pool about the size of a hot tub where the children would swim for therapy for 20 minutes. There was also a gravel box in which the children walked back and forth for a few minutes a day in order to stimulate their feet to help them walk. We saw no playground equipment outside.

The caregivers appeared very loving toward the children and the facility appeared clean although somewhat bare.

Russian Reading List

There are lots and lots of books on Russia. Here are a few suggestions.

For travel information see the Lonely Planet guides as well as their phrasebook. They cover a lot of cities in Russia. Fodor's also has a decent guide to Moscow and St. Petersburg.

If you want to know more about the Russian Mafia than you ever cared about, read *Comrade Criminal: Russia's New Mafiya* by Stephen Handelman.

For the Gorbachev era there are several from which to choose. You can try David Remnick's *Lenin's Tomb* or his *Resurrection; The Struggle to Build a New Russia*, or Dobbs' *Down With Big Brother: The Fall of the Soviet Empire* or Hedrick Smith's *The New Russians*.

For books on current life there are many such as *Waking the Tempests: Ordinary Life in the New Russia* by Eleanor Randolph, *Moscow Days: Life and Hard Times in the New Russia* by Galina Dutkina, or for a funny one read *Moscow Madness: Crime, Corruption, and One Man's Pursuit of Profit in the New Russia* by Timothy Harper.

There are also books that describe some of the cities in which adoptions now occur. Vladivostok, for example, is described in *Open Lands: Travels Through Russia's Once Forbidden Places* by Mark Taplin.

If you want to read the daily Russian news, you could try "Russia Today" at *http://www.russiatoday.com/* or "Moscow Times" at *http://www.moscowtimes.ru/*

Two other interesting slice of life sites are *http://solar.rtd.utk.edu/~asebrant/life/ml.html* and http://www.glasnet.ru/glasweb/gate/media.html And for a real oddball view of Russia you could try the "Exile" at **http://www.exile.ru**

If you want to read about your particular Region or city, all of the Regions and most of the major cities have websites.

One of the best Russian history sites is *http://www.russianhistory.org/*

This site has monographs on subjects that do not appear anywhere else. Also, see http://www.departments.bucknell.edu/russian/chrono.html

Adoption Reading List

For general adoption issues read *Twenty Things Adopted Kids Wish Their Adopted Parents Knew* by Sherrie Eldridge. This is a good laymen's outline of adoption issues. Others include *Being Adopted: The Lifelong Search for Self* by David Brodzinsky; *Talking With Young Children About Adoption* by Susan Fisher and Mary Watkins; and *Journey of the Adopted Self: A Quest for Wholeness* by Betty Jean Lifton.

For attachment issues, read *Facilitating Developmental Attachment: The Road to Emotional Recovery and Behavioral Change in Foster and Adopted Children* by Daniel Hughes; *Holding Time: How to Eliminate Conflict, Temper Tantrums, and Sibling Rivalry and Raise Happy, Loving, and Successful Children* by Dr. MarthaWelch; *Give them Roots, Then Let*

them Fly: Understanding Attachment Therapy by The Attachment Center at Evergreen. Their web site is at *http://www.attachmentcenter.org*
    There are many other books as well.

CHAPTER XIII

Ukraine and Kazakhstan

Ukrainian Process

Many people who are interested in Russia are also investigating Ukraine. Most of the chapters written in this book apply equally to adopting and traveling in Ukraine. The major procedural differences are described here.

In 1999, 323 visas were issued to Ukrainian adopted children. For more detailed information on the process I recommend reading the 1998 State Department's bulletin on Ukranian adoptions at *http://www.travel.state.gov/adoption_ukraine.html* and for more current information visit the Ukrainian list at the EEadopt web site. One of the very best web sites which also includes forms is at *http://www.adopt-sense.com/fees&forms.htm*

Here are some other very helpful sites:
http://www.geocities.com/Heartland/Shores/4447/index.html
http://www.usemb.kiev.ua/consular/Adoptions.html
http://www.usemb.kiev.ua
http://www.adoptukraine.com
http://www.usaemb.pl/Consular/iv_adopt.htm#1

Ukraine is a former republic of the Soviet Union and has been an independent country for over 6 years. It is economically tied to Russia and has suffered the same sort of financial meltdowns. One large difference from the Russian adoption process is that the child's visa is issued by the American Embassy in Warsaw, Poland and not Moscow. Indeed, it is to Warsaw that your I-171H cable is sent. Adoptive parents visit the US Embassy in Kyiv, Ukraine to verify that they have followed all of the correct steps for a legal adoption in Ukraine and then travel to Warsaw, Poland to obtain the child's visa.

Another large difference is that you can not receive any pre-referral information on children available for adoption. Therefore, families can not obtain photos, videos, medicals, names and birth dates of children or any other information about children until they actually arrive in Kyiv. If an American agency says they can provide such information, then that is an agency you need to stay away from. One similarity with the Russian process is that the Department of Education oversees the children's homes. As in Russia, singles can adopt and the age difference between a mother and a child is not as great as in Russia.

Time spent in Ukraine is generally longer than in Russia, although this will not always be the case. It can depend on how long it takes you to find your "forever" child and whether the court waives the 10-day appeal period. The shortest period in country is probably 10 days and the longest 4 weeks. As in Russia, there are regions that are very adoption friendly and some that are not. Some regions waive the 10 day wait, and some do not. Some will only waive it if you pay an "expedite" fee, and some do not charge anything. Some families obtain passports for the child in one day, and some wait weeks. The cost is less than in Russia. Generally the cost is around $12,000 which includes travel costs, although some have completed the process for less. Also, as in Russia, one parent may obtain the immigrant visa in Warsaw, Poland by power of attorney with the other parent simply having a Consular Officer at the Embassy in Kyiv witness his signature on the I-600.

The databank wait is longer than in Russia which means that a child 15 months old is about the youngest you can adopt, as opposed to 6 months in Russia. Families have adopted children under the age of 12 months, but these infants must have a diagnosis that appears on a list authorized by the Ministry of Health (lactose intolerant, heart murmur, cleft lip/palate, etc.). The complete list can be found at *http://www.adoptukraine.com/med.asp*

The Ukrainians are more lenient regarding the age of adoptive parents vis-à-vis the age of the child. It might also be slightly faster to adopt from Ukraine than from Russia. You can travel about 6-8 weeks after the dossier is complete. There is no wait for a referral.

There are approximately 141 children's homes in Ukraine. The typical age ranges are from 0-3 or 4 from 3-7 or 3-17 or 7-17. It can vary greatly. There are a few that are 0-17, 6-17, 0-7, 0-5, 3-8, and 4-9. Numbers of children in a home can be as little as 21 children and as many as three hundred or slightly more. The status of the children depends on why they are there. You might find yourself in a home filled with children, but only a few are available according to the registry. This is because Ukrainian children's homes are also used for foster care. The Russians do the same thing. If a family is having a particular problem they can place their children with their local children's home until they are better able to care for their children. In years past, these placements might be for abuse, drugs or alcohol, but more and more frequently it is because of the poor economic circumstances of the Ukraine. Another reason children may not be available is because they simply haven't been registered. This could be because of lack of diligence on the part of the home director or in many cases because they are having trouble terminating parental rights. For example, perhaps there was a child who was placed for foster care, but the family never came to visit and they cannot be found. Therefore, there is no relinquishment letter in the child's file and the child must have the court terminate his parent's rights. Most of the homes have a director and a senior physician with whom you will meet to discuss the available children. You may also meet with a senior educator or a specialist like a speech pathologist.

Ukraine is described as an "independent process" although there are agencies in the US that will help you on the American side. Many people find their own facilitator by word of mouth. Your dossier paperwork must be translated into Ukrainian, not Russian, although most Ukrainians speak Russian, and documents must be "authenticated" which is different than "apostilled." The notarized dossier documents are first stamped with your state's seal, which is the state's authentication of your notary, then sent to the US State Department where they get a federal stamp or seal of authentication and then these are authenticated by the Ukrainian Embassy where they receive an official Ukrainian stamp before being returned to you. There are fees. The State Department charges $5 per document, but call both to verify before sending any documents.

Now the Ukrainian Embassy has become rather difficult and expensive about authentications. Some families, after having their documents authenticated by the State Department in Washington, send them on to the Ukrainian Consulate in New York. The Ukraine Consulate in New York is a little easier to deal with and will accept documents from any state, as long as they are first authenticated through the State Department. They also accept bundled documents. This can save you quite a bit.

Some families have used a dossier courier group to make the rounds called Pata Group. Their address is: 617 K Street NW Washington, DC 20001 and their telephone number is: 202-789-1330. Another one is Jeff Doyle, P.O. Box 3239, Arlington, Virginia 22203-6134; phone is 703-298-2382. A courier that some families have used is Patti Urban at http://www.Legal-Eaze.com Her email address is Patti@Legal-Eaze.com and her phone is 914.362.4630;fax: 914.362.4637. Another courier service is Laura Morrison. Her email address is laura@asststork.com and her website is http://www.asststork.com

Some of your dossier documents may include: 1) Powers of Attorney for your facilitator and translator, 2) Commitment Letter or Petition To Adopt, 3) Application, 4) Affidavit for INS 171-H (and copy of 171H), 5) Home study, 6) Agency License, 7) Affidavit for Passport (and copies of passports), 8) Medical Forms for you and your spouse, 9) Criminal Record checks for you and your spouse, 10) social worker's license, 11) Letter from agency about social worker, 12) Certified Copy of Marriage Certificate or Divorce Decree, 13) employment letters, 14) self employed persons usually add a CPA letter on letterhead mentioning annual income.

One of your dossier documents to be sent to the NAC will be a "Petition To Adopt." It might read as follows: "We, Barney and Betty Rubble, petition the Center for Adoption of Ukraine to register us as candidates for adoption of an orphan or abandoned child. We ask permission to visit orphanages and state-run children homes to select, make contact with, and get acquainted with children that we desire to adopt. We desire to adopt two children male or female between four months to six years old, with minor surgically correctable condition or a minor chronic medical condition of any race."

It used to be that some of these documents could be bundled so that the cost of authentication was reduced. If you are using the Ukraine Embassy in Washington you need to check with them for their latest bundling requirements prior to sending them to your State for authentication. As an example, they will now not allow bundling of the two police clearance reports for husband and wife. The two reports should be two documents at the state and federal level of authentication.

Once your dossier documents are complete you will need to send them to the NAC. If you are having them translated in Ukraine, your translator can obtain them from the NAC. Otherwise translate them in the States before sending them. Express mail to Ukraine takes about a week. Once the NAC has the translated dossier documents, it takes them about 10 working days to approve you for adoption. When working with an agency, it is likely that their facilitators probably only know certain regions of Ukraine and will lean toward adopting from those. One disadvantage of this is that it may actually limit you. For example, many parents adopt from Simferopol, as it is very adoption friendly. Yet, there are other regions which allow adoption but which few people visit such as Ivano Franko. In interviewing an agency you should ask their references from which regions did they adopt. If it seems they all go to one or two regions, ask the agency why it is limited.

In contrast to the Russian process (the way it used to be anyway) you do not actually receive a "referral" of a child but rather your dossier is first approved for adoption by the National Adoption Center (NAC) in Kyiv who issues you an appointment. Do not go over without an appointment. You then fly to Kyiv and meet your facilitator. Now there are certain facilitators who have very good relationships with some of the children's homes and the NAC and may be able to guide you as to which region you should travel based on information they may have on the available children. However, this is not normally the case.

You will pay your facilitator for your housing, local transportation, legal fees and the services of the facilitators and translators. There are few hotels so you will likely stay in a homestay.

Upon arriving in Kyiv, you travel to the National Adoption Center with your facilitator and translator and meet with the physician and

Center Director and describe what kind of child you wish to adopt. The NAC is located at 27 Taras Schevchenko Blvd., Kyiv, Ukraine 252032; phone: 380-44-246-54-31/32/37;fax:380-44-246-54-52/62. NAC personnel speak Russian and Ukrainian. You will discuss what type of health problems you would accept. You are then recommended a number of children according to your parameters of health, gender, and age. It is not uncommon for the NAC to gently try to guide you toward boys. If you want a girl, be ready to insist politely, but firmly on that choice. Your experience at the NAC may likely vary from that of someone else for a variety of reasons. You are likely to be shown lots of referrals if you have no gender preference and are willing to adopt a child as old as the age of four. Requesting a relatively healthy girl under 18 months of age will likely limit the number of photographs. You are shown the children's pictures and a brief abstract of their medical condition, description and family history. The information may be a lot if the child is older or less if an infant. It varies. The information is probably not as current as the information at the home itself. If you do not find any of these children suitable, then a phone call to the orphanage can be made to determine if other children are available for adoption. You will likely see all of the available children in your age range that the NAC has on that particular day. On another day there might be more, or less. The more restrictive your criteria, the less children you will see. The NAC also probably steers you a little toward the more adoption friendly regions. If you are made of stern stuff, then tell them you will go to any region. A difficult region means that the timeline could be longer as there will be less time periods waived and less service expedited.

At the children's home itself you are likely to see additional available children that have not yet made it into the NAC photo albums. As in Russia, the anecdotal evidence is that there are more boys available then girls. Notwithstanding, many people have adopted girls. Ukrainian law requires both parents to meet the child and attend court. Although most parents prefer to meet the child and choose whom to adopt together, that can be done by one parent.

After narrowing down your search, you are sent by the NAC to a region and you travel to the children's home accompanied by the facilitator and translator. Which orphanage and the region you travel to depends entirely on the location of the child that you picked from the photo album shown to you in Kyiv. Make sure that your facilitator does not influence your choice. Some facilitators only want to go to certain regions. You must have Adoption Center approval to see children and review their medical files. Once you decide which children you will go to see the Adoption Center issues a letter of approval. Most often the letters list specific children. But if there is a children's home that has a number of children who have come available within your criteria, then you will be issued a letter that is general and permits you to see all available children.

At the children's home you interview the recommended children. Present are probably their caretaker, your translator, the facilitator, and the home's pediatrician. Your translator may have translated the medical records and all history known about the child from the records. You ask questions of the director; the caretaker and the children based on the information in the file. If you have made arrangements, you can now have this information sent to the US for evaluation.

There are different ways of handling the interview process. Some parents have asked to see the children in their environment. They go into the room where the children are playing, and ask the director to go around to the available children and lay her hand on their heads. This way the children are not disturbed, and the parents can see the children without them feeling like they are 'on display'. The director just tells the children that the parents are there to visit the children's home, thereby removing any potential anxiety. The parents watch the children and interact with the ones who are available for adoption. This also gives parents a chance to see the children interact with one another. By this method, no one particular child feels the sting of rejection by you saying 'no' to he/she particularly, but that you say 'yes' to the one that you feel best will fit into your family. The problem with seeing one child at a time, and saying 'no', and then seeing another is that it may make a child feel so rejected. Seeing the children in a group setting eliminates that.

Of course, some directors have their own ideas about how it will be done. Indeed, sometimes all the available children are not in the same group. Also, in some homes the caretakers bathe and have the children's hair washed once a week. However, when you come they may bathe them specially and pick out nice outfits for them to be "presented" in. The caretakers want the children to have the best chance of being adopted.

You have the option in Ukraine of bringing a doctor with you to the orphanage to evaluate the children you have been referred. There are both western-trained doctors and locally trained doctors who will travel with you to the orphanage. Your facilitator will help you arrange for a doctor prior to your trip. For example, some parents have taken a pediatrician from the American Medical Center in Kyiv. You may also be able to have the other medical establishment in Kyiv, the Clinic of the Oil and Gas Industry, provide pre-adoption physicals (including blood tests, etc.) at their clinic in Kyiv. Their number in Kyiv is 277-4144. The doctors are all Ukrainian, but most of them speak basic English. Just in case, you might take your translator with you. They can also help move you to the front of the line. The hospital doesn't look Western from the outside, but it has modern lab and x-ray equipment. It may also be cheaper than AMC. The Clinic is located on a hill in a park-like setting. You can also have your child's US visa medical evaluation completed at either the Clinic or at AMC prior to flying to Warsaw. The physical is about $26 US, which is likely cheaper than in Warsaw.

In addition, a number of the US based adoption clinics as well as the usual adoption medical specialists will review medicals sent to them while you are in Ukraine, or consult with you by phone from there. You

may be given a number of days to decide, and may be allowed to actually have blood testing done by the doctor you hire. One line of thinking
is that conducting another blood test may actually increase the risk that
the child will be exposed to infection from an unsanitary needle. If you
want to run a blood test, you may want to bring your own needles. Also,
there is always an issue as to whether the diagnostic results are accurate.
Some families have foregone the whole medical evaluation and relied
on their "gut" feeling when meeting their child. What these families say
is that love is love and we chose the daughters that were meant to be
ours. Others have taken actual tape measurements of a prospective
child's head. A great benefit to the Ukrainian process is that you actually
meet and interact with the child, which provides a lot of information
that you just can't get from a medical record, picture or video. At the
same, emotionally it is probably more stressful. Even if you do not go
through all of the medical evaluation when meeting your child, there is
absolutely no reason not to be prepared to do so. The medical knowledge to help you evaluate is easily accessible on the web or in articles.

Here is a description of one Ukrainian children's home. The
Stroganofski Orphanage in Simferopol, in the Crimea, is for children
ages 5 to 8. It has a capacity of 80. The children are kept in groups of
approximately 10 with three caretakers assigned to shifts to provide 24-
hour coverage. These same caretakers usually stay with "the group" as
long as they are there. The children are assigned to groups based on age,
development and size. The children's home is clean, the caretakers
friendly and warm people. Some caretakers have been there as long as
15 years with wages paid only intermittently. The home has no heat and
electricity and water only part of each day. The children are fed cabbage,
potato soup and a slice of bread with sugared tea several times a day.
Milk and meat is not normally part of their diet.

After choosing your child, and with the recommendations of the
home director, you submit your adoption petition to the court and the

hearing is placed on the judge's calendar. At the same time the papers are sent back to the National Adoption Center in Kyiv for approval.

As you might expect, since Ukraine was part of Russia for so long, its courts run pretty similar to those in Russia. Present in court are normally your facilitator, translator, the Inspector representing the Ministry of Education, the Prosecuting Attorney representing the State and the court reporter. This is very similar to the way the Russian court hearing is handled. The judge and Prosecuting Attorney ask you questions to make sure you know your responsibilities under Ukrainian law toward the child and the Ukrainian government. (The child keeps Ukrainian citizenship until age 18 and you must send annual letters to the embassy on how she is doing in school and her health.)

The prosecutor will ask you about childcare provisions you have made and about school. They will ask about your ability to provide the child medical care. The questions are similar to the Russian Courts. You may also request a waiver of the 30-day wait. After the decision, you have it recorded in the jurisdiction's records at the "Notary's." This is the equivalent to the county clerk where all official records are kept of municipal government transactions. You then may have to travel to the regional city to get a new birth certificate with you named as the new parents. You will need this to get the child a Ukrainian passport.

You then travel back to Kyiv with your child and take the final adoption decree to the National Adoption Center, then to the Ministry of Education, and Ministry of Foreign Affairs. Your facilitator should take care of all of that. If one parent needs to leave early, then the leaving parent should go to the US Embassy in Kyiv and sign the I-600 in the presence of a consular official. The Embassy's holiday schedule is located on their web site. The spouse remaining with the child must also go to the Embassy so they can complete Form I-604, Report of Overseas Orphan Investigation. This will become part of your visa package that you take to Warsaw. They will ask you some general questions about the child and your knowledge of what was told to you. The

Consular officer will also inspect the adoption papers. As with the Russian process, you will need to have your child medically examined before you can receive a US visa. This can be done in Kyiv or in Warsaw. The US Embassy in Warsaw will need the same sort of "pink" sheet as is described in the Russian process. You leave Kyiv with your child and fly to Warsaw, Poland to get the child's American visa from the US Embassy there. Immigrant visas are not issued in Kyiv which is why you put "Warsaw" on your I-600A as the consulate office. It is to Warsaw that the INS will send the cable confirming that they have issued the I-171H. The Embassy web site in Warsaw has a list of approved doctors. Some have used a Dr. Wanda Korulska, whose fees appear reasonable.

The Embassy in Warsaw opens at 8am and although you should make an appointment you can also just show up. You should be able to leave by late morning and then return in the afternoon for the visa. A good explanation of the US Embassy procedure is at *http://www.usaemb.pl/Consular/iv_adopt.htm#1*The US Embassy in Ukraine is located at Kozubinskoho 10, 254053, Kyiv, Ukraine Phone: 380-44-246-8048, 246-8559 and 246-9549 Fax: 380-44-246-8382.The contact is Landon Taylor, Consular Officer.

In Kyiv some families have stayed at the Brataslova. The rooms are clean and there is a nice breakfast every morning. The hotel is a very short walk to the metro, which you can use to quickly travel to downtown. Also there are several markets just outside, including a huge baby market. Some have also stayed in the renovated section at the Libid Hotel at Ploshad Pobedy (or Peromogi) meaning Victory Square(in Russian and Ukrainian). It is at the end of Shevchenko Blvd, just down from the Adoption Center on the same side of the street. It goes for just over $100.00 per night and it is less than a block away from the Adoption Center.

In Warsaw, families have stayed at the Hotel Polonia; ph.—011-48-22-628-72-41; FAX 011-48-22-628-66-22 The rooms are generally about $78.00 per night and include a huge international breakfast buffet. The hotel is very centrally located. There is a McDonalds and Pizza Hut near by. The metro station is less than 1/2 block away. This hotel is within about a 7 block walking distance from the US Embassy. Others like the Sheraton, which is just a few minutes walk to the US Embassy. It is very nice and luxurious. There is also a very nice Marriott. Always ask for the adoption discount when checking in or buying an airline ticket. If you don't ask, you don't get!

As in Russia, your laptop will work in Ukraine as long as your modem is compatible with their phone jacks. You can also use a cyber-cafe. There are several in Kyiv such as one on Prorizna str., 21, up from the Kreshchatik metro stop; phone number is (+380-44)2280548, http://www.cybercafe.com.ua and on the fourth floor of the Doetske Mir department store. There are at least two in Simferopol and at least one in Kramatorsk. As to US money, it should be the usual clean crisp variety. There are money exchangers located in every city.

Most of the discussion relating to preparing to travel to Russia applies equally to Ukraine. Most parents fly into Warsaw, Poland first, as that is where they will be leaving from eventually. They then take a plane from Warsaw to Kyiv. Delta does have a codeshare arrangement with Air France whereby you fly from Paris to Kyiv direct. As with Russian customs, declare all of your money and keep your customs form. You will need a visa to go to Ukraine. Some types of travel like business and private do not require a letter of invitation. You should check with the Ukrainian Embassy or Consulate to verify whether you need an invitation for your adoption trip. Invitations generally come from a travel agency. The visa process is similar to that of Russia except that you must send in your US passports with the application. They put a visa stamp in the passport and then send it back to you. No visa is required to travel to Poland whether flying from the United States or Ukraine. An excellent website that explains how to fill out the visa application form is at: http://www.adoptukraine.com/travel-prep_visa.asp and at http://www.ukremb.com/confr1.htm

For those living in Illinois, things are a little different in relation to how the I-171H is handled. There is a state requirement in Illinois that you identify your child before they will permit INS to send your cable onto Warsaw (or Moscow or anywhere else). Thus, your 171H notice reads that you are approved but that INS is holding your cable. Obviously, you cannot pre-identify for Ukraine, so families have been contacting the DCFS intercountry coordinator, Muriel Shennan, to work out a solution. This solution consists of notifying her that you will fax identification information from Ukraine to her and request that she contact Jennifer West at Chicago INS as soon as possible after receipt of your identifying information. Then, Jennifer West cables Warsaw and if all works well, your cable has been received in Warsaw before you arrive from Ukraine. The National Adoption Center of Ukraine requires a letter explaining why your 171H is being held. You can ask for a letter of explanation from Jennifer West, or from Landon Taylor, the vice-consul at the American Embassy in Kyiv. Here is the contact information: Muriel Shennan: phone-217 785 2692; Jennifer West phone: 312-385-1819, fax: 312-385-3404; Landon Taylor at TaylorLR1@state.gov, phone Consular Section (380) (44) 246-8048. 380 is the country code for Ukraine.

There is no particular format for the Ukrainian home study. If your home study agency follows the normal international format, as is done for Russia, that will be fine. Here are just a few items of which to be aware. There needs to be a notarized copy of the license of the person(s) who signs your home study. Make sure that the agency license is current and will be valid for as long as it takes to complete your adoption. Meaning

that their license cannot expire before the Adoption Center approves you. Sometimes where it is the agency not the social worker that is licensed, the agency provides its notarized license with a notarized letter stating the social worker is an employee. The notary needs to say that "the submitted copy of so and so's license is an exact photocopy of an unaltered original document." This is similar to what is described in the Russian paperchase.

There should be at least 3 notarized copies of the home study. Do avoid using the words "the Ukraine" in the home study. It is not proper and can be considered rude. The country name is Ukraine not "the Ukraine." Avoid placing information concerning adoption costs and household budget into the home study. They are not needed. Do not mention why these children are available for adoption i.e. "the circumstantial events that usually relate to adoption as poverty, unwed mothers and the presence of birth defects". Ukrainians would read this information and think they were being called whores and monsters. There is an extremely high intolerance for unwed mothers. This intolerance extends to talking about the issue. Ukrainians are highly sensitive to birth defects due to the nuclear accident in 1991 at Chernobyl. The name on the social worker license must match exactly the name on the home study. The address on the license and home study must also match.

There should be a statement that the couple is approved for a certain number of children, age range, gender type, and with minor surgically correctable conditions or minor chronic medical conditions of any race. Your annual income must be stated in home study and the word "annual" must be used instead of per year. The home study must state adoptive parents are healthy and free of syphilis, TB and AIDS. The home study must state that adoptive parent have never been given an unfavorable home study and that they have cleared the state's child abuse registry (assuming your state has one).

Ukraine requires a statement that the adopted child will have the same civil rights as any American born child. The language is similar to the following:

"Pursuant to (state's) law and the law of the United States of America, children that qualify as orphans and are legally adopted by an American citizen shall have equal rights as children originally born in the United States and his/her civil rights will not be restricted in any way."

When you return to the States your child must be registered with the Ukraine Embassy in Washington. This is not an unreasonable request if you follow their line of thinking that since the child has Ukraine citizenship until they are 18, then they should be registered as they would be if they were adult Ukrainians. Russia is now moving to such a rule as well. This registration requirement does not stop your child from becoming an American citizen, or give Ukraine any rights over your child.

Kazakhstan

After Ukraine, Kazakhstan is probably the next most popular former Soviet Republic from which to adopt. Kazakhstan has the second-largest land mass in the former Soviet Union, yet its population of 17 million makes it one of the most sparsely populated regions in the world. More than 100 nationalities live in Kazakhstan, with Kazaks and Slavs (about 40 percent of the population each) constituting the two largest ethnic groups. Kazakhstan became independent from Russia on December 16, 1991.

Kazakhstan is notably different from the other four Central Asian republics of the CIS in that a majority of its citizens are Russian speakers. The Kazak language is spoken by over 40% of population, but Russian is the language spoken by two-thirds of the population and is used in every-day business. Your dossier is actually translated into Russian. The country is composed of Kazak 46%, Russian 34.7%, Ukrainian 4.9%, German 3.1%, Uzbek 2.3%, Tatar 1.9%, other 7.1% (1996). Because of its large Russian population in the north, there is always some underlying tension between the two countries. The country is religiously divided between Muslim 47%, Russian Orthodox 44%, Protestant 2%, other 7%. It has a very high literacy rate with some 98% of the population able to read and write. Kazakhstan relies on commodity exports, particularly oil, for its hard currency. Many of its manufacturing industries have closed. It has 14 regions with a geography ranging from mountains to steppes to desert.

Many adoption agencies have started Kazakhstan programs since a new law allowing foreign adoption was passed in Kazakhstan in December 1998. Foreign adoptions fall under the Ministry of Education's international adoption committee although the Regions seem to really run things. There are about 20 agencies working in the country and this number will definitely increase. There have been over 300 adoptions from Kazakhstan. Generally the cost is between $18,000 to $23,000. The usual length of time on the registry database is 5 months. Children can not be adopted until after they are off the registry. Foreign adoption is permitted throughout the country. The dossier documents are similar to those needed for Russia (birth certificates, marriage certificates, medicals, employment verification, bank reference, passport information, home study, post placement agreement, agency license).

Newborns remain in a maternity hospital until they are 5 months old, then they are transferred to a baby house. Waiting time for a referral used to be minimal although the time is beginning to lengthen. Reports indicate that there are some 5000 children living in the children's homes. Not all of these may be available for adoption. More than one child can be adopted at the same time and there can be other children in your family. Your notarized dossier documents are apostilled.

The length of time you must spend incountry can vary. Kazakhstan requires a 14 day visitation before you can go to court and then a 15 day appeal period before the decree is final and you can pick up your child's passport and exit visa. Families who adopted soon after the Kazakhstan law was revised in December 1998 experienced more delays in their process as the regions worked their way through the new process.

Notwithstanding the mandatory 14 day period, some adoptions have been completed in as short a time as 8 days. The average appears to range from 10 days to 3 weeks. The shorter time frames may be related to whether you adopt from a large city like Almaty or Astana or from an outlying region. As in Russia, there seems to be some variety in how each region handles adoptions. Some regions apply the 15 day appeal period strictly and at least one parent must wait out this time after the court hearing before the court decree is final. Other courts will routinely waive this period as well as the pre-adoption time. As in Russia, the waiver is determined on a case by case basis and is solely up to the judge. There are cases where the 'prosecutor' has requested verification of some of the documents presented to the court such as the child being born outside a major city and the mother's letter of abandonment being legalised by a notary unknown to that particular court. The judge may well then enforce the waiting in that case.

You should always ask the agency you are considering using, regarding the length of stay in the region in which they work. This should be verified by the reference families. Both parents do not have to be there the entire time, although they both must attend court. You may receive a referral with medical information and a video while still in the United States although some families have received very minimal information. It varies by region and children's home. You can sometimes call and ask additional questions of the children's home doctor before accepting the referral. Once at the home, you may receive a lot of additional information regarding the background of your child. If the city is relatively small, the Director may know quite a bit about the details of the lives of the birth parents. This information is always very helpful and can be passed on to your child when the time comes.

The children's homes seem generally to be in better shape than the Russian ones. The caretaker to child ratio seems to be lower. Generally children from infant to age 3 are housed together and older children are housed according to age as well. Anecdotal evidence is that the homes are very clean and the doctor/director and caretakers love the children. The children seem to be within their average for weight and look to be very healthy. They eat a lot of "Kasha" which is like cream of wheat and borscht soup. One parent has described a children's home as being very clean, very well staffed, very organized and very well run. The Director was a pediatrician who had worked there for many years. The staff had a genuine interest in the children. Caregiver to child ratio was pretty good, at about 2 to 12-15 children. The interior was very brightly decorated with murals painted on the walls by local artists. There were plants, birds, music and toys.

Here is a description of a children's home in Atyrau, Kazakhstan. The children's home consists of a row of white buildings, in a nice secluded area near a park with a lot of trees. Outside there is playground equipment. The entrance is at the top of a skinny, metal row of stairs. There are several long, thin rooms, all connected by doors to other rooms. It is like a maze. The place is very clean, and every room had hard wood floors covered by bright rugs. There are about 50 children, ages birth to three in this baby house. It is very quiet. Inside one room are about 15 little children, about 2 to 3 years old. They are sitting in little chairs around the edge of the room.

While FAS/FAE is always a concern, because Kazakhstan has a large Moslem population, generally there is less alcohol consumed.

The number of foreign airlines flying to Almaty, Kazakhstan has grown from 3 in 1993 to more than 12 in 1998. Today you can take direct flights to Almaty from Amsterdam (KLM), London (British Airways), Frankfurt (Lufthansa), Vienna (Austrian Airlines), Moscow (Aeroflot, Transaero), and Istanbul (Turkish Airlines). A lot of parents fly into Moscow first as that is where you have to fly from after visiting the US Embassy for the child's visa. Another advantage to Moscow is that you can fly from Moscow's domestic airport to the city in Kazakhstan nearest your children's home. Remember that the Kazakhstan customs declaration form will be in Russian. A suggestion is to copy the one you filled out for Russia as that should be in English. The forms should be very similar. Do not lose your Russian or your Kazakhstan forms. You will need them when you leave. Both Russia and Kazakhstan require visas so you will need two for your trip. If you travel through Moscow, your Russian visa will have to be double entry.

After spending some time at the children's home, you then go to court. Court may be a local civil court or a regional court. Joining you will be your translator. You are asked the same sort of questions as in a Russian court. After you have obtained your Court Decree, the same steps as in Russia are required in that you apply at ZAGS and OVIR for your child's amended Kazakhstani birth certificate and passport. After obtaining these, you must travel with your child to the US Embassy in Almaty. Its address is 99/97A Furmanova St. and phone numbers are 7 (3272) 63-39-21 and 7 (3272) 63-28-80. Faxes may be sent to: 7 (3272) 50-62-69 and email sent to consularalmaty@state.gov. The US Embassy web site is at: http://www.usis.kz/

Almaty is a very large and lovely city. If you have a few days, you might take a short tour into the surrounding mountains. Almaty is the former capital of the country. You can see some really beautiful pictures of Almaty at: *http://welcome.to/kazakhstan* This site also has pictures of Astana and Aktau. Astana was officially named the new capital in December 1997, however most foreign missions are still based in Almaty. At the Embassy they will explain the documents and make a copy for you and another copy for the Embassy in Moscow. The Embassy will complete Form I-604, *Report of Overseas Orphan Investigation*. This must be completed before you travel back to Moscow to obtain your child's US visa. The US Embassy in Almaty does not issue immigrant visas. Your child's medical evaluation (pink form)is normally completed in Moscow, not Almaty. A review of the whole process can be found at *http://travel.state.gov/adoption_kazakhstan.html*, however, be aware that the information at that site is current as of the end of 1999.

You then leave Almaty for Moscow. Moscow is 3 hours behind Almaty. In Moscow, you go through the same brief medical evaluation and US Embassy visa visit as you would if adopting from Russia. Then you catch a plane and you are on your way home.

More information on Kazakhstan adoption can be found on the Kazakhstan email list at the EEAC web site. A great map of Kazakhstan in the May 1999 National Geographic.

Information on Kazakhstan generally can be obtained from these web sites: *http://www.president.kz/main/mainframe.asp?lng=en* *http://www.kazakhstannews.com/* *http://www.kazakinfo.com/*

0-595-13194-8